The Road to Tourism

skills for the
new professional

VIVIENNE O'SHANNESSY

DEAN MINETT

GEOFF HYDE

Pearson Education Australia
Unit 4, Level 2
14 Aquatic Drive
Frenchs Forest NSW 2086

Publisher: Matthew Coxhill
Project Editor: Jane Roy
Copy Editor: Jennifer Coombs
Indexer: Caroll Casey
Cover and internal design: Ramsay Macfarlane
Typeset by Midland Typesetters

Printed in Malaysia, PP

2 3 4 5 05 04 03 02

National Library of Australia
Cataloguing-in-Publication data

O'Shannessy, Vivienne, 1962– .
The road to tourism: skills for the new professional.

Bibliography.
Includes index.

ISBN 1 74009 612 6.

1. Tourism – Vocational guidance – Australia.
2. Hospitality industry – Vocational guidance – Australia.
I. Hyde, Geoff, 1953– . II. Minett, Dean, 1960– . III. Title.

An imprint of Pearson Education Australia

Foreword

The Australian Tourism Industry requires skilled employees to meet the changing and growing needs demanded by both our domestic and international markets.

The Tourism Industry can be labour intensive and at times operating up to 24 hours a day, seven days a week and may be subject to seasonal fluctuations. Tourism operators service the demands of local interstate and international tourists and the industry is heavily dependent upon quality and consistent customer service in order to meet the ultimate expectations of the consumer.

With increasing leisure time coupled with growth in international visitations, the Australian Tourism Industry is a rapidly growing and expanding industry offering a vast range of challenging and rewarding opportunities.

The higher demands and expectations of the consumer in the tourism industry identifies the increasing need for more highly skilled and qualified operators. Multi-skilling across a number of sectors within the industry together with multi lingual and cultural skills in some areas support the quality and growth in tourism in Australia and contribute to our increasing recognition in world markets.

Whilst all operators and establishments have their own unique features, niche and attraction, they all have the common requirement for quality consistent friendly service to support that memorable event or occasion.

The 'Road To Toursim' is professionally framed in a user friendly language and format to underpin and support the education of entrants into the tourism industry and to ideally compliment the Tourism Training packages which encompass the training needs for the broad spectrum of the tourism industry—tourist attractions, tour guiding, wholesale tour operators, retail travel, tourist information, services and meetings.

I encourage fellow Australians to consider a career in the tourism industry for a most rewarding, satisfying and challenging career. With the appropriate skills, commitment and dedication, your career path within the industry may well exceed your expectations.

To entrants into toursim studies and into the tourism industry, I wish you well and trust that you find 'The Road To Tourism' an ideal companion throughout your studies and your career. To those already established in the tourism industry, 'The Road To Tourism' provides a handy reference for some of your day to day requirements as you progress through to supervisory and management opportunities.

I wish you well.

John Sweetman AM
Chairman, Tourism and Hospitality Industry Training Board
Vice Chairman, Tourism Training Australia
Chairman, Tourism Accreditation Board of Victoria

Contents

Preface

The human race was destined to travel ever since fish developed legs and decided to walk instead of swim!

Following this first epic journey, it was discovered that people not only travel, but have needs along the way. The industry that has grown up around servicing these needs is called the Tourism Industry.

Whilst the provision of food and lodging met the basic needs, there has now developed a vast array of additional areas such as the provision of transport, insurance, visitor information, and ancillary services.

Following the success of our first publication, *The Road to Hospitality*, this latest book has been written to explore the far broader area of tourism in a similar manner.

This book will introduce you to the exciting, dynamic and challenging world of tourism—one of the oldest industries in the world. The book complies with the knowledge aspects of the Tourism Industry National Competency Standards up to certificate II level and provides opportunities for practical application in the form of case studies, file notes, and a series of questions.

The world is a great book, of which those that never travel read only one page! Enjoy the journey!

Dean Minett   Vivienne O'Shannessy   Geoff Hyde

Acknowledgements

My thanks to Kellyann Frederick who kept my mind focused on the job at hand and to Professor Brian King for his usual helpful comments and hints. Also to my children Oliver, Julian and Genevieve who always inspire me and put up with my busy writing moods! GH

Thanks to Fiona, Douglas, Melanie and Alec for the constant reminder of what is important in life, and to Ruhi Yaman for his intellectual challenges! DM

Develop and update tourism industry knowledge

CHAPTER 1

LEARNING OUTCOMES

On completion of this chapter you will be able to:

- identify and access tourism industry information;
- define tourism and identify the tourism industry sectors;
- describe the factors affecting a tourism enterprise;
- describe the economic impact of the tourism industry;
- describe the social and cultural significance of tourism;
- describe the environmental issues of tourism;
- list the major industry bodies that impact on the industry and explain their purpose;
- identify career opportunities in the tourism industry;
- list the relevant legislation affecting the industry;
- know where to access tourism data; and
- identify how to keep in touch with trends affecting the tourism industry.

This chapter complies with the Tourism Industry National Competency Standards, unit THTTCO01A, 'Develop and Update Tourism Industry Knowledge'.

There is no doubt that the tourism industry today is one of the most diverse, exciting, challenging and important in Australia and the world. Tourism offers career opportunities that are as dynamic as the industry itself. The possibilities include work with travel agents, tour wholesaling companies, tour operators, airlines, cruise lines, government tourism commissions, regional tourism associations, hotel chains and companies that manage and operate tourist attractions and special events. The skills and abilities required generally fall into the following categories: automated ticketing and reservations; sales and marketing; information and customer services; administration and accounting; policy advice and strategic planning.

New markets are also arising, creating windows of opportunities for well-trained, highly motivated people to complement existing organisations or to start their own businesses. In order to succeed in tourism, however, it is essential to possess a driving enthusiasm for customer service and satisfaction combined with a strong sense of professionalism.

To be successful in the tourism industry we need to develop and maintain tourism industry knowledge that relates not only to the sectors in which we work but the entire industry and we need to understand how each sector is linked. We need to know what tourism is, understand its economic, environmental, social and cultural impacts, its relationship with other industries and the roles and responsibilities of individual staff members in a successful tourism organisation.

Access tourism industry information

In order to develop and update our skills and knowledge of the tourism industry we need first to understand what is meant by the term 'tourism'. Indeed, tourism means different things to different people and few can agree on precisely what it is. We also need to identify sources of information on the tourism industry where we can gain further knowledge that will help us to perform effectively in the industry.

SOURCES OF INFORMATION

To have a better understanding of tourism and its sectors, it is important that we know how to identify and access additional information on each of the sectors and the industry in general.

Our information sources can be people or places. They include:

Media • Local and national newspapers, trade magazines, specialist magazines and travel programs on television and radio provide information about destinations and the facilities and services available at those destinations.

Reference books • Travel guides and textbooks can provide in-depth coverage of specific destinations, sites to see, costs, how to get there, places to stay and the main attractions.

Libraries • Access to newspapers, magazines, the Internet, reference books and computer databases relating to the tourism industry are frequently available in local libraries, schools and academic institutions.

Visiting attractions • Site visits and personal experience provide opportunities to experience at first hand the value of a tourist facility.

Leaflets and brochures • Many destinations/regions provide information about the area including what to see and do and places to stay. Tourism companies and organisations also advertise their own individual products through this medium.

Tourist offices and tourism commissions • These organisations provide up-to-date information on tourist numbers, attractions, infrastructure, strategic plans for the region and other tourism-related information.

Internet • Almost anything you ever wanted to know about the tourism industry can be found on the World Wide Web.

Personal experience • Throughout our lives we participate in a range of activities and events that may be classified as tourism based. These experiences give us a valuable insight into the tourism industry and how it operates.

Colleagues and associates • Our colleagues and associates are a valuable source of information and are usually willing to share their knowledge.

Industry associations • These organisations collect and compile up-to-date tourism data which they make available to their members and other industry professionals.

The next important question is: What sort of information do we want, and what do we do with it? The sort of information we want will vary for each of us depending on how we intend to use it and share it. In whatever role we hold in tourism, our customers and clients constantly seek information from us relating to their tourism experience. They expect us to be able to give them useful and helpful information. The rest of this chapter looks at the sort of information we need in order to understand how to provide excellent service in the tourism industry.

Defining tourism

Tourism occurs as a result of the different types of businesses that provide a range of products and services to visitors. It also involves the input of the public sector (governments, politicians and bureaucrats) through policy formulation, regulation, legislation and funding assistance for marketing and investment. The explanation we give here is simply one view, which attempts to convey the basic principle that defines tourism.

Tourism encompasses those activities that take people away from their usual place of residence for pleasure or a holiday and for reasons other than going to their normal place of work. Most definitions of tourism will, however, preclude business travel, as tourism generally implies travel for leisure and pleasure. That is not to say that business travel is never pleasurable.

> **Tourism**
> Those activities that take people away from their usual place of residence for pleasure or a holiday, other than for work.

In Australia the journeys we take that contribute to the tourism industry, whether within Australia or overseas, are variously referred to as holidays, trips, travelling, visiting friends or touring. Strictly speaking, we should categorise tourists as those travelling solely for leisure or pleasure purposes. All other categories can be called visitors. But many of these tend to have an element of leisure or pleasure in their trip even though this may not be the main motivation for the trip. It doesn't matter what we call it, we are tourists or visitors when we meet the above criteria of tourism; and we will require a range of products and services to meet our needs during this time. Put simply, virtually all travellers become part of the business of tourism.

The Bureau of Tourism Research (BTR), for the purposes of statistical analysis, defines a **trip** as 'a stay of one or more nights but less than three months, involving a journey of at least 40 kilometres away from home'. A trip can be taken for any reason, except where the journey is related to taking up employment. A **visit**, as a component of a trip, is defined as 'being made to each place where one or more nights is spent while on the trip'. There may be many visits on a trip.

It is generally accepted that these activities are temporary, whereas a permanent relocation becomes migration.

Into this definition would exclude, for example, families on day trips, such as to the country or the zoo, and would also indicate that these daytime activities do not contribute to tourism figures. This would not be correct, as day trippers spend money on many other activities other than overnight accommodation.

Into this definition, however, we have introduced other factors, such as **attractions** and transportation. Tourism could therefore be said to be the umbrella under which these industries operate. These other industries are usually referred to as **sectors,** and the people using the umbrella are mainly tourists.

TOURISM INDUSTRY SECTORS

Tourism sectors refer to those industries or business enterprises that provide goods and services to tourists, visitors and all types of travellers while they are travelling. In other words, a tourism sector is one area of an industry, often a specialist area that is part of and contributes to the entire tourism industry.

The tourism industry is therefore the umbrella term used to describe the three interconnected sectors of travel, hospitality and visitor services, as described in Table 1.1, which highlights the different types of businesses and organisations that operate within that sector.

TABLE 1.1 **Tourism sectors**

HOSPITALITY	TRAVEL OPERATIONS	VISITOR SERVICES
Accommodation	Retail travel agents	Attractions (built and natural)
Restaurants	Tour wholesalers	Special events organisers
Cafes/bars	Tour operators	Government tourism commissions
Club venues	Airlines	Regional tourist associations
Gaming facilities	Cruise lines	Visitor information centres
Conference facilities	Railways	Duty-free shops
Catering services	Coach companies	Souvenir outlets
Entertainment	Car rental companies	Recreation/sports facilities

RELATIONSHIP BETWEEN TOURISM AND HOSPITALITY

When people travel away from home overnight, they need a place to stay. A large percentage choose paid accommodation (as opposed to staying with friends or family), with the choice of accommodation depending on several factors:

- cost;
- standard or quality;
- availability;
- length of stay;

- destination/location;
- purpose of travel;
- star rating standard; and
- types of services and facilities available.

In addition, travellers also needs food and drink, which they usually obtain from services in the hospitality industry. However, the relationship between tourism and hospitality does not end there. The two are intrinsically linked and need to work together to help sustain each other. For example, a travel agent may book a **package holiday** for a client, which can include travel arrangements, accommodation, meals, tours, transfers, activities and entertainment for one all-inclusive price.

While from a travel operations perspective tourism is mainly concerned with getting people to a destination, the role of hospitality is to provide not only accommodation but also food and beverages, entertainment and activities (such as in a resort) and to offer a range of other services and facilities that tourists seek.

If a client wants to travel to a particular destination, but the destination cannot offer all the hospitality services and attractions required, this may effectively stop the person from visiting that place.

RELATIONSHIP BETWEEN TOURISM AND TRAVEL OPERATIONS

How do people get to their destination? They travel there: by car; by bus; by train; by air; by sea. Therefore we have a travel industry which helps to arrange and assist people to travel from one place to another.

When people travel they choose a mode of transport that meets their requirements. Their requirements may be affected by time restraints, budget, and transport comfort, convenience or preferences. Travel arrangements can usually be made directly with the transport organisation, that is, a flight can be booked directly with the airline, a train seat can be booked directly through the railway operator, and so on. Alternatively, transportation can be arranged through a retail travel operation, that is, a travel agent.

A travel agency often provides a link between the tourism sectors. A travel agency can book all travel requirements, transport, accommodation, attractions and tours and can assist with travel insurance, passports and visas. It acts as the retail outlet or shopfront for people to buy their travel products. It can provide the knowledge and information required to allow consumers (tourists) to make their decision about holiday destinations. It also sells packaged holidays to suit the required budget for a variety of different consumers.

RELATIONSHIP BETWEEN TOURISM AND VISITOR SERVICES

When a person reaches their chosen destination what do they do? Apart from sleeping, eating, drinking and relaxing, they also tend to visit attractions, take part in recreational activities and tours, shop for souvenirs and visit information centres. Each of these services contributes to the enjoyment a visitor receives from visiting a particular destination.

Without these facilities and services in place, a destination may not hold the right mix of services to attract visitors. This is why Government Tourism Commissions and Regional Tourist Associations (together with local government) spend large amounts of money on the marketing and promotion of particular destinations. They also assist with investment in basic infrastructure and other facilities to service tourists. Moreover, most people involved in the tourism industry at these destinations want these visitors to return again in the future, so it makes sense to make them feel welcome and offer them an interesting, relaxing and enjoyable holiday experience.

RELATIONSHIP BETWEEN TOURISM AND OTHER INDUSTRIES

Tourism as an industry is only sustainable through the existing mechanisms that support a community as a whole. That is, the tourism industry is reliant on and usually has a direct linkage to other industry sectors that supply part of the infra-structure and other goods and services for a destination. For example, hotels must be built and fitted out so that visitors have a place to stay. Other industries are then required to supply the hotel with furnishings for the rooms and other public areas, food and beverages, linen hire, cleaning, and kitchen equipment and utensils. Tourism establishments are also large consumers of public utilities such as power, water and gas. The industry relies on the availability and suitability of all these industries in order to survive and prosper. Other services and facilities needed within the community to maintain appeal for visitors include local transport services, a labour market, theatres, events, retail shopping outlets, banks, chemists, doctors and so on.

How the relationship between tourism and other sectors and industries works is shown in Figure 1.1.

FIGURE 1.1 *DIRECT AND INDIRECT RELATIONSHIPS OF TOURISM, HOSPITALITY AND OTHER INDUSTRIES*

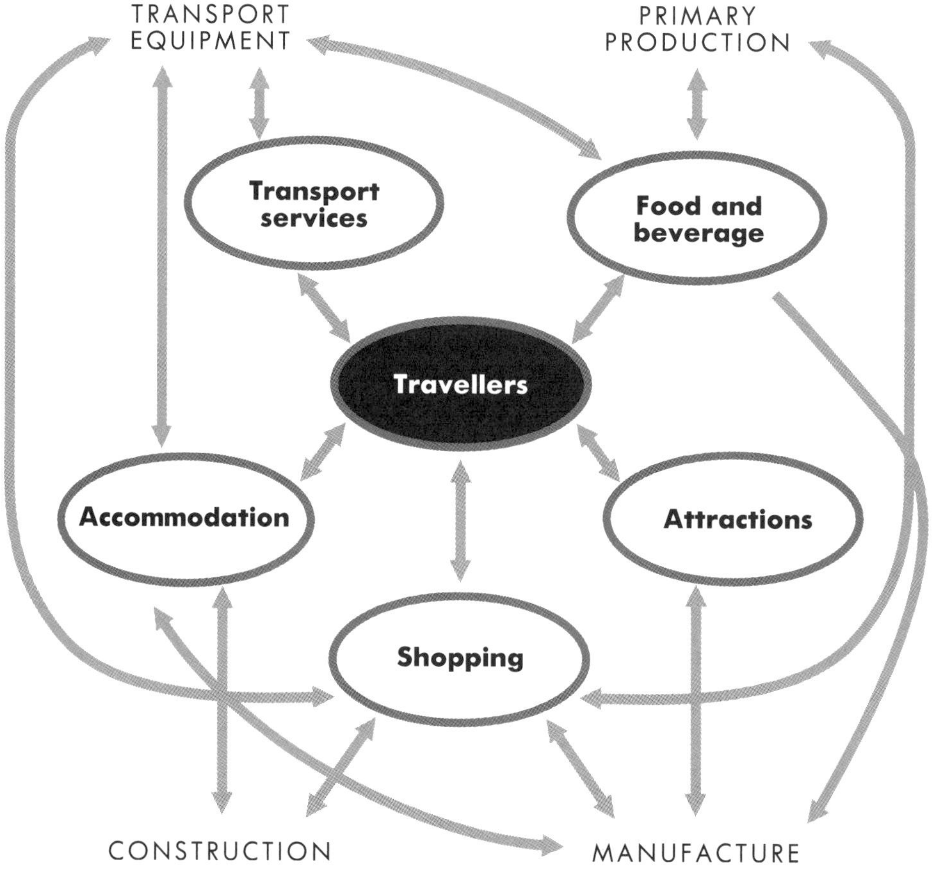

Source: Reproduced with permission of the Tourism Forecasting Council, 1999.

WHO ARE TOURISTS?

As we've seen, tourists can be anyone travelling away from home for reasons other than for work. To help tourism-based enterprises attract tourists, it is helpful for them to understand where tourists come from.

It is generally accepted that tourist markets are divided into three groups:

International • Visitors whose main place of residence is outside Australia are referred to as **inbound** tourists. Australian residents travelling overseas are referred to as **outbound** tourists.

Interstate • These are Australian tourists travelling within Australia, to a state other than where they usually reside, for tourism purposes.

Intrastate • These tourists are travelling within the state in which they usually reside. Together with interstate tourism, this comprises the Australian **domestic tourism** market.

Within each of these classifications are target markets and target segments. A **target market** is defined as a category of people who have been identified as potential customers because of their income, age, place of residence and other factors. Marketing strategies for organisations usually target specific markets. Identifying a target market is sometimes referred to as **market segmentation,** in that it identifies a portion (or segment) of the market that has similar traits, needs and desires that the organisation wants to attract to buy its product.

PURPOSE OF TRAVEL

Irrespective of where tourists originate, there is always a purpose for the travel. The purpose of travel refers to the visitor's reason or main motivation for travel. This becomes important when we are passing on information or wanting to attract a specific type of person. By knowing why people travel we are better able to provide information that meets their specific needs for their tourism experience. Table 1.2 shows the purpose of travel according to the market segment and probable market demographics.

> **quick thinker**
>
> ▶ Make a list of all the services and facilities, apart from accommodation and food, that visitors may require while at their destination.

Factors affecting a tourism enterprise

Not every establishment is in a position to offer every conceivable service or facility available in tourism. Many establishments and organisations choose not to offer everything but instead specialise in a given area, while others are not able to offer certain services or products because of factors outside their control.

Factors that can influence an operation are either internal or external. Internal factors, such as pricing policies and marketing strategies, allow for some control by

Inbound tourist
Visitor to Australia whose main place of residence is not in Australia.

Outbound tourist
Tourists, whose main place of residence is in Australia, travelling outside Australia.

Domestic tourism
Tourism undertaken by Australian residents within Australia, either interstate or intrastate.

Demographics
Identification or segmentation of the market according to age, gender, family size, income, occupation, education and marital status, which allows us to prepare more specific marketing programs for each segment.

Target market
Category or group of people with similar characteristics and buying habits that an organisation wants to attract.

Market segmentation
Separating of the market into distinct groups or categories according to their traits, needs and wants.

TABLE 1.2 **The purpose of travel and the market segment**

MARKET	PURPOSE	DEMOGRAPHIC
Corporate (i.e. travel for business)	Business/sales trip interstate/overseas meeting	Male/female usually over 18
Leisure	Holiday, either group or free independent traveller (FIT)	Single/married/families
	Visiting friends and relatives (VFR)	All categories
	Coach groups on tour	Older age group, more leisure dollars
	Honeymoon	Just married, mixed age group
Educational	Special interest	School groups Aged
Religious	Pilgrimage or church celebration	Religious groups of all ages and genders
Sports	Tour/competition End-of-season holiday	Mixed
Conference/ Convention	Work-related Personal development Education	Predominantly male Single/married
Entertainment	Theatre, opera, concerts	Depends on the production

the enterprise, whereas external factors, for example government regulations and seasonal influences, are beyond the control of the enterprise. How organisations respond to the factors that impact on them can determine their level of success.

Trends in tourism are an external factor that can impact on an organisation and influence how it operates. Why is it, for example, that two resorts, located in close proximity to each other and offering similar tourist products at similar prices, may have varying degrees of success as a business? Trends, fickle though they may seem, have a significant effect. A business must never forget that the customer has a choice.

Trends influence that choice. For example, we have seen a significant shift in our dining-out habits, which has taken us away from more conventional, formal styles of dining to the 'café' set, as the tables and chairs have tumbled out of the restaurants onto the pavements. The onslaught of the fast-food industry, changes in drinking habits and a new consciousness about what we consume in terms of health and diet are all trends that can have us frequenting one side of the street this week and crossing the road the next.

Some of the other factors that influence the operations of a tourism enterprise include:

Competition • With the deregulation of the airline industry, increased competition has forced competitors to offer better pricing and service levels.

Market needs, expectations and demand • Modern technology has increased customers' knowledge and understanding about what is available to them and thus influenced their choices of the products and services they buy.

Seasonality factor • Many tourism-based operations are influenced by seasonal weather conditions and changing climate patterns which are out of their control.

Location of the establishment • The location of an enterprise may make it more vulnerable to trends. It might also be affected by increased competition in the area.

Environmental issues • This is particularly relevant to tourism operations as the awareness of environmental issues increases. Environmental issues can also provide new marketing opportunities.

Economic growth • The strong economic growth in the 1990s influenced the level of spending by consumers on tourism-based experiences.

Industry regulations and legislation • Changes in regulations and legislation can affect a tourism enterprise both negatively and positively.

Availability of skilled staff • The attractiveness and location (city or regional) of the enterprise can significantly influence the availability of skilled staff.

Standard of service/working conditions • The standard of service and working conditions are determined internally. Failure to consistently achieve a high standard will negatively influence customer expectations and repeat business.

Pricing structure • Pricing structure, while usually determined internally, is also influenced by demand (for the service or product), supply costs, competition and location of the enterprise, among other things.

Financial support • This may be by the owners of the enterprise or government funding.

Products and services offered • These are selected by the individual enterprise but may be influenced by other factors such as location of the business and therefore availability of services and products.

Keeping up to date with trends and other important factors that affect the tourism industry is discussed in more detail later in the chapter.

QUALITY ASSURANCE

Like professionalism, quality is not a simple concept to define and is a very subjective issue. Quality can mean the degree of excellence provided, or a relative comparison of certain standards. Assurance, on the other hand, means that each time we buy or receive that same good or service we are assured of exactly the same standard. Quality assurance, therefore, could be said to be the control of the variations in the provision of goods and services to customers to ensure consistency.

Standards for quality vary throughout tourism operations. Some standards are aligned with minimum industry expectations while others are enterprise standards. An actual **standard**, or **standardisation**, is a minimum level at which output is to be produced to assure a consistent quality. By setting standards we are able to measure or judge the quality of the output against a predetermined level.

Standard* or *standardisation
The setting of a minimum level of performance for completing each task.

Successful organisations don't usually get that way by accident. They have in place systems and controls that consistently achieve the standards set. They work on a principle of continuous improvement in their performance and cultivate quality within the culture of the organisation.

Quality assurance programs are not new and are variously referred to as Total

Quality Management (TQM), Quality Management Systems (QMS), Quality Circles and Teams, and a range of other names. They all have a common theme and goal—providing quality products and services to consistently meet customer needs and expectations.

Quality assurance requires commitment to the quality process. To achieve quality, everything we do as an operation must be quality focused. We cannot buy high-grade products to sell today and expect customers to be happy tomorrow when we serve them second-rate products. What is the point of a fantastic marketing strategy if we cannot deliver the goods and services as promised? Quality must permeate the whole organisation, not just parts of it. Quality is also expected in everyone's work performance—in grooming, in attitude and in skills.

Our customers expect quality each time they visit: by our employers, who create an environment in which we want to provide quality service; and by our colleagues, who expect us to be equipped with the knowledge and skills to be a professional. Quality is expected of ourselves so we can achieve our career goals.

Cost of not providing quality:
· Time
· Money
· Loss of customers
· Lack of consistency

The importance of quality and quality assurance programs to tourism organisations lies in the cost of not providing quality. In other words, if we fail to consistently provide quality services and products we potentially waste time and lose money and customers.

QUALITY CUSTOMER SERVICE

As with any service we use—transport, retail, professional and so on—there is the expectation that the people offering that service are able to do so efficiently, knowledgeably, skilfully and courteously. For example, when we go to the doctor we expect him or her to be qualified, to identify the cause of our illness and to help us get well. When people use our services they expect us to be all of these things also—skilled, knowledgeable, courteous and efficient.

The expectation of this in the workplace is not restricted to our visitors or customers. Our colleagues expect it, as do our employers, and if we are unable to perform according to the established standards we are not meeting expectations, which may affect our employment.

If a product or service does not meet quality expectations, time and money will be lost. Customers will complain, the work may have to be done again or the product remade. The costs associated include excess labour, wastage and loss of customers and loss of business. Although implementation of a quality system is costly for an organisation, not establishing standards and a quality system can ultimately cost more. For example, a reputation for poor-quality service spreads quickly by word of mouth and hence impacts negatively on the business.

Remember, the reason for all this quality is the customer. There is a distinct difference between just providing services and being in the business of satisfying customer and client needs. Anyone can provide service, but not everyone can provide quality.

file this

▶ It is good business to attract customers but it is much better business to attract repeat customers.

1. According to the introduction to this chapter, what do we need in order to be successful in the tourism industry?

2. List five sources of tourism information. What sort of information might these sources provide?

3. In your own words, define 'tourism'.

4. What is the difference between a 'trip' and a 'visit'?

5. Why does a definition of tourism usually exclude business travel?

6. What is meant by the term 'tourism sectors'?

7. What is the relationship between tourism and hospitality? Tourism and travel operations? Tourism and visitor services?

8. What is a tourist?

9. Explain the difference between an 'inbound tourist' and an 'outbound tourist'?

10. Domestic tourism involves intrastate and interstate tourism. What is the difference between these types of tourism?

11. To what does the 'purpose of travel' refer?

12. How can the purpose of travel be useful to tourism operators?

13. What is the difference between internal and external factors that can influence a tourism operation?

14. How does competition influence an enterprise? The availability of skilled staff? The economic climate?

15. What is 'quality assurance'? Why do you think quality assurance in tourism-based operations is important?

16. Do you think quality assurance is important in the service industries? Why? Why not?

Economic impact of tourism

Tourism contributes significantly to the economic development of Australia, employing more than half a million people, either directly or indirectly, and generating almost $60 billion per year in revenue (Bureau of Tourism Research). This means tourism becomes a major factor in federal, state and territory government economic strategies, with unlimited potential as a growth industry. Due to the positive impact of tourism on the economy, the government is usually very willing to research, plan and promote it. Tourism will continue to expand, creating wealth and job opportunities.

Each state and territory can and does benefit from the promotion of their many attractions, tours and events that encourage visitors, irrespective of visitor origin, to generate a flow of spending in the community. Overseas visitors bring 'new' money into the economy when they exchange their foreign currency for Australian dollars and spend it at the destinations they visit. Hence, tourism is regarded as a service-based **export**, earning foreign currency that can, in turn, be used to invest or purchase **imports**.

Tourism operates under the same economic principles as any other market—demand and supply. Some attractions and events—Grand Prix, Olympic Games, festivals, AFL grand final, Mardi Gras—will always affect tourism trends, but permanent features such as the Sydney Opera House, Uluru, Kakadu, Phillip Island, the Barrier Reef and the Outback create ongoing benefits for the health of the economy through long-term employment and business opportunities, income, infrastructure, support services and more.

There is no disputing the positive impact that tourism has on the Australian economy, but distance from major tourist markets and cost have proved major obstacles to its growth. The exchange rate of the Australian dollar also has an effect on the demand for tourism services. In 1997 the onset of difficulties in many Asian financial markets impacted on Australia's tourism. For example, the devaluation in some Asian currencies not only boosted tourism to that country by Australian tourists (which took money away from Australian domestic tourism) but also caused a shift in the patterns of tourists visiting Australia from those countries. In the year 2000, on the other hand, the record decrease in the value of the Australian dollar against the American dollar and other major currencies made Australia a more affordable destination, resulting in an increased number of visitors from Europe and North America. In other words, their currency could buy more Australian dollars and became more valuable in Australia.

Naturally, each market segment will react differently to the economic trends, depending on length of stay, reason for travel and country of origin. For example, people travelling for business purposes usually stay only a short time but spend more per head, per night, than any other market. Backpackers are usually the longest in visitor nights, spending a small amount each day but the most overall as a result of the length of stay. Irrespective of the length of stay, however, all tourists will be affected by the value of their currency compared with the currency of their destination.

file this

▶ Visitors from the UK and Ireland usually stay longer, primarily because of distance travelled, but spend less than their Asian counterparts because they more often stay with friends and relatives.

Table 1.3 shows both the actual and the forecast arrivals from the main source markets (origin), as well as the forecast average rate of growth of international visitors.

file this

▶ Actual overseas visitor arrivals to Australia in 2000 were 4.88 million visitors with average annual growth over the next decade expected to be 7.8% (Tourism Forecasting Council, 2000).

TABLE 1.3 **Inbound tourism forecast**

			VISITOR ARRIVALS (THOUSANDS)					
YEAR	NEW ZEALAND	JAPAN	OTHER ASIA	EUROPE	NORTH AMERICA	REST OF WORLD	TOTAL PREVIOUS	CHANGE ON YEAR (%)
1991	480	529	389	531	325	117	2370	
1992	448	630	506	577	312	131	2603	9.9
1993	499	671	704	637	332	154	2996	15.1
1994	480	721	927	721	344	168	3362	12.2
1995	538	783	1118	752	363	171	3726	10.8
1996	672	813	1311	799	378	192	4165	11.8
1997	686	814	1350	874	394	200	4318	3.7
1998	709	751	1081	951	446	229	4167	−3.5
1999	729	707	1211	1072	495	245	4460	7.0
2000	**803**	**701**	**1351**	**1181**	**577**	**268**	**4882**	**9.5**
2001	**804**	**720**	**1520**	**1313**	**639**	**290**	**5288**	**8.3**
2002	**811**	**749**	**1723**	**1436**	**683**	**314**	**5715**	**8.1**
2003	**818**	**791**	**1963**	**1540**	**733**	**339**	**6184**	**8.2**
2004	**827**	**835**	**2214**	**1638**	**783**	**366**	**6663**	**7.7**
2005	**844**	**881**	**2493**	**1729**	**833**	**394**	**7174**	**7.7**
2006	**861**	**926**	**2798**	**1822**	**881**	**423**	**7711**	**7.5**
2007	**878**	**973**	**3132**	**1917**	**926**	**455**	**8280**	**7.4**
2008	**893**	**1020**	**3502**	**2014**	**972**	**488**	**8889**	**7.4**
2009	**907**	**1069**	**3912**	**2113**	**1015**	**524**	**9539**	**7.3**
2010	**918**	**1119**	**4365**	**2213**	**1055**	**562**	**10231**	**7.3**
Average annual growth (%) 1999–2010								
	2.1	4.3	12.4	6.8	7.1	7.8	7.8	

Numbers in bold are forecasts.
'Other Asia' includes all Asian and Middle East countries except Japan.

Source: Tourism Forecasting Council, 2001.

MULTIPLIER EFFECT

Many businesses within the tourism industry rely on each other to support their services and products, each generating a flow of spending through the community as a result of tourism. This flow of spending is called a **multiplier effect** and works in stages as the money is passed from one business to the next and on to the next as each supplies a different service or product to meet the initial demand from the tourist. It is not difficult to appreciate how large a contribution tourism makes to the economy as the money filters through these stages.

Multiplier effect
Flow of spending through the community as a result of tourism activities.

The stages of the multiplier effect do not necessarily flow in the same order each time and not all industries are going to benefit from every tourist or visitor. Also, it is not only tourists who support the tourism industry. People who travel for other reasons—such as on business, for a conference or for educational purposes—use the industry because of the need to travel away from home, creating a need for food, accommodation and other services and products while they are away.

EMPLOYMENT

In 1997/98 tourism was directly responsible for the employment of over 513 000 persons which was 6% of all those employed (Bureau of Tourism Research). This equates to 389 000 equivalent full-time jobs. The more visitors a destination attracts, the more people that are needed to service these visitors. As mentioned previously, the tourism industry is an umbrella of different sectors and numerous businesses and organisations and these businesses must continue to employ more people to service their growing number of customers. Many tourists in certain market segments, particularly within hotels and resorts, also demand very high quality service standards, which often means high staff-to-guest ratios.

Thus, tourism-based operations offer substantial employment opportunities, both ongoing and seasonal, in many destinations. This in turn improves the overall economic welfare of that area and generates a new flow of spending through the community, as the employees themselves often have to spend their income on a place to live, the use of local services and amenities and indeed also visit local attractions.

INFRASTRUCTURE DEVELOPMENT

To make any tourist destination functional, attractive and appealing for the visitor, the infrastructure of roads, bridges, airports, transport systems, telecommunications, water systems, waste disposal and so on needs to be developed and/or upgraded to a certain standard. This requires a massive investment in financial and human terms. Often tourism can act as a catalyst for this and can be of enormous benefit to local

file this

▶ Tourism employs 6% of the Australian workforce and represents 11.2% of total export earnings.

communities and residents as well as their visitors. Tourists also require accommodation and in 1998 $1.2 billion was invested in the construction of new hotels and similar establishments in Australia (Australia Bureau of Statistics).

check please

17. How does tourism contribute to the economic development of Australia?

18. What do we mean when we say that tourism is a service-based export?

19. In 2000 Australia was a more affordable destination for inbound tourists. How did this come about?

20. Explain in your own words the multiplier affect.

21. What relationship exists between employment opportunities and the tourism industry?

22. How is tourism infrastructure affected?

Social and cultural significance of tourism

The tourism industry is often described as a 'people industry', meaning that the very nature of the activity or the experience ensures that you will meet new people in new places. As workers in the industry we will also have plenty of face-to-face personal contact with our customers and clients, particularly the visitor or guest using our services. Even people who know each other well can often find out new things about each other when travelling together and sharing a tourism experience. Tourism actually encourages such social interaction, particularly when people are in holiday mode.

Tourism can also cause considerable social and cultural costs to a community. Too many tourists to a destination can cause overcrowding to the extent that local people feel their lives are being disrupted as access to services, facilities and sometimes even land becomes more difficult. However, such problems can be curtailed with more responsible planning, management and promotion of tourism. **Responsible tourism development** attempts to balance the needs of local communities with those of the tourists. It is the job not only of governments but of tourism professionals in the industry as well.

Responsible tourism development
Balancing the needs of local communities with those of the tourists.

BETTER QUALITY OF LIFE

The economic benefits of tourism (such as increased business activity, employment opportunities and improvements to facilities and infrastructure) can also be classed as social benefits as they help to improve the quality of life in local communities. Community pride can also be reinforced, as was witnessed at the Sydney Olympic Games of 2000, when Australians generally were proud to showcase their country, culture, attractions and facilities to the many visitors. The cultural heritage of a destination, expressed through its language, arts, crafts, food, wine, music, architecture and general historical development, can be viewed as part of an authentic tourism product and should be enhanced, maintained and preserved as part of a destination's tourism assets.

UNDERSTANDING OTHER PEOPLE

Cross-cultural understanding
Learning about and understanding other people's cultures and lifestyles.

The very nature of tourism means that there has to be a host–guest relationship. People travelling from their normal place of residence are bound to meet other people from different countries or regions within a country: fellow travellers, local residents or tourism and hospitality workers within the destinations visited. Tourism encourages us to learn about and perhaps attempt to understand the different lifestyles of other people. The depth and extent of such experiences will depend on the motivation for the travel. 'Cultural tourism' is a term used nowadays to describe the many tourists who wish to participate more fully in and learn more about other cultures and lifestyles. International tourism can help promote cross-cultural understanding, as is happening now between Australia and many of our Asian and Pacific neighbours.

Cultural differences are discussed in Chapter 3, 'Work in a socially diverse environment'.

check please

23. Briefly explain the social and cultural significance of tourism.

24. What is 'responsible tourism development'?

25. How can tourism result in a better quality of life?

26. Why is tourism called a 'people industry'?

27. How does tourism help us to understand other people?

Environmental issues for tourism

Some of the reasons tourists visit particular destinations is because of the climate, the natural scenic attractions and the unspoiled beauty. The natural environment is a major factor in making destinations attractive to visit. Many tourists seek a nature-based experience for their holiday as an escape from city-based life.

PROTECTING OUR ENVIRONMENT

Sustainable development
Balancing limited tourism use of sensitive natural environments with conservation management principles so that future generations may also enjoy these areas.

It is often argued that environmental assets are the very foundation for a tourist destination and should be developed and made more accessible for the enjoyment of tourists. Conversely, too much tourism development can have harmful effects on the fragile environments found in coastal areas, mountains, national parks or islands and should be protected at all costs. The challenge is to balance the use of such areas through careful planning, sensible management policies and proper conservation techniques. The term used to describe such an approach is **sustainable development**—achieving a balance between tourism development and natural environment protection to maintain the integrity of the area for future use. Limited development and certain types of tourism usage are allowed while the sensitive environment is protected for the enjoyment of present and future generations.

ECOTOURISM

Over the past decade a specialised type of tourism has emerged called **ecotourism**. The *eco* is short for ecological, which refers to the biological study of living organisms and their relationships with their surroundings. In simple terms, it can be defined as learning about the lifecycle of plants and animals, or **biodiversity**. Thus, ecotourism is the marriage between the local eco-systems (relationships between the natural environment and the life forms) and the desire of tourists to visit and enjoy these areas in a way that causes minimal harm. Ecotourism has also been more loosely described as 'green tourism', 'environmental tourism' and 'nature tourism'. Thus, ecotourism is concerned with maintaining the natural and cultural integrity of certain tourism areas.

Throughout the 1990s ecotourism grew from being a buzzword to an international movement promoting all types of travel to experience and learn about our natural surroundings. The Ecotourism Association of Australia was formed in 1994 to promote these ideals and to implement a code of practice for ecotour operators.

Although there are conflicting viewpoints as to what types of tourism products should use the term 'ecotourism', strictly speaking ecotourism as a special-interest tourism market should possess the following characteristics:

- be a nature-based experience;
- be low impact and small scale;
- promote a conservation ethic;
- support local communities; and
- provide a learning experience.

Ecotourism is an attempt to provide a link between the economic development of tourism and the conservation and protection of natural areas. It attempts to derive the economic benefits from tourism while helping people to appreciate, understand and protect our environment.

WASTE MANAGEMENT

Waste management refers to how we manage the disposal of the millions of tonnes of waste generated each year through tourism-based activities. Waste is anything that is no longer of any use in its current form.

Much of the waste we generate, however, can be recycled. This means that it can be converted into something new and thereby be of use again.

For most enterprises, as well as the benefits of managing waste effectively there is effort involved. This effort lies in educating staff and even users of the services and products to dispose of waste in a way that is thoughtful and intelligent. For example, organisations can provide facilities for sorting waste according to the following categories:

- plastic
- glass
- paper-based products
- biodegradable materials
- contaminated and non-contaminated waste

Waste management can also include the reduction of pollution generated by equipment and processes. This can be achieved by:

- maintaining plant and equipment regularly;
- using environmentally friendly cleaning products;
- reducing the frequency of changing and washing the linen used by guests; and
- using environmentally friendly packaging.

ENERGY-EFFICIENT OPERATIONS

'Energy' refers to those resources used by an enterprise to provide services such as heating, cooling and lighting. Electricity is primarily used to provide these services. Efficient and responsible use of energy resources helps reduce the potentially negative effects on our environment. It can also reduce operating costs for the enterprise. Other forms of energy include solar power and hydro and wind power, all of which are renewable (can be used again), cost effective (cheaper than electricity) and environmentally friendly.

Accordingly, many enterprises are introducing energy-efficient methods of operation. To help minimise negative environmental impacts, many facilities are converting to alternative power sources such as solar power. Some facilities also reduce their electricity usage with a power-source room key—the guest's room key is required to gain electrical power in the room. The key is inserted into a power slot in the room, thus turning the electricity on. When the guest leaves the room he or she removes the key from the slot, thereby switching off all services in the room that function through electricity, and unnecessary usage of electricity is avoided.

Logically, an awareness of environmental issues is beneficial for all—for tourism-based enterprises, for users of the services, facilities and products, and for the environment. Efficient waste and energy management reduces costs, protects the environment and saves our precious resources. As a greater awareness of these environmental issues develops, more and more people will use an enterprise's attitude to environmental issues as a selection criterion for using that enterprise's services and facilities.

check please

28. Why are environmental issues impacting more and more on tourism-based operations?

29. Why do you think it is important for us to protect our environment?

30. Ecotourism is a rapidly growing industry. Explain what ecotourism means.

31. What are the key characteristics of ecotourism?

32. What is 'waste management' and why is it increasing in importance?

33. What can tourism enterprises do to manage their energy resources more efficiently?

activity 1.1

► Compile an itinerary for an ecotour, outlining the types of attractions to be visited and the activities to be undertaken.

Major tourism industry organisations

The diverse nature of the tourism industry and its fragmentation into different sectors and even subsectors has seen the proliferation of tourism industry organisations and professional associations throughout Australia. Many are mentioned throughout this book and others are listed for your information in 'A few useful contacts' at the end of the book. Key tourism organisations in Australia include:

- Australian Automobile Association
- Australian Federation of Travel Agents
- Australian Hotels Association
- Australian Tourism Export Council
- Council of Australian Tour Operators
- Ecotourism Association of Australia
- Meetings Industry Association of Australia
- National Restaurant and Catering Association
- Pacific Asia Travel Association
- Tourism Task Force
- Tourism Training Australia
- United Federation of Travel Agents

Many of these organisations act as professional industry associations to advance their own causes and tourism in general. They will lobby state governments and the federal government to influence decisions on policy issues that tend to affect their members. They provide many business-networking opportunities through their annual conventions and various travel expos, business seminars and social events. They also help to promote excellence within the industry through annual tourism awards and support for industry training and accreditation schemes.

AUSTRALIAN TOURIST COMMISSION

The Australian Tourist Commission (ATC) is a statutory authority of the Commonwealth government and its main purpose is to market Australia overseas as a tourist destination. Under the *Australian Tourist Commission Act (Revised 1987)* the objectives of the commission are to:

- increase the number of visitors to Australia from overseas;
- maximise the benefits to Australia from overseas visitors; and
- ensure Australia is protected from adverse environmental and social impacts of international tourism.

The ATC works in partnership with tourism industry organisations and Australian states and territories to promote and sell Australia as a tourist destination. It does not undertake the marketing of specific tourism products on an individual basis.

STATE AND TERRITORY TOURISM COMMISSIONS

All Australian states and territories have their own tourism commissions which operate as government-funded statutory authorities or corporations. The state and territory governments are keen to maximise employment opportunities and other long-term benefits of tourism. The tourism commissions are responsible for marketing and developing their respective states and territories as competitive tourist destinations both nationally and internationally. They develop marketing strategies and campaigns to attract visitors from within Australia and overseas.

They are also involved in activities to stimulate investment in infrastructure projects, tourism product development (tours, special events, accommodation, attractions, major conferences and exhibitions) and tourism training programs in the major cities and regional areas.

check please

34. What is the role of professional tourism industry bodies?

35. What is the role of the Australian Tourist Commission?

36. Why do some organisations use the term 'tourism' in their title while others use the term 'tourist'?

37. Why are there state- and territory-based tourism commissions in addition to the ATC?

activity 1.2

▶ Visit the website of two state or territory tourism commissions and/or your regional tourism association. Find out what their roles and activities are. Check any differences.

Tourism career opportunities

Careers in travel and tourism are quite diverse and can include a range of employment areas spread between the private and public sectors. A more comprehensive overview is given in Chapter 9. Careers in the hospitality sector (accommodation, food and beverage outlets) are dealt with in our sister book *The Road to Hospitality* (Prentice Hall, 1999).

Although closely connected with the hospitality sector this section will deal mainly with the travel operations and visitor services sectors. The latter also includes the government-funded and/or government-operated tourism agencies. Refer to Table 1.1 on page 4 to review the sectors of the tourism industry.

SERVICES

Tourism is a service-based industry. Each sector offers different products and services; however, unlike goods or tangible products, a characteristic of service is its intangibility. That means we cannot physically touch or hold a **service**, and it is not something that can be stored for future use. A service is an action, an activity. It is a task performed by employees that contributes to the visitors' experience or the customers' comfort and enjoyment. It is something we do for the visitor or customer.

Each tourism sector also offers services that vary between enterprises within the same sector. These will depend on the market each enterprise is trying to attract, its location and the infrastructure already in place in that location.

Service is offered to clients and customers in the form of information. For example, retail travel agents provide information on destinations, tours and travel options. The service provided by visitor information centres relates to information about the region, attractions, events and facilities, among other things.

Services
Intangible products that cannot be touched, seen or felt. Services have the potential to lack consistency and a great potential for variability.

TRAVEL OPERATIONS

The travel sector includes those companies and businesses that manufacture, promote, sell and distribute travel products. These include retail travel agents, inbound and outbound tour wholesalers (also called tour operators) and transport operators like airlines, cruise lines, coach companies and railways. It is important to understand the roles of each of these travel companies in order to understand how the travel product is distributed to the consumer (tourist). The three main players in the distribution chain are:

- principal—the owner and/or operator of a travel/tourism product or service (an airline, hotel chain, theme park, island resort);
- tour wholesaler—company that purchases tourism products and services (airline seat, hotel bed, travel insurance, airport transfer, car rental and theatre ticket) from the principal and packages them into a single tour product for sale normally through a retail travel agent; and
- travel agent—retail intermediary who links the suppliers of travel and tourism products with the consumer through travel advice, reservations and ticketing services for direct sale to the consumer.

Career paths for retail travel agents are defined in the Australian Travel Agents Qualifications (ATAQ) program introduced in 1992. The levels include:

- Australian travel consultant
- international travel consultant
- senior travel consultant
- travel sales supervisor
- travel manager

People progress through these levels as they gain on-the-job experience and a level of competency together with successful completion of examinations at certificate and diploma levels. Transport operators, particularly airlines, who sell direct to the public also employ people with these qualifications.

VISITOR SERVICES

This sector comprises a host of companies, businesses and organisations that are involved in attractions management (including special events), tourist information services, tourism agencies involved in destination marketing and those involved in promoting the **MICE market** (meetings, incentive travel, conferences and exhibitions). State and local governments play a significant role in many of these activities. Regional tourism associations are now partnered with private tourism operators and local councils to develop and promote their particular regional destinations.

SALES AND MARKETING

Everything an enterprise does to promote itself can be considered a sales and marketing activity. This includes sending staff out to call on potential clients, special offers, brochures, displays, paid advertisements, public relations exercises, sponsorship deals and business cards—or almost anything that brings a name, brand, services or facilities to the attention of the public.

The sales and marketing department coordinates these activities to ensure maximum exposure to the target market in line with the objectives and goals of the organisation. They usually liaise with other departments to determine suitable activities but are primarily responsible for increasing sales through attracting new and repeat business.

POLICY AND PLANNING

With the continued involvement of all levels of government in Australian tourism there is always a need for tourism policy analysts and technical advisers. Tourism policy and planning refers to the way governments regulate and legislate for the development of the tourism industry. Governments provide direct support for market research and the collection and analysis of statistics for use in the planning of tourism projects and programs. State and territory governments and many local governments are also involved in stimulating and facilitating investment opportunities to develop tourism projects, facilities and services.

THE PROFESSIONAL WORKER IN TOURISM

There are many definitions of a 'tourism professional'. The reason for this is because the requirements placed on staff vary within the industry in terms of the organisation's size, sector type, the services provided and target markets. Any definition must, however, include a focus on the customer.

One definition of a tourism professional that attempts to encompass all aspects is 'someone who is able calmly, courteously and effectively to meet customer needs and expectations while maintaining or achieving the objectives of the organisation'. They should at all times be ethical, honest, considerate and efficient in the performance of their duties, and demonstrate a complete adherence to the **service ethos**.

Service ethos
The outstanding qualities, attributes and characteristics a tourism professional inherently possesses in the delivery of service to customers.

PERSONAL ATTRIBUTES

The debate surrounding the desired personal attributes of the tourism professional is very subjective. What is acceptable to one organisation may not resemble the expectations of another. Usually, the target market of the enterprise will dictate the expectations, but an essential quality of all service professionals is the ability to communicate effectively and provide service in a timely and helpful manner.

Knowledge of the product we represent is usually also an essential requirement. The qualities that are of most value to an employer are dedication, honesty and a positive attitude and excellence in personal presentation. Chapter 2 discusses many of these attributes in detail.

check please

38. Who are the three main players in the distribution of the travel product? How do their respective roles differ?

39. Why are governments involved in tourism?

40. What types of businesses are involved in 'visitor services'?

41. What role does a sales and marketing department play in a tourism enterprise?

42. What is tourism policy and planning and why is it important to tourism?

43. In your own words explain what is meant by a 'service ethos' and how this relates to tourism professionals.

44. What essential qualities should all tourism professionals possess?

Legislation and tourism

Various courts and parliaments make laws in Australia. Local government or councils make rules, regulations and by-laws. Laws governing the operation of every tourism-based operation are enforced in each state and territory. And while the laws at state level may vary in detail, they are fundamentally the same.

The laws bind employers and employees, which means that penalties can be imposed on individuals or organisations for breach of any law.

Where an employer has a **duty of care** for the public their liability is extended to the actions of their employees. This is called 'vicarious liability'. A duty of care is the responsibility one person has for the safety and wellbeing of another.

Controls are in place for a variety of areas including those listed below. For specific information refer to the relevant legislation and regulations in your state or territory.

CONSUMER LAW AND TRADE PRACTICES

Laws that regulate trade exist to protect the rights of the consumer, who is defined as a person who purchases goods and services. Legislation provides for the way an organisation conducts business and guards against unfair practices (including fraud and unsafe products, anti-competitive practices or misrepresentation of goods and services) and lists penalties and remedies.

Consumer rights are protected by the *Trade Practices Act 1974* (Commonwealth) and the Sale of Goods Acts (Goods Act in Victoria) in each state and territory. The primary difference between state and Commonwealth legislation is that state legislation regulates all transactions for goods and services, including those available for resale, at a state or territory level. However, where similar regulations exist between the state and Commonwealth legislation, Commonwealth law overrides the state-level law.

The Trade Practices Act regulates business dealings between consumers, competitors and suppliers operating in the Australian marketplace. The Act's main aims are to:

- prevent anti-competitive competition;
- promote fair trading; and
- protect consumers.

INDUSTRIAL RELATIONS

A slightly different approach to industrial relations exists in each state and territory. The primary objectives are the recognition of rights and duties of employers and employees as defined by the relevant **awards, enterprise agreements, industrial agreements** or **Australian workplace agreements**, and other legislation that impacts on the workplace, such as occupational health, safety and hygiene.

In November 1996 the federal parliament passed the Workplace Relations Act. This Act provides for major reform to the federal industrial relations system. The objectives of the Act are extensive but aim to provide 'a framework for cooperative workplace relations, which promotes the economic prosperity and welfare of the people of Australia'. Many workers in the travel operations sector are members of the Australian Services Union (ASU). This **'trade' union** monitors the awards and conditions of its members and can also assist with enterprise bargaining agreements.

OCCUPATIONAL HEALTH AND SAFETY

Legislation for occupational health and safety (OHS) has as its purpose the safety and protection in the workplace of all employees and extends this protection to the general public. OHS legislation provides a framework for employers within which to develop a safe and healthy work environment. Overseen by state and territory WorkCover authorities, the provisions in the Act allow for flexibility in meeting obligations to account for the varying conditions in the workplace and the types of work carried out.

The OHS legislation is guided by three principles: prevention (safety rules); workers compensation for work-related injuries; and rehabilitation (treatment and retraining).

EQUAL EMPLOYMENT OPPORTUNITY

This legislation impacts on industry on two levels—in employment and in the provision of goods and services. Equal employment opportunity (EEO) is designed to ensure that people are not discriminated against on irrelevant characteristics. In other words, employment opportunities must be granted on merit, irrespective of gender, race, religion, sexual preference, disability, nationality and so on.

In the workplace, two of the most important pieces of legislation concerning equal opportunity are the *Federal Affirmative Action Act 1986*, which aims to promote opportunities for minority groups (primarily women) based on merit, not on gender or other discriminatory factors, and the anti-discrimination legislation enacted in each state. This legislation extends to the provision of goods and services and makes it illegal to discriminate based on race, age, marital status, gender, sexual preference, religious beliefs and so on, except where allowable under legislation. An example where it is allowable is the refusal of service of alcohol to a person under the age of 18.

TRAVEL AGENTS ACT

Most retail travel agents and tour operators providing travel services are now required by law under the Travel Agents Act (1974 and 1986 NSW, 1985 WA, 1986 Vic and

SA, 1987 Tas, 1988 Qld and ACT) to hold a licence to conduct such a business. This Act is administered in most states and territories by the Department of Consumer Affairs and was introduced to protect the travelling public after numerous rorts and scams by unscrupulous operators led to a public outcry. According to Cordato (1999), the Act has three main purposes:

1. to set standards of experience and qualifications for members of the travel industry and to set professional standards in management and marketing for travel agents and tour operators;
2. to set continuing financial requirements in conducting their business as travel agencies; and
3. to protect the public's money by setting up a Travel Compensation Fund to compensate the members of the public who lose money through the default of a travel agent or tour operator.

To obtain and retain a travel agents licence it is necessary to be a member of the Travel Compensation Fund by way of an annual contribution payment. When purchasing travel services or products it is still advisable to check that the travel agent has their licence displayed and has some form of accreditation from a professional tourist industry body.

OTHER RULES AND REGULATIONS

There are numerous other rules and regulations that impact on tourism-based operations. These vary depending on the types of operation and the sector. It is beyond the scope of this book to discuss all legislation affecting every sector, but in general other legislation affecting various sectors of the tourism industry includes:

- liquor licensing controls
- gaming regulations
- public health legislation (Health Act, Food Act)
- accident compensation
- innkeepers Act

Keeping in touch with industry trends

Now that we know the sort of general information we need to perform effectively, irrespective of the sector we work in, it is important to keep up to date with changes that may affect us in relation to tourism. Change takes the shape of customer preferences, business practices, new legislation and social or economic trends, among others, as we saw earlier when we discussed factors affecting tourism.

Trends develop for a variety of reasons and, as we have seen, with a range of influencing factors. A favoured destination, a particular attraction or even a special event may be a trend. Next year, those trends may change. Marketing plays a significant role in creating and sustaining trends, as does demand by the target market. That is, having created a trend, it is only sustainable through demand. And demand will only be maintained while expectation is met (or until a new trend begins).

Identifying trends is often a confusing aspect of the industry that can make the difference between success and failure for an enterprise.

Discrimination
This occurs when one person is treated less favourably or differently from another in the same situation based on a difference between the parties. This difference may include race, sexual preference, gender or another characteristic that has no relevance to the situation.

check please

45. What is a 'duty of care'?

46. What is meant by vicarious liability? Do you think vicarious liability is a fair practice or expectation?

47. How are consumer rights protected at the state level? Commonwealth level?

48. What does the Trade Practices Act regulate? What are its main aims?

49. Describe the difference between an award and an enterprise agreement.

50. How might Australian workplace agreements affect the tourism industry?

51. Briefly outline how equal opportunity legislation and the Workplace Relations Act impact on the tourism industry.

52. What is the purpose of occupational health and safety legislation? What are the three principles of this legislation?

53. Give an example of allowable discrimination.

54. What are the three main purposes of the Travel Agents Act?

55. Why do you think it was necessary to introduce legislation requiring travel agencies to hold a licence to conduct business?

56. List four other types of legislation that may affect various tourism industries and give an example of the type of business that may be affected.

Keeping in touch with trends, innovation, change and other influences on the industry requires staying in touch with the sources that report on the industry. Working in the industry will give us access to certain information that keeps us current. Membership of industry bodies, such as those listed at the end of this book, will also keep us up to date. If unsure, ask questions. Someone will know the answer.

Other substantial sources of timely and relevant information are the industry sector associations who publish regular newsletters, and various trade magazines and the daily newspapers in each capital city. Many newspapers dedicate a section to tourism and/or travel on a weekly basis.

It would not be a practical exercise to source and read every available piece of information relevant to tourism. However, to stay in touch and gain benefit from what we do have time for, it is necessary to identify and analyse the relevant information for the sector in which we work and how changes impact on our area of expertise.

ACCESSING TOURISM DATA

Earlier we learnt that to find out more about the tourism industry we need first to source information. Sources of information come from a variety of areas, such as the media, books and the Internet. Because most of the information we need has already been collected and analysed, it is referred to as **secondary sources**. **Primary sources** include research that requires us to collect the information (usually through interviews and questionnaires) and analyse it ourselves. There are three major secondary sources of information that can assist us in researching the tourism industry:

- Australian Bureau of Statistics
- Bureau of Tourism Research
- Tourism Forecasting Council

The **Australian Bureau of Statistics** (ABS) is the Commonwealth government agency that collects and collates data for all industry categories, including the tourism industry. In particular, data can be accessed on visitor numbers, tourist accommodation, occupancy levels and expenditure. In 2000, the ABS introduced the Australian Satellite Account for Tourism, which provides for a more accurate reporting on the economic contribution of tourism in terms of total consumption figures, gross domestic product, employment and export earnings.

The **Bureau of Tourism Research** (BTR) was established in 1987 and is an intergovernmental agency administered through the Commonwealth Department of Industry, Science and Resources. It conducts national travel and tourism surveys, in particular the International Visitor Survey (IVS) and the Domestic Tourism Monitor (DTM). The bureau undertakes detailed analysis of tourism markets, economic research into the tourism industry and special studies on the outlook for tourism. These statistical and market research reports are made available to the tourism industry at a nominal charge.

The **Tourism Forecasting Council** (TFC) was established in 1993 to provide present and potential tourism investors, tourism operators and governments with forecasts of activity across all tourism sectors including domestic, international and outbound tourism. It builds on the data supplied by the ABS, BTR and other industry associations and specialists to predict future trends in the tourism industry.

USING THE INFORMATION

The information collected is used in a number of ways by tourism enterprises, primarily for planning future activities, and is usually shared with customers and colleagues. For example, a tour operator offering guided tours to Yulara may want to know how many tourists visit Uluru each year, from where they originate, how much they spend, how long they stay, their demographics and their accommodation and transport preferences. This information can assist in the planning of future tours to the region, the prices charged, how long each tour will be, frequency of departure, accommodation options, market segments to target and a number of other factors.

If, on the other hand, a retail travel agency specialising in 'adventure' holidays wanted to find out which destinations or specific adventure activities were increasing in popularity, they could find this information out through research. In turn, they could promote that destination to its target markets, through various marketing activities.

Your skills and knowledge about the tourism industry is most useful when you have an opportunity to share it. In tourism, our customers and clients are seeking as much information about tourism as possible in order to make informed decisions about the destinations and attractions they visit, the types of accommodation venues they stay in and the types of activities they are likely to participate in. Our role is to provide the knowledge and information to help them with these decisions.

57. Keeping up to date with changes that may affect the sector we work in is an important part of effective performance. What types of changes are likely to affect the tourism industry?

58. List three organisations that provide us with up-to-date information.

59. Give an example of how this updated information may be used.

Work with colleagues and customers

CHAPTER 2

LEARNING OUTCOMES

On completion of this chapter you will be able to:

- define interpersonal skills and state their relevance to the tourism industry;
- recognise the need for and develop effective communication in the workplace;
- explain the three components of effective communication—verbal, vocal, visual;
- explain the principles of non-verbal communication and its relevance to effective communication in the workplace;
- explain how we develop effective listening skills;
- describe the barriers to effective communication in the workplace;
- demonstrate a high standard of personal presentation;
- describe the key features of teams and team development and state the importance of teams in the workplace;
- define who our customers are and identify how we meet their individual needs; and
- identify and manage customer dissatisfaction.

This chapter complies with the Tourism Industry National Competency Standards, unit THHCOR01A, 'Work with Colleagues and Customers'.

Communication is more than just talking; it involves all of our senses—sight, sound, touch, taste, smell—and the more senses we use the better we are able to communicate our message. Most of us assume that 'talking' means we are communicating, and while talking is a form of communication, it doesn't mean that effective communication has in fact taken place.

Communication, to be successful, must be two-way. Communication is about passing information from one person to another. It can be up or down, as in a chain of command, or sideways, as in a conversation with a friend. Effective communication exists when what is passed from one person is received by another as intended. It is most readily received if it is relevant to the receiver's needs and interests.

Communication takes place every day between a variety of people and in various ways. Its effectiveness is often determined by how we communicate and the relationship we have with each person with whom we communicate.

Whichever way we look at it, communication is about someone sending a message, and the receiver indicating—by giving us feedback—that the message is understood. Or is it?

Defining and acquiring interpersonal skills

paint a picture ▶ **Interpersonal skills**

David and Rani wanted to book a cruise for their honeymoon, and decided to use their local travel agent who had been advertising in their local paper. As they walked into the agency, one of the consultants was talking on the telephone, staring out the window, and the other two were at the back of the office having coffee and chatting. Both of them looked at David and Rani then back at the first consultant before returning to their conversation. The first consultant was clearly exasperated with the caller and was saying 'Look, we can only go by what the reps tell us, I didn't realise that it was so bad'.

When she hung up, she looked at David and Rani and said 'Some people!'.

How do you think you would feel in this situation?

WHAT WE SAY OR HOW WE SAY IT?

Our ability to communicate effectively is measured not so much by what is said but by how we say it, and by our actions or behaviours. Communication skills are a part of our overall interpersonal skills, which underpin our working life. What has the receptionist above demonstrated in terms of her ability to communicate effectively with other people?

Let us put interpersonal skills into a tourism perspective. Tourism is a 'people' industry. We can work in it, play in it, dabble in it, use it, love it and many of us make a career from it.

Tourism professionals are required to use every ounce of their energy to please, to perform, to satisfy, to pacify, to assist and to serve customers. (In this text, the word customer can be interchanged with guest, client or visitor, according to the context in which it is used.) Our ability to achieve this ideal of 'being all things to all people' depends on our interpersonal skills.

Interpersonal skills are, therefore, defined by our actions, words, personal presentation, behaviour and ability to communicate in the workplace with colleagues and customers. We achieve this through our work, both as individuals and as team members.

Interpersonal skills
Skills required by all tourism professionals that enable us to communicate and interrelate effectively with others.

CHOOSING TO BE EFFECTIVE

We can choose to be effective communicators. We know how to groom ourselves, speak, read and write, and we know the difference between appropriate and inappropriate actions through *learning* these behaviours. We learned these skills from our parents, from friends at school and from colleagues and associates at work. All our behaviours are therefore ultimately by choice. This means that not only can behaviours be learned and unlearned but they can be developed, and this includes our communication behaviours.

In the workplace, we demonstrate our interpersonal skills through our attitudes and assertiveness, our self-confidence and open-mindedness. What skills we lack, we can develop. Some of the communication behaviours (interpersonal skills) we can develop include:

- effective communication through body language (non-verbal communication) and listening skills;
- improved personal presentation, through poise, deportment and personal hygiene;
- being polite and courteous;
- teamwork; and
- effective social interaction.

It is how we use these skills that determines their effectiveness and impact on others, and it is our successful application of these skills in the workplace that determines our professionalism.

The strategies for developing interpersonal skills need not be complicated; however, they do require honest self-evaluation and an acceptance that change may be required in some of our behaviours.

DEVELOPING INTERPERSONAL SKILLS

Improving our interpersonal skills takes time and effort. However, having recognised a need and acted on it, we are able to improve on one of the most essential skills for a tourism professional—effective interpersonal communication.

Our interpersonal skills can be developed through:

- formal study or short courses;
- workplace experience and observation;
- mentor programs; and
- personal development.

check please

1. 'Our ability to communicate effectively is measured less by what we say than by how we say it.' What does this statement mean?

2. What are interpersonal skills? Why are interpersonal skills important for tourism professionals?

Workplace communication

Internal customers
Those people in our organisation with whom we interact, such as our colleagues.

External customers
Those people outside our organisation with whom we interact, including paying or potential customers or clients.

Workplace communication is between ourselves and our colleagues, whom we refer to as **internal customers**; and between ourselves and customers or clients, whom we refer to as **external customers**. Even if we do not have direct contact with customers (e.g. we work in accounts), every day we will deal with someone who does (e.g. a travel consultant). Therefore, effective communication skills are required no matter where we work.

The concept of *internal* and *external* customers is certainly not new, but reinforces the idea that every role in tourism can potentially impact on customer expectations and satisfaction with their tourism-related experiences.

Effective communication in the workplace promotes goodwill, trust and personal satisfaction between everyone and can contribute to the quality of our working life. It builds respect and rapport between employers, employees and customers and creates a more team-oriented environment.

file this

▶ If you are not serving a customer, remember, you are probably serving someone who is—the same level of professionalism should extend to every person.

STAGES OF COMMUNICATION

All models of the communication process aim to provide effective communication through the correct use of the model's various stages.

Stage 1 The sender. This is the person sending the message. How this person communicates is determined by the influences on them, including education, self-image, background, family and friends, attitude, feelings and emotions and so on.

Stage 2 The message. This is the link between the sender and the receiver. The message is passed from one to the other by means of a *channel*. A channel used for delivering a message may be written, verbal, non-verbal or a combination of all three.

Stage 3 The receiver. This is the person receiving the message. Like the sender, the influences on the receiver determine interpretation, as does the channel used. It is not necessarily relevant whether the receiver agrees with the message or likes the channel that has been used; what is important is that the message is understood as intended.

FORMAL, INFORMAL OR THE GRAPEVINE

Communication in the workplace can be both formal and informal. **Formal communication** is usually structured and will include information passed on through accepted channels such as memos, letters, procedures, policies and meetings. Examples of these forms of communication are shown in Chapter 5, 'Perform clerical duties'. It can travel *down* through the channels, such as from supervisor to employee, or *upwards*, as from the employee to the supervisor. It may also travel *laterally*, that is, sideways, as between two colleagues.

Informal communication is generally unstructured and the information is communicated orally. Although this is an accepted channel, it is often harder to follow up. Informal communication may include messages, instructions or the passing-on of general information. It can also flow up, down or sideways.

Of course, informal communication is also what takes place as a general conversation. This can be considered gossip, or the grapevine. It may be simple banter between two colleagues or a discussion with a customer.

The **grapevine** is an informal communication channel whereby information is passed on by word-of-mouth. The general perception of the grapevine is that it is a negative aspect of communication in the workplace. However, it can be an effective means of communicating information quickly.

Unfortunately, with gossip or the grapevine, by the time the information travels around the organisation once or twice, it has probably been embellished, altered and adulterated. In situations where a lot of gossip exists or an extensive grapevine is working, there is a clear indication that poor communication between the parties exists. Establishing effective channels for the distribution of relevant and timely information can stifle speculation and reduce the gossip.

Formal communication
Structured communication such as letters, memos, procedures, etc.

Informal communication
Information communicated through unstructured means, such as that which is communicated orally.

Grapevine
Informal communication channel. The information is often not reliable or accurate.

---

check please

3. Why do we consider internal customers as important as external customers?

4. What is meant by 'If you are not serving a customer, you are probably serving someone who is'?

5. What factors influence the stages of communication?

6. What is meant by the *channel* when communicating? Give examples.

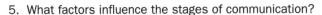

Effective communication

Effective communication can be *oral* (verbal, vocal, visual) or *written* (writing and reading). Which one we use will depend on the situation. Most information communicated in the workplace will be oral *and* written. For example, a customer who makes a reservation on the telephone may later receive a letter of confirmation. A departmental meeting will be oral but the agenda and subsequent minutes will be written. Job-related instructions can be communicated orally but the procedure is usually written in policy guidelines or procedures manuals.

quick thinker

▶ Write down the names of three people with whom you regularly communicate and how you communicate. What channels are used? Do you always understand what is communicated to you? If not, how do you go about clarifying the meaning of the information?

ORAL COMMUNICATION

Every time we speak, three elements of communication are involved which must be synchronised to convey the same meaning:

1. The *verbal* element is what we actually say—the message, the words.
2. The *vocal* element is how we say it—our tone, our pitch, our accent, our diction.
3. The *visual* element is what the receiver sees—posture, facial expression, movement.

If these elements do not convey the same message, at the same time, then the message may not be believed and communication has not been effective.

REFINING OUR VERBAL COMMUNICATION

Verbal communication is the *what* component of speech. That is, it relies on the *words* used to communicate the message.

Most industries have a language peculiar to themselves, and this is also the case with tourism. While it is important to learn the jargon, there are times when its use is not appropriate and when it may act as a barrier to effective communication. For example, it is usually not appropriate to use jargon with customers and often it is inappropriate to use jargon when a new colleague begins work, as the newcomer may not have yet learned what it means.

For example, a customer has just booked a flight for two people to Los Angeles. The travel agent, following procedure, confirms the details with the customer: 'Mr Jenkins, I have booked QF 123 for two pax departing 16.45, arriving LAX at 23.50 on the 13th of November'.

How much of this information do you think the customer understood? Do our customers know that the international airline code for Qantas is QF? Do our customers know that 'pax' is industry jargon for 'passengers'? Do our customers know that LAX is the international airport code for Los Angeles airport? And do all customers understand the use of the 24-hour clock? Probably not.

Effective communication in this case would have resulted if the travel agent had said: 'Mr Jenkins, I have booked Qantas flight number 123, for two people, departing at 4.45 pm, arriving in Los Angeles at 11.50 pm on the 13th of November'.

When we speak we do not want to risk offending and alienating customers or colleagues by the words we use. Therefore, we need to:

• speak clearly;
• avoid slang and jargon;
• develop our vocabulary;
• make the content appropriate and relevant; and
• put the words in the correct context.

REFINING OUR VOCAL COMMUNICATION

Vocal communication is the *how* component of speech. Vocal communication includes our voice projection, tone, pitch, speed and breathing techniques. Although the words are important, how we say them is often more important. We should:

- vary our tone to give the words emphasis or appropriate meaning;
- be aware of the pitch—put in context to the situation;
- project our voice as much as is necessary for clarity and for it to be heard;
- speak at a consistent speed (not too fast and not too slow) to aid understanding; and
- remember to breathe! If we forget to breathe, the words don't come out!

It is very easy to speak down to, or become impatient with, people who may not immediately understand the message being communicated. It is important to take some responsibility for this lack of understanding, as it may be us who are not being clear (see Figure 2.1).

FIGURE 2.1 *ONE-WAY COMMUNICATION*

REFINING OUR VISUAL COMMUNICATION

The *visual* element of communication is arguably the most important element for getting the message across.

We are often unaware of the visual messages we communicate, so when interacting with others we need to ensure that the visual communication does not conflict with the verbal and the vocal. Visual communication includes our personal presentation and hygiene and specific body language, all of which will be assessed by the person with whom we are communicating. Therefore we need to:

- be aware of individual personal space;
- maintain eye contact and be aware of facial expressions;
- maintain strong posture and develop appropriate hand and body movements; and
- maintain a high standard of personal presentation.

Individual cultures respond differently to each of these elements. This is discussed in Chapter 3 in greater detail.

As with all skills and behaviours that are learned, the more we apply the techniques, the more confident we become and ultimately the more professional.

WRITTEN COMMUNICATION

Like verbal communication, effective written communication is reliant on the words we choose, how we express them, how we present them and the proper use of grammar. Written communication is only sometimes appropriate. Deciding when it is appropriate will depend on our judgement, skill, employer and, most importantly, the receiver.

paint a picture ▶ **Communication**

Nerida had recently been promoted to sales manager with a professional conference organiser. She was eager to impress and wanted to ensure that her communication was prompt and effective. She had always felt that morning sales meetings were a waste of time and that the time could be better spent out on the road selling the company's services. So she mostly communicated with her staff by e-mail. After a few weeks, Nerida was surprised to learn that many in her team were not bothering to read the information she sent and would regularly call her to seek clarification on issues covered in her e-mails.

Why do you think Nerida's team stopped reading her e-mails? What suggestions would you make to Nerida about how she could improve her communication skills?

Good written communication depends on several elements:

- clarity;
- conciseness;
- tone (serious, light-hearted, demanding);
- presentation;
- reason for writing;
- correct language (i.e. the words used) and grammar; and
- ability of the receiver.

If any of the elements are missing or could be misinterpreted, then written communication may not be the most appropriate way to deliver a message. The characteristics of people will determine how they respond to the different forms of communication. Many people like formal, written communication, whereas others prefer to receive information orally.

Irrespective of our preference for written or oral communication, much of the communication we send or receive during our careers will be written because it is a permanent reminder of what has been said and can always be rechecked as to its meaning.

The types of written communication include:

- personal or business letters;
- reports and proposals;
- business plans;
- facsimiles or e-mail;
- memorandums;
- stock orders;
- résumés and job applications; and
- policies and procedures.

Each type of written communication has formal and informal styles for presentation. Which one is chosen will depend on the context in which it is required. However we deliver written communication, it is important to:

- use appropriate words;
- date all correspondence;
- spell a person's name, title and company correctly;
- check that the address is correct;
- check the spelling and grammar—a good dictionary and thesaurus is essential (a computer spellchecker is not reliable because it does not notice if we have used the wrong word, only if we have spelt a word correctly); and
- determine if the tone is consistent with the message and proofread before sending—have we said what we mean?

Written communication and format styles are discussed in detail in Chapter 5, 'Perform clerical duties'.

---

file this

▶ Once something is communicated in writing, there is a permanent reminder of what we have said and when.

ELECTRONIC COMMUNICATION

With the rapid development of information technology, it is almost impossible to convey concisely the advantages and uses of computerisation. From a communicator's perspective, the computer age has effectively reduced the world to a manageable chunk of technology that fits snugly into our workplace or the privacy of our home. E-mail, the Internet and newer software all combine to meet or exceed our communication needs.

E-commerce
Conducting business transactions via the Internet.

Some of the most exciting applications now available revolve around the use of **e-commerce**, that is, doing business over the Internet (World Wide Web). Businesses can now display their products in a variety of ways, from static pictures to three-dimensional tours through sites. Hotel rooms, resorts, cruise ships and a variety of destinations can now be inspected in 'real time' (virtual) without having to rely solely on the word of travel consultants or promises in paper brochures. Consumers can select and purchase a holiday and receive receipts electronically, while businesses operating at their chosen destination can purchase almost everything they need over the Net as well. And although there is still only a small percentage of consumers who purchase tourism products this way, there is no doubt that the number will increase and hence we need to ensure that we understand the technology involved and how best to use it for our own benefit.

While technology will undoubtedly continue to astound and confound many of us, it will not replace the minimum skills required for effective interpersonal skills.

check please

7. Of the three elements of communication—verbal, vocal, visual—which has the greatest impact and why?

8. Why is written communication not always appropriate? Give two examples of when it is appropriate.

9. 'Once something is communicated in writing, there is a permanent reminder of what we have said and when.' What are the implications of this statement?

Non-verbal communication— body language

Body language is the non-verbal signals, movements and gestures we use to aid or hinder communication. The way people interpret our body language has a major impact on how they *hear* our message.

Interestingly, until recently many people denied the importance of body language as a factor in the communication equation. Thanks to extensive research by behavioural scientists and others, body language is now an accepted concept that all good communicators are aware of and understand.

TYPES OF BODY LANGUAGE

Body language is usually classified as either open or closed. *Open* body language indicates we are receptive to the messages being sent and is often an indication of our ability to communicate. Being receptive, however, doesn't always mean we understand! Open body language is identified through the gestures we make, and indicates that we are open to what people are saying and confirms (usually) what we are saying to our listener. Palms open and upwards, nodding, smiling, body facing sender/receiver, good poise and eye contact are all examples of open body language.

TABLE 2.1 **Some of the more basic signs of body language**

SIGNAL	MESSAGE	OPEN/CLOSED
smile	pleasure, happiness	open
frown	disapproval, anger	closed
shrugging shoulders	don't know, doesn't understand, don't care	closed
nodding head	yes, agree, understand	open
shaking head	no, disapproval, don't understand	closed

but it is not

By contrast, *closed* body language says we are not interested in the message or the person and is often indicated by arms crossed, legs crossed or by looking away. Closed body language does not necessarily mean that the receiver doesn't understand, just that they are not open to the message being sent.

Body language signals should not be interpreted in isolation, and we should take into consideration the diverse cultures in the workplace of both colleagues and customers because of variations in cultural interpretation that may influence the use of body language.

Most gestures or signals are usually accompanied by other gestures (or clusters) and a verbal message that allows us to interpret the message in its entirety.

All body language needs to be put into context in the same way as we do for other forms of communication. In the workplace, our body language will be different for each experience and will depend on who we are dealing with (i.e. colleagues or customers) and our relationship with them.

quick thinker

▶ Fill in the gaps for these body language signals:

SIGNAL	MESSAGE	OPEN/CLOSED
tapping finger	impatience, boredom	
crossed arms		closed
slouching	bored, tired, uninterested	
hands by the side	relaxed, listening	
rolling the eyes	disbelief or 'here we go again'	
maintaining eye contact		

What other body language signals are you familiar with?

FACIAL EXPRESSIONS

According to the Bible the 'eyes are the window to the soul'. Experts in the field of body language claim that the face is the window to the mind and it is 'possible to read someone's thoughts by looking at them'.

We can often tell from a person's face when they are happy or sad, surprised or shocked, in a bad mood, in pain, or whether they have understood what we have said or are entirely confused. When reading facial expressions, we rely on the eyes, mouth and expressions as well as the angle of the head. In context, we also interpret the hand gestures and other body movements. Many faces give away what the person is thinking, although some people master the art of controlling facial expressions so as to give no indication of their feelings or thoughts (poker faced).

PERSONAL SPACE

Personal space can be defined as the distance we require between another person and ourselves when we are interacting to feel comfortable. This distance will vary depending on who that person is, our relationship to them, the difference in our cultural influences, and the situation. We are usually more aware of personal space once someone has invaded it.

The closer our relationship is with someone, the closer we allow them to us physically. When interacting with people we don't know or don't like, we prefer them to remain further away from us. At these times, it is not unusual to see someone take an involuntary step backwards, or, if this is not possible, put a hand out to try to stop the person coming any closer.

Being aware of other people's space is an important part of effective communication. Experience will tell us how close we like to be to others and how far away we like others to be from us.

PHYSICAL CONTACT

A similar principle to personal space applies to physical contact. There are written and unwritten rules about what is appropriate or acceptable which vary from country to country, culture to culture and person to person when it comes to physical contact.

Of course, there are exceptions to these rules, for example if we are helping an elderly customer walk, shaking someone's hand or helping them to sit. The upper arm is usually acceptable for us to touch, but only if really necessary.

Body language is a complex process that requires time and experience to master. Understanding its complexities gives us an advantage in the communication stakes.

---

file this

▶ In relation to our customers we should generally be close enough so they can hear, and never touch them.

check please

10. What is the difference between open and closed body language? Give four examples of each.

11. Why should body language not be interpreted in isolation?

12. What do some of our facial expressions say about us?

13. Why is personal space an important consideration when interacting with customers?

Effective listening skills

Nature has given us one tongue but two ears, that we may hear from others twice as much as we speak.

Epictetus (Greek philosopher)

What is the difference between listening and hearing? Surely they are the same thing?

Hearing we can do without thinking. Hearing, as one of our senses, aids communication and often occurs unconsciously. Listening, however, needs concentration and requires us to actively participate in the communication process.

Listening is a learned behaviour and has many distinct advantages—it is polite, aids understanding, helps us make intelligent decisions, improves our vocabulary, helps us maintain an open mind and makes us better communicators.

quick thinker

▶ When someone is speaking to us, how do we let them know we are listening? When we are speaking, what do we expect of our listeners?

If we can identify the elements of communication—verbal, vocal and visual—we can determine when people are listening. Conversely, they will know if we are listening to them!

The visual response is often the most important indicator of whether or not we are listening:

- Are we looking at the speaker and focussing on them, paying attention?
- Are we offering feedback—nodding or shaking of the head?
- Are our facial expressions indicating understanding?

Verbal and vocal responses to the speaker are also clear indicators of listening:

- Did we get our message across without interruption?
- Does the listener ask questions to clarify meaning?
- Is the response what we expected? Is it appropriate?
- Are we allowed to finish our own sentences?

When we are listening:

- Do we actively work at listening and ask questions to clarify understanding?
- Do we judge the content, not the delivery?
- Do we listen for the real meaning, keeping our minds open?
- Are we concentrating on the listener and resisting distractions?
- Are we providing appropriate feedback?
- Do we let the speaker finish without interruption?
- Do we wait for the speaker to finish before formulating our response?

Barriers to effective communication

Barriers to effective communication are those things that inhibit or get in the way of communication. Apart from the background influences on the sender and receiver, there are many other reasons why there may be a breakdown in the communication process, whether oral or written. The breakdowns often occur because of interference during communication, which causes barriers.

Examples of interference include:

- Selective listening: we may 'tune out' because we are bored or we don't like what we are hearing—especially when the message doesn't confirm our views and attitudes.
- Jumping to conclusions about the meaning of the message: we think we already know what the message means.
- Inconsistency in the delivery of the message: the words chosen, the tone, context or channel may be inappropriate.
- Cultural differences: because of our different backgrounds, our understanding, interpretation and analysis of what is being communicated will vary.
- Lack of confidence: if we are not confident in what we are saying, or unsure of what we are hearing, people's understanding and interpretation will be affected;
- Physical barriers: this may include distance or people or objects that are between the sender and the receiver. It can also include a hearing disability.
- Lack of time: when we are in a hurry, we may not take the time to listen or deliver the message appropriately.
- Thought speed: because we talk at a different speed from how we think, we are often planning what we are going to say next while the speaker is still talking, so we may miss the meaning of what is said.
- Impatience: usually with others; this makes us poor listeners. The result is that the information 'goes in one ear and straight out the other'.
- Prejudice: personal prejudices affect our judgement in that we hear only what we want to hear. Prejudices can involve the way a person looks, speaks, acts, their culture, age, gender, sexual preference, colour, among others.
- Bad habits: these include doing something else while someone is trying to communicate with us. For example, when using the telephone, just because the person on the other end of the telephone can't see us doesn't mean they don't know if we are listening or not. Another bad habit is interrupting the speaker and finishing sentences for them.
- Noise: this can be other people around you, outside noise, music and so on.

OVERCOMING THE BARRIERS

Good communication is not very difficult but it does take practice to be an effective communicator, to break down the barriers and to ensure that the messages we receive and send are what are intended.

There are many other reasons why communication may fail to be effective. When we identify any of the above behaviours as our own, we are more easily able to overcome those barriers. Understanding the influences on the sender and receiver, selecting the correct channel and appropriate words or mannerisms, and using them in context to the situation, will place us well on the way to becoming effective communicators.

The first step to overcoming communication barriers is recognising that barriers do exist for each of us. Once we are aware of the barriers we are better able to overcome them. We may have recognised our own barriers from the list above, thought of others that are a specific barrier for us or had someone point them out for us. However barriers are recognised, it is important to make plans to overcome them. To succeed we need to set in place a conscious personal goal to change that behaviour. This is the second step to overcoming barriers.

The next steps involve an understanding of the influences on the sender and receiver, selecting the appropriate words or mannerisms and correct channel to communicate our messages and using them in context to the situation. This will help us become effective communicators and reduce barriers.

Standard
The minimum level of quality or output.

check please

14. Why is the development of effective listening skills an important quality in a tourism professional?

15. How can we break down the barriers to communication?

Personal presentation

First impressions are very important in tourism, as in any service industry, because both customers and colleagues demand a high standard of personal presentation and behaviour.

When people look at us, they immediately begin to form an opinion about us. This is their *perception* of who and what we are. They will perceive us as having a certain level of intelligence, personal standards, integrity and personality, based on how we look. This then impacts on the way we are received and treated.

Industry standards
Standards that are expected across the entire industry, irrespective of the sector. They will apply, for instance, in health, hygiene and safety issues.

quick thinker

▶ How we look is often the first chance we have to make an impression. It is important to make it a positive one. It is a moment of truth. What sort of first impression do you think you make?

PERSONAL PRESENTATION STANDARDS

Standards refer to the minimum required level of quality or output. In terms of personal presentation, we are talking about the way we look and present ourselves. There are minimum **industry standards** that apply with regard to personal presentation, and expectations that exist in specific organisations, which are **enterprise standards**. Standards vary between organisations and depend on location, style of operation, image and customer base.

Enterprise standards
Standards set by the individual organisation that determine the level or quality of service provided by the organisation.

PERSONAL PRESENTATION AND HYGIENE

Hygiene legislation, council regulations, codes of practice and food standards impact directly on tourism-related industries. Some of these regulations dictate personal hygiene standards that must be observed. However, many rules about personal hygiene are self-imposed. It is reasonable to expect, then, that we have sufficient professional pride to ensure that our personal presentation is of a high standard and is not offensive. We have influences, of course, but the biggest factor affecting personal presentation is societal expectations.

In tourism there can be no question about our personal hygiene because a high standard of personal hygiene is implicit in customers' expectations of us. Like our behaviour and communication skills, the way we look and smell is all part of the bigger picture when it comes to interpersonal skills.

GROOMING

Another way to think of personal presentation is grooming. Before we go to work, go to an interview, go to a party or just about anywhere else, we take the time to groom ourselves. Grooming is the attention to detail we give to how we look. When working in the tourism industry the standard of grooming and hygiene expected includes:

Bathing—To bathe or not to bathe? There is no doubt! A high standard of personal hygiene and grooming cannot be overestimated. Neglect in this area can have far greater implications than our colleagues not wanting to sit next to us at lunch!

Clothing—Do clothes maketh the person? Well, maybe, and certainly many establishments take considerable pride in how their staff dresses. A uniform is often an indicator of the standard of the enterprise and many organisations are noted for the style of uniform worn. Whether or not we have a uniform, however, is irrelevant to the presentation and cleanliness of our clothes. Like us, our clothes need a set routine for hygiene: they need to be regularly laundered and ironed, worn correctly and treated with respect. If a uniform is required it should be worn appropriately, with pride and not embellished. A name tag, if issued, is considered part of the uniform.

Shoes—Sadly, many people neglect their shoes, both in terms of purchasing good quality and in caring for them. There are certain aspects of tourism that make our feet potential injury targets. We may be on our feet for long periods (as a flight attendant, a tour guide or guest service officer in a theme park), things may be spilled on our shoes, they may get kicked or are just worn *ad nauseam*—all good reasons for taking care of our feet and wearing shoes that afford support and protection in the event of an accident. Polished shoes are an indication of our personal presentation standards and indicate our degree of pride in ourselves.

Hair—Clean shiny hair is a sign of good health. Constantly touching our hair is not only unhygienic but can be quite distracting to the person we are communicating with. If we have long hair, it should be tied back and off the face. Hair also needs to be washed regularly.

Hands—Our hands work very hard and keeping them in good shape is often difficult. Fingernails should be manicured and if nail polish is worn it should not be chipped.

Body odour—Bathing daily is essential in any service industry. So is the use of deodorant. However, perfumes and aftershaves can be unpleasant for others.

Oral hygiene—No one likes to admit they have ever had bad breath, but most of us have had it at some time. Good oral hygiene means cleaning our teeth at least twice a day and using a breath freshener, especially after eating and smoking.

16. People's perceptions of us often determine how we are treated. Why?

17. What is the difference between an industry standard and an enterprise standard?

18. What relevance does our personal hygiene have to our interpersonal skills?

Teams and team development

There exist a considerable number of definitions of what a team is, how it is formed and developed and its key features. However, whatever the definition, a team has as its main objective the achieving of a goal through the combined efforts of the members of that team. The discussion in this book on teams and team development is a very simplified version of the subject, on which more extensive research exists elsewhere.

Team spirit is inherent in successful teams. Team spirit means that members of the team encourage and support each other, working together to achieve their common goals. Team members who have team spirit demonstrate, through their actions, commitment to the other members, the job and themselves.

GROUPS

Teams are sometimes confused with **groups**, which exist in the workplace. Groups are a collection of people who are brought together with a common link or purpose. Groups can be *formal* or *informal*, and can strongly influence the performance levels of individual members. Each of us has a role to play in every group we belong to and each role contributes to the success of the group.

Formal groups are made up of people who work in the same department and have the same supervisor and perform similar duties. From this larger group, subgroups will develop and these are *informal groups*. Informal groups are composed of people who have similar tastes, ideals, personalities and so on.

The distinction between formal groups and informal groups is that in the former the members are forced together, whereas in the latter members are chosen. A group of any sort does not necessarily mean there is a team, however.

The effectiveness of all groups is dependent on the **group dynamics**, that is, the way people operate together and interact with each other.

Teamwork, on the other hand, is the collective effort of all to achieve the common goals. Teamwork depends upon several factors:

* common commitment and dedication to objectives;
* the right mix of technical and interpersonal skills;
* group cohesiveness and flexibility;
* effective communication skills;
* tolerance and understanding;
* honesty and trust; and
* motivation and morale.

Like a chain, a team is only as strong as its weakest link (member). If any of the factors is missing then the team becomes weak because of the interdependence of each team member.

Group
A collection of people in the workplace who are brought together because of a common link, for example similar skills.

Teamwork
When the members of a group collectively contribute to the achievement of goals set by the team.

TEAM DEVELOPMENT

We can throw a group of people together, toss in a bunch of goals, provide explicit instructions about the task to be accomplished, set the standard of quality to be achieved and even hold their hands, and say 'we have a team', but we would be mistaken. A team develops gradually; it evolves. A team has its ups and downs, finds the right track, loses it, and then finds it again. A team takes time.

STARTING OUT

A team usually starts out as a group. We are put together to achieve a goal—a project, a sales target, customer satisfaction, increased revenue. If, as a group, we are able to contribute to establishing the goals, already we are learning to interact with each other, and we feel ownership of this goal because we have contributed to its design.

During this early stage of team development we are establishing relationships with each other but we probably feel a little tentative about our role and contribution.

THE JOURNEY

Of course, we all possess skills, strengths and talents that contribute to the team's success. We also have weaknesses that can hinder progress. Teams work through stages whereby they determine who is best suited to complete what function. This is sorting out the roles we play. The interaction here is defined by the group's dynamics. There may be conflict, disappointment, frustration or even power struggles. But there will also be conflict resolution and respect for alternative points of view, as long as we keep in mind the purpose of the team—achieving the goal—and that everyone's input is important.

We can use our communication skills to resolve problems, deal with issues, make decisions and reinforce the team goals. We do this by sharing information, allowing all team members to contribute, acknowledging our own weaknesses and doing our best.

THE DESTINATION

Weeks, even months can go by before a group becomes a team. It takes time to find the right mix of skills for achieving each task, to settle into the roles and confirm the relationships. Eventually, though, teams gain strength, achieve a few minor goals on the way to the main goal and then, one day, we instinctively know where we fit, what is expected of us and that our contribution to the team is vital. We are one of the links, without which the team cannot be strong.

When teams are effective there is no doubt that the organisation will benefit and our work life will be considerably more enjoyable. When the work environment is pleasant, employees are generally happy. When employees are happy, the customer will benefit.

In all effective teams, trust, support and respect is shown within the team in day-to-day work activities. Cultural differences within the team are accommodated, tasks are completed within designated time frames and team members seek and offer help when required.

check please

19. What is 'team spirit' and how can it make a difference?

20. What is the difference between a team and a group?

21. Explain briefly the three stages of team development.

Putting our skills to good use— the customer

A customer is a person who pays for goods or services. In the tourism industry we also commonly use the terms 'guests', 'clients' or 'visitors' when referring to our customers.

A person who visits a tourism establishment for the purpose of dining, being entertained or seeking accommodation is often called a **guest**. By definition, guests are also customers because they pay for these services and products. A **client** or **customer**, on the other hand, may be someone who relies on our advice to assist in a buying decision, for example which countries to visit and which airlines and which hotels to use.

Our customers are drawn from a variety of markets and will choose an organisation according to their particular needs and wants.

Customer
A person who pays for our goods or services.

Client
A person who seeks our professional advice.

Guest
A person who visits a tourism establishment for the purpose of using its facilities and services.

---

file this

▶ 'A customer is not an interruption to our work—he or she is the reason for it.'

Anon.

One of the best ways to put into perspective the 'what and who' of customers is to consider our own experiences as a customer:

- Did we feel important and welcome?
- Were we assisted promptly and efficiently?
- Did we feel satisfied?
- What special needs did we have and were they met?

Excellence in service is achieved when the customers' perceptions of the service provided consistently meets or exceeds their expectations. This is generally achieved when all are working hard to provide service that is timely, courteous and efficient, through the use of effective interpersonal skills.

TAKING RESPONSIBILITY

The responsibility for the customers' satisfaction lies directly with us as the serving staff, through our ability to read the signals that every customer gives, indicating what they want, and being flexible enough to respond appropriately.

On the other hand, if a customer is dissatisfied, or conflict has arisen, we have a unique opportunity to turn that negative impression into a positive experience. Developing our skills in handling difficult situations takes practice. The success we have will depend on what the issue actually is, the skills we have to deal effectively with the situation and what an employer will allow individual staff to do to rectify a situation. If in doubt, seek assistance from colleagues or a supervisor.

SATISFYING CUSTOMER NEEDS

In order to satisfy customer needs we first have to determine what those needs are. Market segmentation will help identify some of those needs, but we must remember that each customer is an individual.

Customer expectations are affected by their cultural background, socioeconomic factors (how much they want to spend or can afford), their age, their personality or frame of mind and their areas of interest. Their expectations of our organisation will differ from their expectations of us.

Possible customer expectations of the *organisation* may include:

- professionalism;
- a pleasant atmosphere;
- cleanliness;
- safety (comfort) zone;
- good value for money (perceived);
- entertainment;
- familiarity with surroundings and the product; and
- quality.

Possible customer expectations of *us* include:

- excellent communication and interpersonal skills, including technical skills, diplomacy, patience and attention to detail;
- confidence, motivation, initiative and enthusiasm;
- good personal presentation;
- product knowledge;
- consistency in service; and
- individual attention.

file this

▶ One of the most important things we can do for customers is use their name! (And it's often right in front of us: on their luggage tag, on their credit card or, in group situations, on their name tag!)

It may be surprising to learn that many customers return to an establishment or operator because the individual service provider was able to meet their expectations, even if some of their expectations of the organisation weren't met.

Although our ability to provide good service may be affected in part by the guidelines of the enterprise, it often just depends on the individual's personal attributes.

file this

▶ If customer satisfaction is the final destination, we will only reach it through the journey of service excellence.

SPECIAL NEEDS

Every customer is special. However, some have needs that are unique to them. Initiative, sensitivity, flexibility and attention to detail will all contribute to the experience of these special customers.

CUSTOMERS WITH SPECIAL NEEDS

Customers with special needs include the disabled, children, women, visitors from other cultures and non-smokers. It is important that they are not treated differently just because they have special needs. We do, however, need to recognise they have special needs that must be accommodated and ensure that all those dealing with them are aware of their challenges (e.g. advising airlines that the customer is blind or deaf).

One of the most common mistakes made is to ignore or speak down to a customer with a disability because we don't know how to communicate with them or lack the confidence to try. Most disabilities we will encounter are physical; there may be nothing wrong with the intellect.

WHEELCHAIR USERS

Most tourism-based operations (accommodation venues, attractions, transport operators, etc.) today have excellent facilities to accommodate people in wheelchairs. If an establishment has stairs it will generally be required by law to provide a ramp for access. In restaurants a wheelchair will require more space than a chair and the customer will need more room to manoeuvre. Wheelchairs in planes need special consideration, as they do in ships, coaches and other forms of transport.

Be on hand to greet people with disabilities at the door, as it is very useful for them to have the door held open.

DEAF AND/OR MUTE CUSTOMERS

When communicating with deaf and/or mute customers remember to look directly at them. Always speak clearly and slowly. Visual communication is important with all customers, but especially with customers who are deaf. The process can be aided with gestures and written notes; however, be specific. We cannot make the usual assumptions made with other customers. Even if there is a third person translating, it is appropriate to look at the deaf customer when talking about them; it is also not necessary to yell!

BLIND CUSTOMERS

Instructions for blind people need to be even more precise because they do not have the benefit of the visual aspects of communication. It is not sufficient to say that the door is 'over there on the left' with a sweeping motion of the arm! Let the blind person take your arm if you are leading them. Don't be afraid to use words like 'see' and 'saw'. When guiding a blind person, indicate not only that there is an obstacle or steps to be navigated, but say how many steps there are or how to get around the obstacle. If the blind person is travelling alone they will require many different written items to be read to them. Also, don't be afraid to ask the customer if they would like any particular item made available for them.

Contracts, itineraries, reservation information and other written forms of communication need to be read to blind people.

CUSTOMERS USING WALKING AIDS

Sometimes walking aids are permanent, such as a walking frame or an artificial leg, or they may be a temporary walking stick. Customers using these aids will require more room to manoeuvre and need our patience and understanding if they take more time to get somewhere. There will also need to be provision made for easy access to each area, as for wheelchairs, and stowage of the walking aid if the customer is to be seated.

file this

▶ We should not assume that all disabled customers want extra or special attention. They will ask if help is required. However, we can assist with doors, personal luggage, getting into or out of a chair or car.

If in doubt, ask them!

CHILDREN

Unlike years gone by, when children were seen but not heard in restaurants, hotels, planes, ships or on tours, the tourism industry is now recognising that the way we treat customers in this category may determine whether their parents return again! Irrespective of age, children are customers and often have a greater influence over their parents' buying decisions than previously realised.

Children's menus, play areas and activities such as colouring books can help to meet their needs and hence meet those of their parents at the same time. Other service points for children include smaller or boosted seating, special seat belts, quick service, smaller food portions and not being patronising.

CUSTOMERS WITH SPECIAL DIETARY REQUIREMENTS

It wasn't so long ago that when a person said they were vegetarian we treated them as though they had a contagious disease! Vegetarians and vegans (who follow a strict vegetarian diet that excludes all animal products) are now part of the everyday tourism experience, along with diabetics, people with food allergies, people with religious requirements and just plain fussy eaters.

However, not every establishment caters for these special needs. Indeed, just having an understanding of these needs and requirements, and trying to accommodate them, goes a long way to achieving service excellence in most cases.

WOMEN

It may seem strange to categorise women under special needs, but many places have not yet caught on to the ever-increasing female market. While we have been used to male business travellers and backpackers for many years, the requirements of female customers can differ substantially.

Women use tourism facilities as much as any other market segment but are often treated as unusual, particularly when travelling or dining alone. Why? Their needs are just as valid as any other customer.

Many women travel for business, or pleasure, alone and may for instance request a room in a particular location (such as near a lift) in a hotel for security reasons. Many women also do not wish to dine alone. On the other hand, they do not want to be the centre of attention either. Like all single people, offer them a choice of where to sit if possible, or ask if they would like to be paired with another single traveller.

SINGLE PEOPLE

For all single travellers it is also useful to have reading material available or a view to look at if possible. Sometimes they may like to strike up a conversation with other single travellers, so ask if they would like any assistance with meeting others.

CUSTOMERS FROM OTHER CULTURES

If there is any industry that brings us into contact with a diversity of cultures it is tourism. Although it is not expected that we are fluent in a multitude of languages or understand all the characteristics of many different cultures, we are expected to make every effort to communicate with and assist people who do not speak English, who have special dietary requirements because of religious or cultural beliefs, or who act differently from us.

We will both work with and serve people from different cultures from our own. Communication between the different cultures is referred to as **cross-cultural communication** and requires sensitivity to the differences to be successful.

Chapter 3 deals with cultural diversity in greater detail.

Cross-cultural communication
Communication that takes place between two or more people from different cultures.

NON-SMOKERS

Almost every type of business has now recognised the needs of this growing market by providing non-smoking facilities. Many accommodation venues allocate entire floors as non-smoking areas and restaurants will divide the room according to demand. Some pub-style hotels are now introducing far more powerful air cleaners to smoky areas, hoping to appease both smokers and non-smokers, and air travel (indeed, all public transport) in Australia has been non-smoking for many years.

Legislation to protect the public and employees against the associated dangers of passive smoking has been introduced in some states, prohibiting smoking in many enclosed, public areas. This is proving to be relatively controversial, with concerns expressed that the impact on tourism operations will severely restrict trade in some sectors. While this remains to be seen, there is no doubt that successful tourism operations need to be aware of all the implications, legal and social. When advising clients on travelling overseas, however, it should be pointed out that smoking is still a socially acceptable pastime in many countries, and is still allowable on many overseas travel routes.

OTHER NEEDS

Special needs can be as simple as requesting a specific seat on a flight or coach, a room with a view, a special meal or a child's portion. Or they can be as complicated as bringing in special equipment and food, providing security or rearranging an entire aeroplane or venue.

Provided a request or special need is not illegal, immoral or dangerous, our responsibility as tourism professionals is to attempt to meet that need.

SINS OF THE SERVER

No customer is 'difficult'; some just seem to present us with more of a challenge. However, let's face it, most of us are guilty of having an 'off' day and in the tourism

---

file this

▶ Nothing is impossible. Impossible just takes a little longer!

industry we will probably encounter someone we refer to as 'difficult' who is also having an 'off' day. Our challenge is in how we manage our behaviour during these encounters. Tourism is a people industry after all, and we need to develop skills to deal sensitively and effectively with all customers.

check please

22. What factors influence customer expectations?

23. Why do you think most tourism-based operations accommodate non-smokers?

24. What should we consider when communicating with deaf or mute customers?

25. Why is greater attention paid to children as customers today than ever before?

Customer dissatisfaction

Customer relations are about how we interact with our customers. Good customer relations must therefore be about satisfying our customers through the efforts we make. However, occasionally there is still cause for complaint. Sometimes it is our fault, sometimes it is not. But as frontline staff, it is most likely we will be the ones to whom a customer expresses dissatisfaction.

How many times have we been to a tourist attraction or a retail outlet, were dissatisfied and did something about it? And how many of our complaints were managed to our satisfaction? How many restaurants or shops do we now refuse to visit because of a poor experience? When it comes to a bigger expense, such as for a tour or a flight, we are more inclined to express dissatisfaction when something goes wrong. How our dissatisfaction is handled will influence whether or not we use that service or product again.

Most people have an eagerness to complain about disappointing experiences on a holiday or on an airline to friends and colleagues, but are reluctant to express this to the enterprise. This means customers go away disappointed; we lose a customer without ever knowing why or getting the chance to find out what was wrong or to fix it.

All too often, establishments that have experienced customer complaints view that customer as difficult, expecting too much or hard to please. It is important to recognise that complaints are usually constructive criticism that indicates room for improvement and are a reminder that we can continue to improve. Complaints reveal weaknesses in the standards of the operation and give the enterprise a chance to retain a customer they may otherwise have lost.

CUSTOMER EXPECTATIONS

When a customer complains, they have several expectations:

- to be taken seriously;
- to get an immediate response;
- to have the problem resolved; and
- to have someone listen to them.

Complaints are also a way for us to develop our own interpersonal skills. Don't be surprised when you do receive a complaint; look upon it as an opportunity to turn a dissatisfied customer into a satisfied customer.

Of course, not all customers are going to complain politely, and some won't complain at all, but a few signs can indicate something is wrong—most of the meal left on the plate, a request to change rooms, or the customer suddenly appearing unhappy. If that happens, we can indicate our concern by enquiring if everything is all right. This gives the customer the opportunity to express their dissatisfaction and for us to fix the situation. And regardless of how a customer complains, we shouldn't take it personally—they are not attacking us but letting us know there is a problem.

HANDLING COMPLAINTS

There are a number of different strategies for handling complaints; however, we can successfully deal with complaints by following these steps:

1. Acknowledge the problem—listen to what is said.
   Stay calm and don't argue. Focus on the problem and never ignore a complaint. Use feedback techniques to clarify exactly what the issue is (e.g. 'You are unhappy we didn't confirm your booking early enough?')
2. Express concern—empathise.
   Use communication skills, be sensitive and polite and don't apportion blame. Accept responsibility for the inconvenience on behalf of the organisation.
3. Indicate what action will be taken.
   Be positive and assertive but don't commit to a solution that can't be delivered.
4. Do what was said would be done—now.
   Of course, there is always the possibility the customer doesn't accept the solution or is still not satisfied, in which case an alternative should be offered. Customers usually don't like to be asked what they would like; they want the problem fixed—now. If still unsure what the issue is, go back to step one and clarify the issue, or seek assistance from a colleague or supervisor.
5. Follow up.
   When the issue has been addressed, check that the customer is now happy.

Each solution is contingent on the authority we have to solve the problem and the policy of the enterprise. If at any time we are not comfortable with handling a particular situation, a colleague or supervisor can help. It is better to get some help than to lose our patience or try to make the customer feel guilty about complaining.

No matter the situation, remember that the customers are just like us; they have feelings and opinions that require consideration whether we agree or not. Proving a customer is wrong will never bring them back again.

file this

▶ The customer is always right—because they think they are right!

check please

26. What are the benefits of complaints to an enterprise?

27. What are the expectations of customers when they complain?

28. Why is it important to 'follow up' all complaints?

29. Why is the customer always right? Explain.

question point

1. Interpersonal skills define our ability to interrelate with other people. What are the essential skills for tourism?

2. Define service excellence.

3. What are the differences between customer expectations of the enterprise and of you?

4. Briefly describe different types of customers and what their special needs may be.

5. How did we learn our behaviours and how do they relate to our interpersonal skills?

6. What personal barriers to communication do you think you have? What can you do to overcome these?

7. List five ways you can improve your communication skills.

8. What is cross-cultural communication?

9. How can the grapevine influence what is communicated in an enterprise?

10. Explain briefly the difference between formal and informal communication. How are they used in the workplace?

11. Why are written communication skills important to interpersonal development?

12. What is the difference between formal and informal groups?

Work in a socially diverse environment

LEARNING OUTCOMES

On completion of this chapter you will be able to:

- define the concepts of culture and describe how multiculturalism has impacted on the Australian workplace;

- identify some of the misconceptions held about different cultures we work with;

- identify characteristics of the major overseas tourist markets;

- explain how the various religious beliefs and cultural influences of our colleagues and customers affect the tourism industry;

- describe issues that cause cross-cultural conflict or misunderstanding in the workplace between colleagues or customers; and

- describe the legislation that protects the rights of all cultures.

This chapter complies with the Tourism Industry National Competency Standards, unit THHCOR02A, 'Work in a Socially Diverse Environment'.

A general awareness of different cultures can contribute to our enjoyment of the workday and enhance the likelihood of exceeding customer and client expectations. It can also teach us respect for other cultures and to value the contribution everyone makes to our family, social and working life.

One of the objectives of this chapter, therefore, is to encourage a better understanding of different cultures and provide the opportunity to develop skills in cross-cultural communication.

There is no expectation for all of us suddenly to get along with everyone, but it is hoped that issues raised in this chapter will engender respect and an open mind. People are different and people's cultural background will influence these differences.

Culture and multiculturalism in Australia

In Chapter 2 we learned that our ability to communicate effectively is measured less by what we say than by how we say it. Our culture and upbringing define what is acceptable and appropriate within our society but does not often teach us what is acceptable or appropriate in other cultures.

Multiculturalism
A situation whereby several cultures co-exist and contribute to the community as a whole.

Cultural stereotyping
The characterisation of all people who originate from a particular culture or background as being exactly the same.

This has changed significantly with the growth of Australia's **multicultural society**, but in many instances it is still not unusual for us to refer to a customer whose needs or behaviours we don't fully understand, or a colleague whose ideas or attitudes we don't agree with, as 'difficult' or 'demanding'. As a result, we sometimes find ourselves in a position of conflict or misunderstanding of the needs of others. Additionally, we sometimes fall into the trap of **cultural stereotyping** which may hinder our efforts to communicate and 'get along' with people.

The major cultural groups in Australia include immigrants, refugees or descendants from all major regions, including Asia, Africa, North and South America and Europe, as well as our own indigenous communities. All bring with them customs and traditions and a rich history that contributes to our multicultural experiences.

APPRECIATING DIFFERENT CULTURES

When we talk about a particular **culture**, we generally mean a collection of beliefs, rituals, morals, values and attitudes among a group of people. Culture can also be defined as a way of life, 'how we do things around here', an accepted behavioural pattern, a religion, law or habits. A cultural definition may also include a people's literature, art, and language or dialect. Irrespective of the definition, what is most important is how we respond to these cultures and subsequently work with them. Valuing diversity is a part of personal development.

Some of the cultural characteristics in Australia can be as simple as the tradition of following the same sport in the family or even the same team; it can be the celebration of Christmas Day (Christian), celebrating Passover (Jewish) or observing Ramadan (Muslim); it may be the celebration of a birthday, a person's name day or bar mitzvah. Others may be the strict observance of a religious belief, such as prayer times, the way a person dresses, speaks or behaves; the way food is prepared; the formalities of greeting other people; or the way in which business is transacted.

All of these elements are characteristics of a culture. Background, family structure, sexual preferences, age and attitude all contribute to the individuality of each person. Cultural awareness and thus value and respect for various cultural groups are required by all of us working in the tourism industry.

In Australia more than 15% of the population speak a language other than English in the home. The most common of these are Greek, Italian, Chinese, Vietnamese and Arabic.

Our indigenous population and the many **nationalities** that live in, or visit, Australia possess distinctive cultural characteristics that can impact on the workplace. There will be some commonalities, but mostly it is the diversity of each group that makes contact with them so rich and rewarding.

Nationality
Belonging to, by birth (place of origin) or by acquiring citizenship of, a particular nation.

AUSTRALIA'S INDIGENOUS CULTURE

An aborigine is defined as one who is an original inhabitant of a country. Hence, as the Australian Aborigines were the original inhabitants of Australia before white settlement they are the indigenous population. Today there are fewer than 400 000 Aborigines and Torres Strait Islanders in Australia.

It is believed that the Australian Aborigines have lived here for over 40 000 years. They were a nomadic people who lived in isolation from other cultures. They learned and developed skills for survival off the land, although they did not depend on agriculture.

Despite an apparent lack of commonality of language, political, legal, economic or social structures, Aboriginal groups did have a structure within tribes in the form of customary laws and rules. However, it was this seeming lack of commonality that led to the settlement of Australia as unoccupied territory—*terra nullius*—as the Aborigines were not recognised as a civilisation. This was later ruled to be inaccurate.

Aboriginal culture is rich and diverse. Central to the beliefs of Aborigines is their spiritual link to the land. Their beliefs originated with the ancestral spirit beings of the Dreamtime. The spirits, both human and animal, were responsible for the creation of the earth and all living things and gave rise to the mythologies passed down through time in oral history and tradition.

Much of the Aboriginal culture is expressed through ceremonies and rituals held for mourning, settlement of disputes, exchanging of gifts, initiation and accessing ancestral powers, among others. No formal writing existed for Aboriginal languages until the twentieth century; however, Aboriginal history, experiences and lives are passed on in verbal lore and recorded in the drawings of animals, plants, the seasons, the family, hunting and other activities. This art contributes significantly to the cultural identity of the various tribes who live in urban and rural Australia.

In the past two decades, non-indigenous Australia has made significant efforts to reconcile its social and political relationship with Aborigines and Torres Strait Islanders. The Aborigines themselves actively seek their own rights and identity through cultural, sporting, political and social identities. Their culture is integral to Australia's own cultural identity.

The growing demand for tourism experiences involving indigenous cultures presents exciting opportunities for greater involvement by Aborigines in tourism and hospitality.

activity 3.1

▶ An international visitor tells you they wish to experience indigenous Australian culture. In small groups, research the availability of tourism experiences in your state or territory that would meet these customer expectations. Information should be provided on outback tours, history, sacred sites, rock art and other sites of cultural significance, bush medicine and bush tucker, handicrafts and tools, museums, traditional dance performances and anything else you think is relevant.

OVERSEAS VISITOR MARKETS

While most of the customers and colleagues we communicate with are English speaking, a large percentage will not have English as their first language. In addition, there are a large percentage of overseas visitors (inbound tourists) with whom we communicate who do not speak English at all. In these instances, our effective verbal and non-verbal communication skills become very important in overcoming any communication barriers.

According to the Australian Bureau of Statistics, the overseas visitor market contributes in excess of 12 billion dollars annually to the Australian economy.

The largest group of visitors to Australia are Asian, more specifically Japanese. The next main sources of tourists are New Zealand, Europe, including the UK, and North America (USA) respectively.

Despite the distance, European visitor numbers continue to rise, but the fastest growing group are tourists from the South-East Asia region, especially China, Korea, Malaysia and Singapore (Bureau of Tourism Research, 2000).

The reason for travel can be to some extent determined by the place of origin. For most, the main reason is holiday. For example, many Asian visitors fall into one of three main categories for purpose of travel: study, holiday (including the honeymoon market) and business. A higher percentage of visitors from the UK and New Zealand will visit friends and relatives, whereas many of the other visitors visit Australia as a holiday destination.

All too often visitors are grouped by region—Asian, European, American, and African—rather than by individual country. This does not allow for a more comprehensive understanding of individual differences, which can be quite significant.

MARKET SEGMENT GUIDE

Segmenting our markets allows organisations to serve their customers better, compete more effectively and ultimately achieve their goals (for example, to make a profit). Identification of specific groups of people (a market) allows for marketing efforts (advertising, packaging, sales promotions) to be specific for the target market.

Each of the countries listed in Table 3.1 forms part of a market segment, each with individual expectations, and can be further broken down, indicating more detailed needs and reason for travelling.

Because of the diversity of the nationalities and their cultures, it is obviously not possible to categorise them as a single market segment. However, many of them will have certain expectations in common, such as respect for their differences and a high standard of service.

TABLE 3.1 **Origins of a few of our colleagues and visitors**

PACIFIC REGION	EUROPE	AMERICAS	AFRICA
New Zealand Pacific Islands (Polynesian, Melanesian and Micronesian) Papua New Guinea	England Ireland Scotland France Germany Italy Spain Scandinavia (Norway, Sweden, Demark) Holland Greece Austria	North America (USA, Canada) South America (Brazil, Argentina) Central America (Mexico, Costa Rica)	South Africa Egypt Kenya Morocco Nigeria Mozambique

SOUTH-EAST ASIA	EASTERN ASIA	SOUTHERN ASIA	MIDDLE EAST
Thailand Vietnam Cambodia Laos Malaysia Philippines Indonesia Singapore	Japan China Taiwan Hong Kong South Korea	India Pakistan Sri Lanka	Lebanon Saudi Arabia Israel Yemen Iraq Iran Jordan Qatar

check please

1. Briefly explain in your own words the meaning of 'culture' and 'multiculturalism'.

2. How does multiculturalism impact on your workplace and social interests?

3. Our indigenous population already contributes to the tourism industry. How else do you see Aboriginal and Torres Straight Islander involvement contributing to tourism?

4. How does Aboriginal attachment to the land impact on tourism? Give an example.

5. What image, if any, do you think our overseas visitors have of Aboriginal culture? Non-indigenous culture? What can we do, if anything, to improve the image we have?

6. What value does market segmentation serve?

7. Do you think it is appropriate to treat all visitors from 'Asia' the same? Why or why not?

Preconceived ideas and misconceptions

While it is important to stress that there are similarities across cultures, many preconceived ideas about nationality or **race** can lead to **prejudices, racism** and stereotyping.

Tendencies to pre-judge will cause communication barriers and stress or anxiety. In overcoming these challenges we need to be aware of our own attitudes, recognise the contribution individuals make to the community, and accept that cultural diversity is integral to the success of the tourism industry, irrespective of the sector.

Race
A group of people sharing a distinct ethnic origin.

file this

▶ The most appropriate greeting in the workplace will be a warm, genuine smile that is welcoming. It is important for us to be 'ourselves'. If we try to copy behaviour of a customer it may be misinterpreted and offence taken.

Prejudice
A preconceived, unfavourable opinion about something or someone, often formed without personal knowledge or experience.

Racism
The belief that one person (race) is inferior to another based on the principle that certain characteristics of particular cultures make it so.

The following list may help identify and clarify some of the misconceptions about various cultures:

- Not all Asian cultures use chopsticks.
- Asia is a geographic region, not a country.
- Many North American visitors expect water to be served immediately (with their meal), refer to the main course as the entree, prefer their salad before the main meal and have high expectations of service.
- Not all cultures use please and thank you. This does not mean that person is being rude. All cultures have a standard for politeness that may not correspond to our own, but there is an underlying expectation of good manners, etiquette and professionalism.
- Accepted forms of greeting and farewell vary between cultures. For many, the greeting ritual is quite significant. Some of these include:
  - a handshake (most cultures);
  - bowing (some Asian cultures);
  - nose-rubbing (Maoris and Inuit);
  - embracing and kissing (many Europeans and Arabs);
  - slap on the back (some Western cultures);
  - touching clenched fists (Caribbean Islanders).
- Table manners vary, and any of the following may be encountered:
  - slurping food (particularly soup—helps to cool it down);
  - lifting plate to mouth (especially when using fingers or chopsticks);
  - eating with fingers;
  - fork used only;
  - belching (sign of appreciation);
  - leaving food on plate (sign that the host has provided ample food).
- Each culture requires different 'personal space'.
- Time as a commodity ('time is money') is not important to all cultures.
- Facial expressions are used to signal thoughts and feelings. In some instances the interpretation may be different from what was intended. Some Asian cultures

tend to control their facial expressions, whereas Westerners tend to use facial expression to convey more meaning.

- Not all cultures will complain if there is a problem. Those that do, do not generally intend to offend. They want the problem fixed.
- Respect for family structure and authority is inherent in Asian cultures.
- Not all Asians bow to each other.
- Not all Western cultures shake hands.
- Not all Europeans kiss on greeting.
- Various cultures (and religions) will observe different holy days or other significant holidays and cultural obligations. This may impact particularly on the workplace when a colleague requires time off to observe a holy day or some other important occasion.
- Special dietary requirements may be requested due to religion, nationality, culture and preference and for other reasons.
- Touching, other than handshaking or in some instances a kiss, is generally taboo across all cultures.
- There does not exist a word in every other language for every English word. Conversely, there exist words and expressions in other languages that do not have a literal translation into English. This can often hinder the communication process. Use of gestures, diagrams and practical demonstrations will assist understanding.

Other issues that are potentially misunderstood are the differences between cultures in how each deals with age, gender, seniority (in the workplace), a person's profession or title and work ethics. An open mind is necessary.

check please

8. What is the difference between 'race' and 'nationality'?

9. Of what use will a better understanding of misconceptions be to us in the workplace?

10. What is likely to occur if we pre-judge people based on our own prejudices?

Characteristics of overseas visitors

It is very easy and convenient to classify all people with similar appearances and behaviours into the same category. We assume that a Western-looking person wants what we want. We assume that Asian people all want and expect the same thing. Nothing could be further from the truth. Not only is it helpful to understand which countries form part of which region as presented in Table 3.1, it is also helpful to understand how each of those countries on the same continent differ, and how the various market segments within each country differ.

SOUTH-EAST ASIAN AND EAST ASIAN CULTURES

Each culture has distinctive characteristics and well-defined needs. From the lists in Table 3.1 it should be obvious that not all the people in South-East and East Asia are referred to as Asian, despite the geographical location.

Visitors from Singapore, South Korea, China, Japan and many other countries represent separate and rapidly growing markets for the tourism industry in Australia, both as tour groups and as **free independent travellers (FITs).**

From the two distinct market segments described above—honeymoon couple and business traveller—it can be seen that although they both originate from the same country, and therefore are going to have some expectations in common due to cultural influences, they will also have many different needs due to personal experience and reasons for travel.

BODY LANGUAGE

Body language and gestures have cross-cultural implications due to a general lack of universal meaning (with, perhaps, the exception of a smile and even a handshake). In service and in the workplace with colleagues, we want to avoid confusion or offence, no matter how innocently it may happen.

When interacting with colleagues and guests from South-East Asian and East Asian cultures:

- Avoid prolonged eye contact as it may give offence.
- Be aware of personal space—usually what is acceptable in Western society is

too close for Asian society. With the exception of a handshake, it is not appropriate to touch.

- Exhibit a high standard of grooming; it represents professionalism and respect—for self, the employer and others.
- It is not appropriate to imitate the bow for Asians, who use bowing as a means of greeting and sign of respect and appreciation, if you are not familiar with the correct way to perform this greeting. A handshake is acceptable.
- Smile appropriately and genuinely.
- Do not point as it is not polite.
- Do not be over-familiar.
- Use non-verbal communication—this can aid understanding and thus communication.

Although each country has its own language (some with several dialects), many Asians speak a second language and often a third. Many of the Asian countries also share the same or a similar language (such as Indonesia and Malaysia, Hong Kong and Singapore), but their food requirements and eating habits vary from country to country.

Similarly, while most Asian cultures are not physically demonstrative in public, handshaking is generally appropriate.

MIDDLE EASTERN CULTURES

As with the other geographical and cultural groupings above, it is not intended to generalise about expectations of guests from middle eastern countries. The countries that are within this region are referred to as the Arab states or the Middle East. Among other Arab countries are Egypt and Morocco (North Africa). With the exception of Israel, the language spoken is Arabic; French is also common.

Possibly the greatest cultural influence in many of these countries is their religion. In Israel it is principally Judaism; elsewhere it is Islam. A person who practises Islam is called a Muslim, whereas a person practising Judaism is Jewish. The culture of each country is strongly characterised by the religions practised, which, in many instances, also determine the law for the country. The position a person holds in the community firmly influences how Arabs deal with each other and other cultures. This can be based on a person's profession, gender, education, religion and other factors.

BODY LANGUAGE

The Arab manner of dress is greatly influenced by religion and in some instances this may hinder communication. For a Muslim woman in traditional dress, often only the eyes can be seen. When we rely on other non-verbal communication to aid understanding, this can create a barrier that needs to be overcome. Some general points are noted below:

- Arab culture places considerable importance on eye contact. It may appear they are staring but this is a sign of respect. Their preference is to face the person with whom they are speaking.
- When greeting each other, many Arab men embrace and shake hands. They will not embrace a stranger and may not shake hands. It is not appropriate to touch a Muslim woman at all.
- Many Arabs do not use dramatic or sudden arm movements.

- The right hand is used for eating, passing items and so on, as the left hand is considered unclean.
- It is considered rude to slouch, lean against walls or put hands in pockets when communicating with Arabs.

file this

▶ Personal space for Arabs is closer than Western cultures are generally used to.

SOUTHERN ASIAN CULTURES

The way of life for many of the cultures in this region is largely influenced by religious or spiritual beliefs. This may also be a considerable influence on how these people deal with others of a different religion, class, profession or gender. The main religion in India is Hinduism. The next main group is Islamic, followed by Christians and Buddhists, and there are many sects. In Pakistan, Islam is the dominant religion.

India and Pakistan have a rich, colourful and often turbulent history. Religions—Hinduism and Islam respectively—play a significant part in separating the two countries. Despite this, they have some characteristics or traits in common.

BODY LANGUAGE

Inhabitants of both India and Pakistan, and other countries in the region, dress in a distinctive manner, with many religious influences. The physical features of the countries' inhabitants are similar, but where Pakistani people are influenced by religion in much the same way as Arabs in terms of body language, dress, culture and laws, Indians vary considerably. Note the following:

- Indians will place their palms together under their chin and bow as a traditional greeting.
- Indian women do not customarily touch but may shake hands, mainly with other women.
- Indians consider whistling in public impolite.
- Indians, usually in their own country, may beckon a waiter by snapping their fingers or hissing.
- As for Muslims, the right hand is used for eating.
- It is not unusual in either country for the men to eat before the women.
- Correct titles are important when addressing people.

WESTERN CULTURES

As distinct and varied as our visitors from countries listed as Western may be, it is not uncommon to assume that because Australia is Western then all traits must be the same between the groups. Nothing could be further from the truth.

It is also not uncommon to hear many service providers complain of the demanding American or the aggressive German. These demands and this seemingly aggressive attitude is the behaviour these visitors would demonstrate in their own country. That is to say, they are placing on the Australian tourism industry the same expectations they hold at home. Are they really making unreasonable demands or trying to be difficult to get along with? The answer is no. They are behaving characteristically of their culture. They are expecting service that meets their expectations.

BODY LANGUAGE

Often the body language demonstrated by other Western cultures is not unlike our own but may sometimes be very unlike our own. Generally, however, there will be less confusion with cross-cultural implications than with many other cultures. Note these points:

- Good eye contact is expected. It indicates the listener is being attentive and is considered polite.
- It is common for both men and women to shake hands on greeting one another or saying farewell.
- It is also not uncommon for some customers, who may come to know us by name, to touch our arm or pat us on the back. The customer does not expect us to do this in return.
- The more intimate the working relationship, the less personal space need be observed.
- Use open, positive body language. Smile genuinely and often.
- Many Western cultures use body language as a distinct form of communication. Remain open-minded about this, as your interpretation may not be what was intended.
- With non-English-speaking Western visitors, the same principles apply as to Asian visitors in the use of gestures and other forms of communication where no common language exists.

In all of these examples, generalisations have been made. You will encounter situations where any or all of the above can occur, and find that many people, especially those who have been exposed to other cultures, may adapt according to the culture they are in at the time.

---

activity 3.2

▶ Research and report on a culture/nationality of a colleague in your class or at work—do not select your own culture to report on, but try to ensure that all cultures represented in the class are researched.

As a minimum, include in your report the following distinctive features and characteristics:

- manner of dress;
- religion(s) practised;
- holidays observed and rituals;
- food preferences (restaurants in Australia);
- forms of greeting;
- service expectations; and
- distinctive behavioural patterns.

VERBAL COMMUNICATION

Our tone of voice and the words we choose will aid understanding and be representative of us and the organisation in dealing with overseas visitors and colleagues with different backgrounds. All the potential communication barriers that exist between people who speak the same language will have even greater importance when communicating with people whose first language is other than English.

The following can be applied to all nationalities and cultures and will relate to both customers and colleagues:

- Formality in addressing people is more appropriate than familiarity.
- Avoid colloquialisms and slang.
- Avoid humour. What seems funny in one culture is not necessarily funny in another.
- Speak slowly and clearly, but not loudly. Clear pronunciation of each word, not a rise in pitch, will aid understanding. Avoid technical jargon.
- Use short sentences. Do not try to convey too much information at once.
- Rephrase a message or question if necessary. Look for signs that indicate the listener has not understood—nodding and smiling or a blank expression. Asking if the person understands will usually result in an affirmative response, even though they possibly don't understand at all.
- Courtesy is important. Everyone likes to feel genuinely welcome and to be put at ease, especially in a foreign environment. Use a formal style in a pleasant tone of voice. The message received in how we say something may be clearer than what we have said.
- Attempt to use a person's name. Even if pronounced incorrectly, most people will appreciate the effort—and correct you.
- When verbal communication is not possible, use gestures and diagrams. If need be, get assistance from a colleague or supervisor.

file this

▶ All efforts to speak another language, even if only a greeting, will be warmly appreciated. However, be wary of using foreign language slang or words picked up from colleagues as they may give offence.

When in doubt, smile. A smile crosses all boundaries.

activity 3.3

▶ A colleague is having difficulty explaining to an overseas visitor who doesn't speak English how to get to a tourist attraction in your area. You go over to help. How do you communicate to the guest what they need to know? Role-play this as a class exercise for feedback on your success.

11. Why would we avoid prolonged eye contact with our South-East Asian visitors?

12. With which culture might prolonged eye-contact be appropriate?

13. Name five countries, and their regions, from where Muslim visitors might originate.

14. Why do you think colloquialisms and humour should be avoided when communicating with overseas visitors?

Religious influences and the link with tourism

Religion plays a significant role in many cultures. An understanding of some religions will help to meet the dietary, spiritual and other needs of many we work with and our customers. For example, we may work with someone who requests a particular day off work for religious reasons and another person who does not celebrate Christmas. We may serve a customer who requests a kosher (Jewish) meal on a flight or someone else who wants to know the location of a mosque.

BUDDHISM

Buddhism is particularly significant in India, Sri Lanka, Thailand, Cambodia, Japan, Vietnam, Korea and China. Buddhism is growing also in many Western cultures.

Buddha, meaning 'Enlightened One', was the title given to Siddhartha Guatama, a Northern Indian prince of the 5th and 6th centuries BC. He founded Buddhism and is the spiritual symbol of today's Buddhists who still follow his teachings and practices. At the core of Buddhist teachings is, among other things, the quest for peace, enlightenment and equality for all living things. Buddhism is philosophically opposed to materialism. Many Buddhists worship in temples.

Buddhists do not have any dietary restrictions although many choose vegetarian or vegan diets.

HINDUISM

Principally practised in India, Hinduism is regarded as the oldest of the major religions in the world today, dating back to 1500 BC. The religion is defined more by what people do than how they think. That is, there is more conformity in behaviour than in belief. Unlike Christians, Jews, Muslims and others, Hindus believe in many gods and that the human soul lives on in animals or other humans. Hindus revere the cow, most abstain from meat (especially beef), they prefer to marry within their caste (a social class or standing) and believe in reincarnation.

Many Hindus are vegetarian and eat Prashad, which is food that has been blessed for Hindus. It is not uncommon for Hindus to pray before eating and they observe strictly the use of the right hand for eating (and many other activities), believing the left hand to be unclean.

JUDAISM

Judaism is one of the oldest continuing religious traditions, and adherents of this religion are called Jews. Modern Judaism integrates cultural and individual ideologies. Traditionally, Jews pray daily: in the morning, afternoon and evening in a synagogue. Every seventh day is the Sabbath when no work is performed. The Sabbath is spent in prayer, study, rest and family feasting and commences on Friday at sunset and ends on Saturday at sunset. The *Torah* outlines the Mosaic laws (teachings of Moses), which most Jews observe.

Practising and non-practising Jews are located throughout the world, principally in Israel, Europe, North and South America, Australia and parts of Africa.

Jewish dietary laws are strict and were originally designed to preserve health standards. Certain animals are considered 'unclean' and therefore not to be eaten. These include fish without fins or scales, pigs and animals that live underground. Edible animals must be properly slaughtered and soaked, salted and washed before the meat is considered fit for consumption. Meat and milk products cannot be prepared or eaten together. Food that complies with Jewish dietary law is referred to as 'kosher'.

Many international-standard hotels in Australia today have a kosher kitchen and there may also be found kosher restaurants, butchers and other food outlets.

Unlike Christians, Jews do not observe Christmas. However, they do celebrate Chanukah (festival of the lights), which generally falls around the same time as Christmas. Their main religious festival is Passover, normally held in April.

ISLAM

Islam is the religion practised by Muslims. Islam is a major world religion based on the teachings of Allah, through the prophet Mohammed (also spelt Muhammad). Muslims are found in diverse cultural regions including North Africa, most Arab states, South-East Asia, America and Australia. Islam is believed to be the second largest religion after Christianity in Europe.

Devout Muslims observe a daily ritual of prayer, usually held in a mosque, and believe strictly in only one God, Allah. Their prayers are offered up to Allah and his messenger Mohammed. Their teachings are written in the Muslim holy book, known as the *Koran*.

Like Jews, Muslims observe a strict diet. Their food must be prepared according to Muslim law; Muslims must not eat pork or decaying meat, the meat of animals that have died violently or food that has been offered as a sacrifice to other gods. Food prepared according to Muslim law is called halal.

Muslims also fast for the month of Ramadan (Ramadan is observed so that believers may cultivate piety). During Ramadan, which falls 10 days earlier each year because Muslims observe a lunar calendar, Muslims are forbidden to eat or drink between dawn and sunset, and abstain from smoking and sexual intercourse. They celebrate the end of Ramadan with the *Eid ul-fitr* festival. Muslims also tend not to celebrate Christmas, similarly to Jews. The Koran forbids the drinking of alcohol and gambling at all times.

SHINTO

Not unlike Hinduism, Shinto is more a way of life than a religion. The principal Shinto sects are divided about beliefs and practices in faith healing, Confucianism ethics (a philosophy that rejects supernaturalism, including the concept of God), purification rites and spiritual worship. Shinto, meaning 'the way of the gods', is widely practised in Japan; the rest of the religious population in Japan mainly believe in Buddhism or Christianity.

Shinto is not an organised religion as such but boasts many shrines; personal worship is often observed.

CHRISTIANITY

Christianity comprises several faiths, or denominations, including Baptists, Presbyterians, Catholics, Anglicans and many others. All have as their central belief the existence of Jesus Christ (as the son of God), that he died and rose again and that there is only one God. The teachings of Jesus are recorded in the *Holy Bible*. For many, Christianity is today more a doctrine of existence, a way of life, than a strict religious observance.

Worship, or attending *Mass*, is often conducted in a church and, like Jews, some Christians observe a Sabbath, being a day of rest. However, the day of rest is usually observed on the first day of the week: Sunday. Christian faiths also worship in private and observe various practices including fasting and receiving of the sacraments, baptism, confession and the Eucharist—a holy communion with God by receiving small portions of bread and wine blessed by a priest, symbolising the body and blood of Jesus. The Eucharist is more important to Catholics than to other Christian denominations.

Christmas (the birth of Christ) and Easter (death and resurrection of Christ) are the two main religious festivals widely observed by Christians and coincide with our main holiday (Holy day) periods.

---

quick thinker

▶ How will your knowledge of the various cultural influences and religious beliefs of your colleagues and customers help you to communicate better?

Throughout Australia, temples, churches, mosques, synagogues and other places of worship co-exist and, although the majority will be found in major cities, the various denominations can also be found in rural areas. From a tourism perspective, our visitors' religious needs are accommodated in the form of places of worship and dietary requirements, among others things. It is helpful to be aware of what services and facilities are available in your area.

Cross-cultural conflict

Cross-cultural conflict is conflict that usually occurs because of cultural differences and ignorance or misunderstandings arising from those differences. This kind of conflict may occur with a colleague or a customer.

One common cause of cross-cultural conflict is communication difficulties. A customer or colleague who is experiencing difficulty in communicating may express frustration through anger or gestures. The frustration is not generally directed at the other person, but it is sometimes difficult not to take it personally.

Apart from verbal communication, many issues may exist that cause conflict or misunderstanding. Some of these include issues discussed above—prejudice, racism, stereotyping, nationality, religion, customs, mannerisms, behaviour—and others that may not be as obvious or as straightforward to understand and deal with, such as when we simply don't like someone or they dislike us.

WORK ETHICS

Most people like to think they have, and indeed many do have, a good work ethic. A work ethic is how we feel about the work we do and therefore affects how hard we are likely to apply ourselves or how much effort we are likely to exert. For most of us, our work ethic is determined by influences such as our culture, family, colleagues and leadership in the workplace. And we have a tendency to measure other people's work ethic based on our own efforts. For example, you may have heard someone say 'she is so lazy' or 'she works like a machine' (works hard). These are both expressions of a person's work ethic.

Many of our Asian counterparts work a six-day week. There is strong company loyalty and considerable respect for superiors. Some other cultures may also work longer hours and have shorter weekends but work at a slower pace and stop for prayer. Others still believe strictly in the rights of the worker, work only the set times and are loyal only to themselves. Some cultures do not observe time as strictly as many Western cultures, so place little importance on a specified start or finish time. None of these is necessarily a better or worse work ethic; they are simply different because of the influences in each person's life.

There will be varying degrees of experience, skill and knowledge in the industry that may indicate a different standard or work ethic. If all achieve the same high standard of customer satisfaction and organisational goals, is any one attitude to work more right than another? Remember, it's the quality of the effort within a certain time frame rather than the overall quantity of time put in that will usually achieve the desired results.

FESTIVALS AND NATIONAL HOLIDAYS

Each country, religion, nationality or other cultural group observes specific festivals and national holidays. In Australia we have seen some of these celebrated with great enthusiasm—for example, the celebration of Chinese New Year. In the workplace many employees may request days off to celebrate their specific cultural or religious festival observation, or request different working hours on that day. Just as Australia observes Christmas Day and New Year's Day—and, in Victoria, even a day for a horse race, the Melbourne Cup—so too do many of the cultures we work with and serve observe days that are important to them.

Discrimination
Treating a person differently from another in similar circumstances.

DISCRIMINATION

In the workplace, discrimination, which is the treating of a person differently from another in similar circumstances, may occur in various areas, for example because of culture, age, gender, race, religion, sexual preference and nationality. Remember, discrimination is unlawful, and frequently leads to cross-cultural conflict, often because we are unaware of our own prejudices.

GENERAL ISSUES

There are numerous other causes of cross-cultural conflict, some of which we may have experienced personally. Sometimes we are not even aware that our behaviour is causing offence or conflict. Sensitivity to and respect for other cultures can help us reduce the likelihood of conflict.

Telling ethnic jokes, colleagues talking in their first language, colleagues mixing in their own ethnic groups, special consideration for rostering, inappropriate body language, expectations that all should conform to 'our' ways, lack of patience, making assumptions and jumping to conclusions are all issues that do arise and can cause conflict. Taking the time to learn about other cultures and people is a good way to start, particularly for a job or a career in the tourism industry.

Applying an open-mind strategy is the first step to resolving the conflict—after all, the many cultures with which we come in contact have as many other cultures to contend with as us. Our supervisors and colleagues are there to support us. Seek out their assistance if needed.

RESOLVING THE CONFLICT

How each person or organisation chooses to deal with issues that cause conflict is personal and not something that can be treated lightly. How we manage conflict is often determined by, again, our cultural and family influences, personality, position in the organisation and ability to cope with the situation. Remember, however, that Australia is a 'free' country, which means we all have the right to practise our own religion, customs and beliefs; we have freedom of speech and the right to live free from harassment and discrimination.

Strategies for managing conflict situations is discussed in Chapter 6, 'Deal with conflict situations'.

---

check please

15. Explain the difference between 'kosher' and 'halal' foods.

16. Where, in general terms, is Buddhism practised? Hinduism?

17. What is Ramadan?

18. Explain how misconceptions arise with respect to cultural differences. What experiences have you had (if any) that arose as a result of misconceptions? How would you now deal with the situation, given similar circumstances?

19. Make a list of all the things you believe identifies your culture. Do you think other people see it the same way? Why? Why not?

20. What is discrimination?

21. How might different work ethics in the workplace cause conflict?

Legislation that protects the rights of all cultures in Australia

If cultural differences in the workplace, and particularly those that may cause conflict, are ignored, the potential harm may affect both the workers and the organisation. If the workplace becomes unpleasant or even hostile, individual work performance can be affected, productivity may be reduced and, ultimately, customer relations may be adversely affected.

Applying the communication skills learned, and being alert to signs that conflict or differences exist, will help in developing positive cross-cultural relationships.

RACIAL DISCRIMINATION

Racial discrimination
Treating a person less favourably than another in similar circumstances because of their race, colour or nationality.

Racial discrimination occurs when a person is treated less favourably than another in similar circumstances because of their race, skin colour or nationality. For example, in the workplace it is against the law to refuse to employ or promote a colleague, or refuse to serve a customer, based on racial characteristics.

The *Racial Discrimination Act 1975* makes it unlawful to discriminate against a person on the basis of their race, colour or national origin and aims to promote equality among all people.

SEXUAL DISCRIMINATION

Sexual discrimination
This occurs when one person is treated less favourably than others, because of their sex, marital status, sexual preference or pregnancy, in otherwise similar situations.

Sexual discrimination occurs when a person is treated less favourably because of their sex, marital status or pregnancy. For example, we cannot offer a product or service to a person and not another, based on their gender. We cannot refuse to employ a person because they are female (who may in the future become pregnant).

Sexual discrimination legislation protects people against sexual harassment, unfair dismissal and other forms of discrimination relating to gender.

Seeking help outside the organisation

There is a vast selection of writings on individual cultures and cross-cultural communication. We may be interested in only one other culture or religion or in several. We may be interested in learning more about our own culture. The tourism industry is all about people: people from diverse cultures. The more we understand these differences the better we are able to communicate with everyone we encounter.

The following list may assist in further research and study:

- reference books
- embassies
- mass media
- industry bodies
- interpreter services
- community and cultural groups
- trade publications
- internet.

RESOURCE FILE

Most of our guests and colleagues who practise a particular religion or who have particular dietary requirements or other 'different' needs look exactly like everyone else! Some are more obvious, for example a priest, minister or rabbi, and some can be identified by their garments, such as Orthodox Jews, Muslim women and nuns.

There are times when information is sought for places other than attractions or shopping, and special needs that need to be met. To provide the best possible assistance, a personal reference book or resource file, alphabetised, can be a useful tool. The sorts of information to include are:

- a list of all nearby churches, mosques, synagogues and other places of worship;
- halal and kosher butchers;
- Asian grocers;
- interpreter services;
- community cultural groups;
- embassies and consulates;
- restaurants (variety of cuisines);
- cultural festivals and religious holidays; and
- sporting activities.

An additional tool to provide the best service is to use observation (learn to recognise the traits demonstrated by each nationality, religion, culture and so on). You can also ask colleagues who have previous experience and those colleagues who come from a different country or background.

All the chapters in this book will provide additional information that can be added to the reference book.

OTHER COMMUNICATION TIPS

As you gain experience you can keep a written or mental note of any situation that you experience that aids communication with either colleagues or customers. As a start, try to remember:

- that competence and professional behaviour is expected at all times;
- to demonstrate patience when communicating;
- if need be, to seek assistance from a colleague or supervisor.

question point

1. How and why does a person's religion impact on the tourism industry?

2. Effective cross-cultural communication enhances the tourism experience. Discuss.

3. Describe six potential causes of cross-cultural conflict. How may these be effectively managed or resolved?

4. What specific legislation exists in your state or territory to protect individuals against discrimination? What are the objectives of the legislation?

5. Do you think all visitors to Australia have any common expectations of their experience here? If so what are they? Explain your answer.

6. Which characteristics of each of the major overseas tourist markets will help you quickly identify potential special needs?

7. Why do you think some cultures are reluctant to complain if a problem arises?

Communicate on the telephone

LEARNING OUTCOMES

On completion of this chapter you will be able to:

- explain the role of telephone systems in tourism environments;

- demonstrate appropriate telephone etiquette;

- demonstrate appropriate skills for responding to and managing incoming calls;

- manage complaints received on the telephone;

- manage emergency and threatening calls;

- demonstrate how to manage requests you don't know the answer to; and

- demonstrate appropriate verbal skills for making outgoing calls including responding to messages.

This chapter complies with Tourism Industry Competency Standards, unit THHGGA01A, 'Communicate on the Telephone'.

The many skills we have learned relating to face-to-face communication with colleagues and customers can be similarly applied to the telephone. The fact that each party to a telephone conversation cannot see the other does not change the basic requirements for courtesy and attention to detail. The three elements of communication—verbal, vocal and visual—are just as important here as with face-to-face contact.

When using the telephone we often form a mental picture of what the other person looks like, we visualise what they are doing when speaking on the phone and whether or not they are paying attention or are even interested in the conversation. We can usually sense if they are smiling or frowning, sitting up straight or slouched.

What we lack in the visual sense we are able to 'read' by a person's voice—their tone, the words they use and the speed at which they speak. All these elements can be the difference between a successful and a poor customer contact experience on the telephone.

We can sense when someone is being impatient, we can sense when they are smiling, and we can sense hand movements, gestures and expressions. We can 'see' on the telephone.

Advances in telecommunications, such as e-mail, video-conferencing and Wireless Application Protocol (WAP), have revolutionised how we interact and, indeed, as technological advances such as video-phones and Internet cameras become more widely used, we will eventually be able to 'see' who we are speaking to.

How did we ever survive without our mobile phone, our facsimile machine, the Internet, answering machine, voice-mail, e-mail and other sundry gadgets and services that have come into everyday use in Australia in our private lives and for business purposes?

The role of telephone systems

Many individual enterprises require their telephone system to perform a variety of functions and they design their own standard procedure for a range of telephone uses, including:

- incoming calls;
- taking messages;
- sales calls;
- transferring calls;
- handling complaints; and
- making calls.

The significance of an effective telephone system can be measured by comparing the telephone we have at home with the one needed by an airline reservation centre or an international hotel. At home we can make and receive calls locally, intrastate and interstate and internationally. We can connect our facsimile machine and computer modem to our telephone line and we can have more than one line and more than one handset. Phone companies are able to provide us with a range of services that meet our individual needs. We can have call waiting, complete financial transactions, use an answering service, or call-divert our mobile phones. The list seems endless.

Now imagine the hotel, with 200 telephones. Each customer may potentially require any or all of the above services. The hotel does not necessarily connect a separate telephone number for each room, and for each department, but often uses a system that will accommodate each and every telecommunication requirement. If they do not, they risk not meeting customer expectations.

Usually, however, each room and hotel department has access to a telephone via its own line or extension and its associated facilities. This gives access to:

- multiple lines and extensions;
- local and long distance calls;
- modem and fax connection;
- hands-free dialling;
- conference call facility;
- message bank;
- message light in room;
- call waiting, call holding, call back;
- multilingual, prerecorded wake-up call facility;
- call diversion;
- night switch (to allow a main switchboard's call to be forwarded to another extension or location; usually after normal office hours);
- Internet and e-mail; and
- room-to-room direct dial.

A multitude of other facilities and services for the customer's benefit and organisational convenience is also available.

Most telephone systems are connected to the organisation's computer system, which allows automatic registration of each call made and, if appropriate, can charge it to a customer's account, or can track the usage of the telephone by a particular department. The system will also record all calls made and received, numbers dialled, the time a call was made or received and the length of time of a call.

Technology now also enables not only the extension of a particular phone to be displayed, but also incoming external telephone numbers, which in the past has been the sole domain of emergency services departments.

It is everyone's responsibility to familiarise themselves with the functions and capabilities of the telephone system in operation at their place of work. We need to take the time to learn its capabilities *before* we need to use it.

---

quick thinker

▶ What telephone system is used at your work/college? What special features does it have? Do you know how to use all its features?

THE TELEPHONIST

The person answering the telephone is always important, irrespective of the size of the organisation and whether it is a single-function role or the duty of another role, such as a receptionist. This person *is* the organisation as far as each caller is concerned. The person who responds to the incoming calls is in an ambassadorial role—they represent the company in the first instance. The caller's first impression of the organisation is based on this first contact.

check please

1. How does telephone communication differ from face-to-face communication?

2. What is the role of a telephone system?

3. List 10 capabilities an international hotel may look for when choosing a telephone system.

4. What is the role of a telephonist? What do we mean when we say this is an ambassadorial role for the organisation?

Telephone etiquette

Telephone tools
· A smile
· Message pads and pens
· List of extension numbers
· List of regularly called numbers

A highly developed telephone technique will convey an impression of professionalism. Being alert, patient, courteous, willing to help, informed and attentive should be consistent throughout the enterprise, even by those employees whose customer telephone contact is secondary to their usual duties.

Apart from 'professionalism', there are a few other basic rules to telephone etiquette.

Before working with a telephone, we must prepare ourselves with the right 'tools'. We must be equipped with:

- pen and paper for taking messages or computer;
- a list of people likely to be called by staff and customers in our organisation;
- a list of all extension numbers within the organisation;
- product and services descriptions;
- special offers; and
- any other relevant information that a caller may request.

Telephone etiquette
· Answer within three rings
· Stop anything else you are doing
· Give your total attention
· Don't use slang, colloquialisms or jargon
· Use an appropriate form of address

It is also important that we stop what we are doing when the telephone rings and that we speak clearly and distinctly. If our mouth is too close to the mouthpiece we sound muffled and difficult to understand. Our posture plays a vital role in projecting our voice; if we are slouched in a chair it is difficult for us to speak clearly.

A smile on our face will come through in our voice. We need to use our listening skills and take the time to be helpful.

Other telephone etiquette standards for all calls include:

- answering the call within three rings;
- answering according to enterprise standard procedure (consistency);
- recording messages legibly;
- using the caller's name when known;
- when the caller's name is not known, using appropriate forms of address—Sir or Madam;
- transferring calls promptly;
- thanking the caller for calling; and
- allowing the caller to disconnect the line first. Never hang up on a customer first!

Responding to and managing incoming calls

Almost every household in Australia has a telephone. For a business, the telephone is a lifeline. The way that businesses respond to incoming calls can be the deciding factor for their success.

Because many customers' first experiences of a tourism organisation is via the telephone, failure to meet customer expectation at this point—failure to make a positive first impression—could be failure to win or retain a customer.

As we learned in Chapter 2, customers can be either our fellow employees (internal customers) or paying customers (external customers), therefore incoming calls can be received from either external or internal customers. Each is as important as the other but responded to differently. Every call received from an external customer is an opportunity for us to promote the product and services of the organisation and it is an opportunity for us to develop our interpersonal skills.

There are four key points to communicate when responding to an external incoming call:

1. salutation—greeting appropriate to the time of day;
2. identification of the *enterprise*;
3. identification of self; and
4. offer of assistance.

For example: 'Good morning, Australian Adventure Tours. This is Douglas. How may I help you?'

Each enterprise will develop its own procedure, but irrespective of what that procedure is it is important for everyone to use it every time they respond to an incoming call. By establishing consistency, the customer's expectations are met and we don't have to think about what to say or in which order we say it.

The above procedure gives an appropriate greeting, identifies that this is the organisation the caller wants, lets the caller know to whom they are speaking and, as a courtesy, offers help. This has the added benefit of being able to establish quickly the purpose of the call. If we do this consistently, the caller can confirm they have the correct organisation and save time asking.

When external calls are received, the caller is likely to request information about the organisation, book a service or facility or ask to speak to a customer or colleague. These requests will require competence in all of the functions listed above—responding, transferring, message taking and so on.

When responding to internal incoming calls it is equally important to be consistent and follow the four key points—an internal call may be a transferred call from an external customer or a call from a colleague within the organisation, an internal customer. To respond to internal calls, the standard procedure is:

- salutation—greeting appropriate to the time of day;
- identification of *department/section of the organisation*;
- identification of self; and
- offer of assistance.

For example: 'Good evening, reservations. This is Sanjay. How may I help you?'

file this

► If you know it, use a caller's name, as you would when communicating face-to-face.

check please

5. List the rules for telephone etiquette. Why is telephone etiquette important?

6. What are the four key points to communicate when responding to incoming calls?

CULTIVATING OUR TELEPHONE SKILLS

The skills required to operate telephones are considerably more involved than we first think. For example, what do we do when the phone rings and we are talking face-to-face with a customer? How do we deal with a complaint that has nothing to do with us or a situation where the caller sounds threatening or it is an emergency?

Each situation can have a standard procedure that ensures consistency, but we still need to inject our own individual personality otherwise we risk sounding insincere or stilted.

TRANSFERRING A CALL

Most calls received by the telephonist will be transferred—to reservations, the check-in counter, the restaurant, a customer, a colleague. Most people accept that when they call an organisation they will not get the person or department they want immediately and so need to be transferred. What most people don't accept is having time wasted when they don't know they are being transferred, being transferred to the wrong extension, being put on hold for a long time, getting lost in the system and asked again who they want or getting disconnected. If we are completely comfortable with our telephone system, and have practised our telephone etiquette and skills, transferring calls will become second nature and our life is made simpler.

Steps for transferring an external call:

- Follow the standard procedure for answering the telephone.
- Ascertain who the call is for—having offered assistance, the caller probably tells

paint a picture

▶ Adam and Sophie Goldberg were planning a holiday to Japan and needed information about flight availability to Tokyo, accommodation, tours, car hire and travel insurance. Sophie tried calling her local travel agency but the number seemed always to be engaged, or it rang out. Finally, after trying for a number of days, she managed to speak with a travel consultant. This is how the conversation went.

'Yes, Timeless Travel.'

'Oh, at last, I've been trying for days to get through to you. Are you having trouble with your telephone?'

'No, we're just busy. Can I help you?'

'Yes. I'd like some information about flights to Tokyo next spring, please.'

'Look, I don't suppose you can come in here to book it?'

'Well, not really. And at this stage we are just looking for availability and prices. We also want some information about accommodation, car hire and travel insurance.'

'I haven't got anything in front of me and it would take time to put together. And besides, I've got someone in front of me right now. Can you e-mail me the information you want?'

'No, I can't e-mail you the information; I just want some prices and availability. Can you help me or not?'

'No, not right now, can you call back later?'

'It's obviously too much trouble for you. I think I'll try someone else.'

'Oh well, please yourself.'

Frustrated, Sophie slammed down the phone, making a mental note never to use this travel agency again. She considered the repercussions of a telephone conversation like this one in her workplace. Surely this travel agency realised that responding this way to telephone enquiries was losing them business.

Clearly, this was a poor telephone interaction. Where do you think the problems began? What do you think the main problems are? How should this telephone conversation have gone? What recommendations, if any, would you make to the travel agency about how to respond to incoming calls?

you they wish to speak to a particular person or department, or would like to enquire about your services or make a reservation.

- Let the caller know you are going to transfer them—apart from this being a courtesy, it doesn't leave people wondering what happened when suddenly they are no longer speaking to someone but listening to music or a recorded message. If transferring first requires placing someone on hold, ask the caller if they mind holding.
- Sometimes it may be necessary to ascertain who is calling before transferring the call. This is known as screening the call.

- Thank the caller for calling and promptly transfer the call to the appropriate extension—a list of all in-house extensions and in-house customers should be kept by the telephone.

file this

▶ Many telephone systems are set up so that if an extension does not answer after a set time, the call will automatically revert back to the switchboard. If this is the case, it is necessary to let the caller know that the person or department they want is unavailable. It is also our cue to offer to transfer the call to another extension or take a message.

If the extension is engaged, then it is necessary to let the caller know this and offer three options, depending on the circumstances: would they like to hold; would they like to speak with someone else; or would they like to leave a message?

Example 1
'Good morning, Evergreen Tours. This is Chung-Lee. How may I help you?'
'I would like to enquire about your Red Centre Tours please.'
'Certainly, Sir. Reservations will be able to help you with our packages. I will transfer you now. Thank you for calling.'

    If the line is busy:
'I'm sorry, Sir, reservations are engaged at the moment. Would you like to hold or can I ask them to call you back?'

Example 2
'Good morning, Tourism Victoria. This is Bryce. How may I help you?'
'Good morning, I would like to speak with the Marketing Manager, Ms Jordan, please.'
'Certainly, Madam, I will transfer you to her extension now. Thank you for calling.'

    The call reverts back to the switchboard:
'I'm sorry, Ms Jordan is not at her desk at the moment. Is there someone else who can help you or would you like to leave a message?'

Example 3
'Good evening, Sea World Nara Resort. This is Jacob. How may I help you?'
'Good evening, I would like to speak with Mr Hallion in room 601 please.'
'Certainly, Sir. I'll transfer you now. Thank you for calling.'

    The line is busy:
'I'm sorry, Sir, Mr Hallion's line is busy. Would you like to hold, or may I take a message for you?'

    Or the call reverts back to the switchboard:
'I'm sorry, Sir, Mr Hallion is not in his room at the moment. May I take a message for you?' (Of course, many enterprises now have voice-mail attached to all extensions, which means the caller can leave their own recorded message.)

SCREENING CALLS

Screening calls is what we do when we want to find out who is calling and why before we transfer the call. Sometimes a call is received for a person who is not available, the department requested is closed or the telephonist may be able to deal effectively with the enquiry. In these situations it is appropriate to screen calls. It can save time for the caller, the telephonist or the person receiving the call if we know who is calling and the reason for the call.

How we manage calls when we are screening is very important. The words we choose can make the difference between making a caller feel important or somewhat suspicious. Remember, every caller is important.

Steps for screening calls are:

- Follow the standard procedure for answering the telephone.
- Ascertain who the call is for.
- Ask who is calling and, if appropriate, what the call is about.
- Follow the standard procedure for transferring the call.

Example 1
'Welcome to Qantas. This is Mark. How may I help you?'
'I'd like to speak to the human resources department.'
'Certainly. May I ask who is calling, please?'
'Yes. My name is Fiona Kirby.'
'Ms Kirby, may I ask what the call is regarding?'
'I'm calling about positions available within the airline.'

At this point, having ascertained who the call is for and what it is about, a decision is made as to whether or not to transfer the call, explain why the call can't be transferred (take a message), offer to transfer to someone else or whichever other option is appropriate.

If the caller is screened in this way, and subsequently transferred, let the other person know who is on the telephone and why they are calling. This gives the receiver of the call the opportunity to greet the caller by name. If we don't do this the caller will have to repeat all the information already given to the telephonist.

Example 2
'Good afternoon, On-line Booking Services. This is JulieAnne. How may I help you?'
'Hi, JulieAnne, can I speak with Thomas in sales, please?'
'Certainly. May I ask who is calling please?'
'This is Graham from Bondi Car Rentals.'
'Graham, may I ask what the call is regarding?'
'Yes, it's about the booking Thomas made for one of your clients.'
'Graham, I'm sorry, Thomas is not available at the moment, but Kendelle is. Would you like to speak with her?'

The advantage of having determined what it is that Graham wants is that instead of having to leave a message he is still able to speak with someone immediately about his query. We are therefore providing better customer service. If Graham doesn't want to speak to another person we can offer to take a message.

PLACING ON HOLD

We already know that most organisations have multiple lines for the same telephone number. This means that several calls can be received, made, transferred or put on hold all at the same time. In reality, there could be anywhere from one person to a large call centre managing all this receiving, transferring and message taking. During the day, there are peak times when several calls can be incoming at once. The person answering the calls needs skill and diplomacy to ensure that all procedures are observed efficiently.

One of the most frustrating things that can happen when we make a call is, without being asked, and without the opportunity to express even a single syllable, hearing 'please hold', click! We then make a decision: listen to computer jingles three times in a row or the company's prerecorded sales pitch, or, if it is an enquiry about products or services, hang up and call another organisation. Potentially an organisation has just lost a sale. Someone else just failed to make a positive first impression! If we do wait until the telephonist comes back to us, we are already feeling a little upset and the organisation has to work that much harder to meet customer expectation.

There is one, single, definitive key to putting someone on hold and keeping them happy: ASK.

Having asked, wait until the caller responds in the affirmative and thank them before doing it, and don't leave them on hold for too long.

Example 1
'Good afternoon, Grampians Visitors Centre. This is Mark. Would you mind holding please?'
'Certainly' or 'OK' or 'not at all.'
'Thank you.'

If we know we will have a person on hold for any length of time, return to the caller every 30 seconds.

'I'm sorry to have kept you waiting. Thank you for holding. Someone will be with you in a moment.'

Of course, if we repeat this a number of times the caller will think we are a recorded message or won't believe us anymore, and we risk losing their confidence or, worse still, their custom.

When we can get back to the caller:
'I'm sorry to have kept you waiting. How may I help you?'
Then follow the standard procedure for what the caller wants.

Rare though it may be, we occasionally encounter, in response to our request to hold, a 'No' or 'I'm in a hurry'. Do we put them on hold anyway or perhaps tell them how busy we are?

Despite the fact that six other lines are ringing and four people are standing in front of us, keep the smile in our voice and offer assistance. Remain positive. Most times the call will be dealt with in under 60 seconds—they need to be transferred, a message taken. What has been achieved is a satisfied caller and we have met their needs.

TAKING A MESSAGE

Telephone messages can be passed on verbally or in written form. They can also be passed on electronically—e-mail is a fast and effective, written form of communicating messages. To ensure accuracy and provide a permanent record, written messages are preferred. Verbal messages may not be accurate, and accordingly may miss important details, can be forgotten and cannot be checked for accuracy.

Messages may be taken for colleagues or customers. It is necessary to record a message when the requested person is unavailable or information has to be sought and the caller called back.

When taking a message:

- establish who the message is for;
- record all relevant details;
- repeat all the details back to the caller;
- tell the caller what action will be taken; and
- pass on the message in a timely manner.

Preprinted message pads are available in various formats, which prompt each stage of taking a message (an example is shown in Figure 4.1). They are usually in duplicate—the original is given to the person being called, the copy remains in the pad (for future reference if required).

For example, taking a message for a staff member:

'I'm sorry, Mrs O'Flaherty is not at her desk. May I take a message for you?'

Record the message details:

- who the message is for;
- date and time;
- name of person leaving the message and contact details;
- what action to be taken—will call back, would like them to call back, etc.;
- message itself; and
- name of person taking the message.

FIGURE 4.1 *TELEPHONE MESSAGES*

CHAPTER FOUR – COMMUNICATE ON THE TELEPHONE

Check the spelling of any names and check all numbers recorded. Repeat all details back to the caller.

'Mr O'Flaherty, I'll repeat the message back.

'The message is for Mrs O'Flaherty. "Please call Mr O'Flaherty on 0418 980303 before 2 pm".'

'Mr O'Flaherty, I will pass the message on to Mrs O'Flaherty as soon as possible. Is there anything else we can do for you?'

'Thank you for calling. Goodbye.'

Allow the caller to hang up first.

Do what we say we are going to do—pass the message on to Mrs O'Flaherty as soon as she returns to her desk. This may be in person or by activating an in-house message service (via an internal network system or intranet) or another system used for passing on messages.

Remember, however, not to make promises that cannot be kept. We sometimes say things like '. . . I'll get Mr . . . to call you back'. Can we really?

Other things we sometimes say imply we can do things we really can't and can sometimes give the caller a poor impression of the organisation.

In Activity 4.1, there is a list of recommended *don'ts* when speaking on the telephone. On the other side, there is a column for *do say*. Next to each *don't*, write an alternative that is more appropriate. The first one has been completed to help get you started. You may find it helpful to work with a friend and to compare responses with others in the class.

DOING TWO THINGS AT ONCE

Most of us are multiskilled and pride ourselves on being able to do more than one thing at a time. But one occasion when we don't do two things at once is on the telephone. On the telephone we need to concentrate on the caller, just as we do when communicating face-to-face.

We now know what to do when more than one call is received at a time, but what do we do if we are on the telephone and someone walks up to us or, conversely, we are speaking face-to-face with a customer and the telephone rings?

It is difficult, but we can't ignore one for the other. If we ignore the telephone when speaking with a customer, they will be glad it is not them on the other end of the line. If we ignore a customer in front of us, they will feel very frustrated if we don't even acknowledge them.

The procedure for handling both situations is simple. If we are on the phone and a customer appears, acknowledge them with a smile, nod or wave. If we are with a customer and the phone rings, we need to excuse ourselves, answer the call, following the on-hold procedure until we are able to take the call.

Example 1
The phone rings and you are having a conversation with a customer:
'Would you excuse me for a moment please Mr Pilger?'
Mr Pilger won't mind, as long as you are brief, therefore not keeping him waiting.

When answering the call, follow the standard procedure for putting someone on hold, but remember not to leave them waiting too long.

file this

▶ Acknowledge a customer in front of you when on the telephone to someone else.

▶ **Telephone etiquette**

activity 4.1

DON'T SAY	DO SAY
'Yeah, he's still at lunch'/'on a tea break'/ 'a busy person'	Mr Smith is not available. Would you like to speak with Mrs Gardner, or may I take a message for you?'
'Call back later'/'tomorrow' /'in an hour'/ 'next week'	
'Look, the manager's walked out'/'The water main's burst'/'I have other things to worry about, too'	
'Are you sure you can afford that'/'I think that is more than you want to pay'/ 'It's very expensive'	
'Gone home sick/early'/'been fired'/ 'is late for work, as usual'	
'Hold on a tic'/'just a sec'/'puttin' you through'	
'What did you say your name was?'/'Who are you again?'/'Gee, that's a strange name, how do you spell it?'/'Mr who?'	
'What was it you were after?'/ 'What were you calling about, again?'/'Who is it you want?'/ 'Do they work here?'/'Have you got the right place?'	
'It's not my fault/problem/department/ responsibility'	
'Don't blame me, I only work here'	
'I can't help you'/'She won't help you'/ 'He won't do that'	

Example 2
You are on the telephone and a customer approaches:
Acknowledge the customer immediately. They can see you are on the telephone, and will accept that you cannot attend to them immediately. You now have an audience—the

waiting customer is able to form an opinion about you based on your actions, body language and telephone technique. They are standing there hoping you are as courteous to them as to the person on the other end of the telephone.

You can acknowledge a person as they approach you in any number of ways, all of which are acceptable; for example, you can look at them, smile and perhaps nod your head. You can look at them, smile and perhaps mouth that you won't be long. Whatever you do, you immediately return your full attention back to the telephone.

If it appears the call may continue for some time, it may be necessary to ask if they mind holding for a moment; you will then be free to look after the other customer.

The key here is not to ignore either someone in front of you or a ringing telephone.

Managing complaints on the telephone

Because the telephone is often located at the front counter of an organisation (especially small businesses), this is the first point of contact for customer complaints, even when it has nothing to do with that person or the department.

Most people aren't interested in whether or not the person answering the telephone is the right person to whom to express their complaint. Generally, people who call to complain consider whoever answers the telephone to *be* the establishment. And not every customer politely informs us they would like to make a complaint, either!

If a person has had a bad experience and doesn't complain at the time, they may stew on it, in which case they may call at the height of their anger and be potentially aggressive and make irrational demands; or they may think rationally about the experience and let us know calmly, so that we have the opportunity to fix the issue.

In Chapter 6, 'Deal with conflict situations', we will learn that when a customer complains they want to be taken seriously. They want an immediate response; they want the situation resolved and they want someone to listen to them. No matter what they say, demand or threaten to do, we must extend them every courtesy. If we respond aggressively, we end up with a lose–lose situation. On the other hand, it is very difficult for them to continue verbal abuse if we are genuinely sympathetic, empathetic and offering to resolve the situation. Remember, don't take it personally and do behave professionally.

file this

▶ Every complaint is an opportunity to win a customer back. It is an opportunity to convince a customer that we care about any incident that does not meet their expectation. It is an opportunity to improve how we do things.

Steps for telephone complaint resolution:

1. Establish the issue—it may be something we are able to resolve. If not, let the caller know who the right person is, why, and then transfer them to that person. We thank the caller for bringing the problem to our attention.

2. Acknowledge the issue—if we are able to resolve the situation, we should express concern and apologise on behalf of the organisation. Do not blame anyone, or pass the buck.
3. Indicate what action will be taken—the caller may want a sincere apology, a complimentary entry ticket, free flight or other product, or a refund. We can only offer what we are authorised to offer. That is, if we do not have the authority to refund the customer, we need to refer the problem to whoever does have the authority and inform the caller of this. We may be able to do this immediately or we may have to call the customer back.
4. Do what we say we are going to do—whether it is referring the complaint to our supervisor, sending a gift voucher or giving a refund—immediately.
5. Follow up—make sure that what was offered was followed through.

All complaints are only resolved when the customer is satisfied that their expectations were met. We look for a win–win situation. If we mishandle a complaint, try to blame someone else or say it is not our problem, we lose the chance to make a positive impression and may lose a customer.

check please

7. Why do we screen calls? How can screening benefit the caller?
8. State the correct procedure for acknowledging another person when on the telephone. Why is this important?
9. Why do you think it is important to develop a procedure for responding to complaints on the telephone?

Emergency and threatening calls

It is hoped that throughout our careers we never encounter an emergency or threatening call, but if we do, it is better to be prepared than to ponder later what might have been.

EMERGENCIES

In Chapter 7 we learn what to do if we discover an emergency, such as a fire. An emergency is any act or event that has the potential to harm people or property and requires immediate action. In this chapter we discuss how to respond if we are the one receiving an emergency call. If we discover an emergency, the first principle is Stop, Think, Act. The same applies if we receive a call telling us there is an emergency or an illness/accident.

Ask the caller:

- the exact nature of the emergency—fire, explosion, gas leak, etc., or illness/accident;
- the exact location of the emergency, or details of the accident/illness; and
- who the caller is, what department or outlet they work in, and what action they have taken or are taking.

Write this information down, and then determine the necessary course of action. This will depend on the nature of the emergency and the enterprise standard procedure. The likely course of action will involve some or all of the following:

- calling the most senior person on duty;
- raising the fire alarm;
- calling the appropriate emergency services department;
- calling security;
- beginning evacuation;
- following procedures for ensuring that a full list of in-house or on-site customers and staff on duty is available for a head count when everyone is evacuated;
- following procedures for securing cash and valuables during an evacuation; and
- following procedures for the administration of first aid.

THREATS

Threatening calls vary. It can be that a bomb is on the premises (refer to Chapter 7), a threat of violence is made against a staff member, a customer or us personally, or a person making a complaint can intimidate or threaten damage to property. Whatever is threatened, remain calm.

If the threat is about a bomb, follow the established procedure for the organisation. When physical violence or property damage is threatened, don't disregard the caller as a crackpot. Do not laugh at a person making a threatening call, and don't treat it lightly. Don't get angry and don't say things that are likely to upset the caller even more.

Take the call seriously and write down everything the caller is saying. As with a bomb threat, try to find out as much information as possible: who they are, who the threat is against, why, when this will happen, how they will do it. Ask if there is anything you can do that will solve the problem. Attempt to calm the person down if they are very angry, but never give the caller any personal information.

If we hang up, it is very likely they will call back. Depending on the enterprise policy and procedure in place, the police may have already been called. Even if the call appears to be only a prank, keep a record of the conversation, inform the supervisor and advise the person in charge of security. In many instances it will be necessary to inform the police. They are unlikely to be able to do very much, but it is important they are informed of the situation, especially if the caller calls more than once and specifically identifies a person they wish to harm.

file this

▶ Treat all threats seriously and immediately advise your supervisor of what has happened.

Managing requests we cannot answer

When we first begin at an organisation it will take time to learn about all the products and services available. It will take time to become familiar with all the people, what is possible and what is not possible.

Several years ago, a Sydney hotel which prides itself on exceeding all customers' expectations had one couple staying who loved their room and didn't want to move, but requested the tree outside their window be cut down so they could better enjoy the view! It may well be expected that the receptionist's first reaction was total amazement, and then to simply say no. Some things, after all, are just not possible.

But saying no is not considered part of the service ethos. Sometimes we genuinely don't know the answer, or it may be that the request has never been made before. Instead of saying it can't be done, or no, we say we will find out. And find out we do. It's amazing how many of these seemingly strange or difficult requests can be accommodated, whether we receive the request over the telephone or face-to-face. And although the tree wasn't removed, it was important that the customer felt they were taken seriously and every effort was made to meet their needs and provide them with a reasonable explanation.

file this

▶ If you don't know the answer, find out. Never say NO.

HELP THE CUSTOMERS—INFORM THEM OF LOCAL ATTRACTIONS AND PLACES OF INTEREST

Whether we work in the local tourist office, a visitor information centre, a large hotel or as a customer service representative in any large tourism-based organisation, we are going to be asked questions such as 'What is there to see and do?' 'How far is it to . . .?' 'How do I get to . . .?' 'What time does that start?' 'Will it rain today?' and any number of other questions. It becomes our responsibility, no matter what sector or department we work in, to know the answer.

Most of the questions are asked by customers or potential customers making enquiries about our location, products and services. We can't tell the customer there is a brochure, so come and get it, or tell them to call the local tourist office, the number is in the *Yellow Pages*. The person they are speaking to *is* the brochure, *is* the local tourist office, as far as the customer is concerned.

The answers to all these strange and common requests and questions can be kept in our own resource book that already contains information about attractions, sites, services and so on. We discussed this in Chapter 3, 'Work in a socially diverse environment'.

If we don't know the answer, we find out.

Making outgoing calls

Outgoing calls are made for a number of reasons depending on the style of operation. We call suppliers to place orders, customers to confirm bookings, or to respond to messages left for us earlier; we make sales calls, calls to employees, calls seeking information and calls to colleagues in other departments.

Whatever the reason for a call, we follow the basic rules for telephone etiquette and we equip ourselves with the right tools. Outgoing calls are just as important as incoming calls because the other party is still able to form opinions and make judgements about the organisation and us.

When making outgoing calls:

- have paper and pen available;
- have the correct number;
- have any relevant documentation or product information on hand that may be required;
- have the correct name of the person you wish to speak to and, if appropriate, the correct department; and
- quickly identify who you are, where you are from and the purpose of the call.

Example 1

Making an external call to a tour operator for a customer:

'Good morning, Sam, this is Scott from OMH Travel. I have a customer interested in one of your guided tours to Rottnest Island. Could you please tell me how frequently the tours depart, at what time, where they leave from and what time they return?'

'Do you have seats available for Thursday? How much is it per person? Does that include lunch? How can my customers pay for that?'

'Thanks for your help, Sam. I need to let Mr and Mrs Brown know the details before I can confirm the booking. Goodbye.'

Example 2

'Mrs Brown, this is Scott from OMH Travel. I have the information you requested for day trips to Rottnest Island. Strada Tours offer a full day trip to the island departing daily, which includes a tour of the island, free time to explore after lunch, and lunch is included. They have seats available on Thursday. They can pick you up from your hotel at 8 am and will return by 4 pm. The cost per person is $75.00.'

'Mrs Brown, we can include the cost in your total holiday or you can pay Strada Tours direct by credit card.'

'Would you like to think about it, Mrs Brown, or would you like me to go ahead and book the tour?'

'You're welcome, Mrs Brown. If there is anything else we can do for you just call me. Thank you. Goodbye.'

Example 3

Making a booking for a customer in a restaurant:

'Good afternoon, Sue, this is Alec from V-Line. I have some passengers who would like to dine with you tonight. Can I make a reservation for Mr and Mrs Fraser, please?'

'They would like a table in the non-smoking section, near the door please, at 6 o'clock. They are going to the theatre, so will need to be finished by 7.45.'

'They will be staying at the Hotel Rendezvous so you can contact them there if you like.'

'Thanks, Sue.'

Internal calls can be a little less formal, but no less polite and courteous.

RESPONDING TO MESSAGES

What expectation do we have when we leave a message for a friend on their answering machine or at work? We expect them to call back. What do we do when *we* receive a message from a friend? We return the call—usually at our earliest convenience.

In the business world we cannot afford to be selective about whose calls we return or tardy in returning those calls. Even if we know we are unable to help the caller, or if we really don't want to speak to the caller, courtesy in business demands we call anyway, in a timely manner.

Most telephone messages are sales opportunities, a repeat customer, a new customer or an unhappy customer. By underestimating the importance of returning calls, we potentially risk losing customers because we failed to give proper service.

---

activity 4.2

▶ Complete this activity with a friend and record yourself so you are able to assess critically your telephone skills. Make up whatever information you think is necessary. Continue to practise until you are comfortable with each scenario. When you are confident with your skills, role-play each scenario with a third person assessing you. This will provide feedback on your strengths and on areas needing improvement.

The situations below give you the opportunity to role-play each of the scenarios presented in this chapter.

The telephonist/receptionist

1. A customer calls enquiring about your company's products and services:
   A. Transfer the call to reservations.
   B. Handle the call yourself.

2. A caller has asked to speak to the sales department:
   A. Screen the caller before transferring.
   B. The line is busy, take a message.

3. Several lines are ringing:
   A. Put the caller on hold.
   B. A customer approaches the desk.

4. A customer is yelling at you about a problem with his flight last night:
   A. Resolve the problem.
   B. Explain who they will need to speak to.

Making calls

1. Responding to messages:
   A. A customer called to complain.
   B. A supplier called about an order.
2. Making enquiries:
   A. What are the visa requirements for visiting Venezuela?
   B. Make a reservation for a day tour.

question point

1. What are the steps to take if we receive an emergency or threatening telephone call?

2. What should we do if we do not know the answer to a customer enquiry?

3. Why is it important to return all messages left for us and in a timely fashion?

4. What is the procedure for: transferring a call; placing a call on hold; screening calls?

5. Why should we 'get back' to the customer on hold as soon as possible?

6. State the correct procedure for taking a message. Why do we repeat the message back to the caller?

7. What is meant by 'mental images'?

8. What are the basic rules for making outgoing calls?

9. Why should we care about internal calls?

10. What is the procedure for handling multiple calls? For dealing with customers face-to-face while the phone rings?

Perform clerical duties

CHAPTER 5

LEARNING OUTCOMES

On completion of this chapter you will be able to:

- describe the range of office documents commonly used in tourism-based organisations;

- identify and use office equipment, and manage equipment malfunctions;

- process a range of office documents;

- write correspondence; and

- maintain correct storage and filing systems for front-office information following enterprise standard procedures.

This chapter complies with the Tourism Industry National Competency Standards, Unit THHGGA02A, 'Perform Clerical Procedures'.

When we think about the tourism industry we mainly think about tourists, attractions, tours, transport, accommodation and visitor services, among others. It is easy to forget that the organisation and provision of services to consumers of tourism products require substantial planning, coordination and administration. This means that no matter which sector we work in we need to undertake a range of clerical and administrative tasks more commonly associated with the conventional meaning of the word 'office'.

We therefore need a range of clerical and administrative skills to be able to meet both the needs of the organisation we work for and our customers or clients. Clerical and administrative tasks refer to those aspects of the job that require us to process a range of documents, understand document-filing systems and use office equipment.

To be able to do this we need to know how to operate different types of office equipment, such as the computer or facsimile machine, compose a range of documents, such as business letters, internal memos and operational reports, and handle administrative tasks related to the customer or client needs, such as accommodation vouchers and itineraries. And we need to be able to do all of this according to enterprise standard procedures.

The main purpose of this chapter, therefore, is to provide the basic skills and knowledge required to perform effectively the clerical and administrative tasks associated with many tourism-based enterprises.

Clerical and administrative tasks
Those aspects of the job that require processing of a range of documents or the use of office equipment.

The range of office documents

Office documents are paper-based records relating to the enterprise's activities. Processing refers to how we accurately and legibly manage those documents. This includes initiating and responding to correspondence, filing of documents and completion of forms.

In most enterprises it is likely that several staff will process the various documents at different times. For example, in a travel agency we may record a client's travel requirements (transport, accommodation, tours) but a colleague may write the itinerary or make changes to it, while another colleague may produce the airline ticket, etc. In an airline one person may make the booking (computer entry) and another will issue the ticket at the check-in counter, or the customers may even issue their own electronic-ticket. Also, additional information is often compiled from the records we generate. For example, a rooming list may be compiled from the bookings we make for our clients. Therefore it is important to put written systems in place to control the flow of information and that all staff be familiar with the systems and follow operating procedures.

We begin by looking at the types of documents we are likely to encounter in a range of tourism enterprises. It is important to note that these are examples only and may vary between even similar types of operations.

DOCUMENTS USED IN TOURISM-BASED ENTERPRISES

The types of documents used in the various tourism-based enterprises vary according to the nature of the business. For example, what a transport company (airline, rail service, coach company) uses and processes will differ from what a retail travel outlet or tour operator will process and use.

However, while the size and needs of each enterprise will differ, as indeed the layout and structure of documents may, similar-use documents will contain essentially the same information, irrespective of the workplace. For example, an itinerary produced by one travel agency may look slightly different from the one used in another travel agency. The format used for writing a letter of confirmation to a client may vary between agencies but the letter is likely to contain basically the same information. The examples used here therefore are representative of the types of documents used but are not the only versions we are likely to encounter.

Documents may be produced manually or by a computer, they may be for internal or external use. **Internal-use documents** refer to those documents used within the organisation. **External-use documents** refer to those documents that are coming into or being sent out of the organisation. External-use documents may be seen and used only by staff or may be seen and used by customers.

Internal-use documents
Those documents used within the organisation.

External-use documents
Those documents that are coming into or being sent out of the organisation.

CUSTOMER ENQUIRY SHEET

Customer enquiry sheets are most frequently used in travel agencies and by reservation staff in accommodation venues, tour companies, transport providers and so on. When customers or clients make enquiries about our products and services, a standard customer enquiry sheet may be used to record the details of their enquiry. The types of information we note down include:

- client name and contact number
- flight/holiday information details (number of seats, room types, number of people, budget, etc.)
- prices quoted (if any)
- conditions of booking (for example, 21-day advance purchase requires an additional cost if dates are changed)
- dates requested
- special requests or details (such as special meal requests, disabilities).

This information is retained until the client either confirms that they want to make a booking or disposed of if the client does not go ahead with the booking. An example is shown in Figure 5.1.

CUSTOMER PROFILES

Many tourism-based enterprises maintain a **customer profile** database. This may be a formal, computerised record of a client's personal details and details on travel habits or a manual file maintained by a clerk or consultant for their own use. Accommodation venues and travel agencies frequently maintain a customer profile. However, good operators also keep detailed databases so that they have an accurate idea of customer needs and wants for the future. A database is likely to contain the following information:

- name and contact details
- details of previous travel/accommodation and other product requirements
- special points about the client (preferences, requests).

Each time the client or customer uses our services or products the profile is updated.

FINANCIAL CONTROL DOCUMENTATION

In all tourism enterprises financial control documentation is used. Financial control documentation is any document that records the financial transactions that take place

FIGURE 5.1 *EXAMPLE OF A CUSTOMER ENQUIRY SHEET*

TRAVEL TRUNK PTY LTD
10 HAY ST, PERTH • TEL: 09 505 5055
for people on the move

CUSTOMER ENQUIRY SHEET

Date:

Consultant:

Customer details	Enquiry	Action

between a client and the enterprise and the enterprise and other businesses. The most common external financial transaction documents are receipts, which are issued to customers after payment for products (even ride tickets used at Dream World may be considered receipts or proof of payment).

Other documents of financial value that are used include travel documents, such as airline, coach and train tickets (and ancillary travel documents), travel vouchers (usually for accommodation and food), confirmation of booking slips and credit card dockets.

Establishments that hold supplies of travel documents are required to observe strict security for the storage of tickets. In addition, the enterprise is required to maintain strict control of ticket issue.

The reporting tool for enterprises that issue airline tickets (travel agencies, airlines) is the **BSP** (Bank Settlement Plan), which is administered by **IATA** (International Air Transport Association). The enterprise is required to complete the report weekly. Revenue raised from a ticket sale is debited from the issuing enterprise's bank account and directed to the respective carrier (airline, coach company, etc.) or tour operator.

Internally, financial records take the form of financial reports. For example, an enterprise needs to keep track of its profitability. It does this by recording what revenue it has received, what costs it has incurred to run the operation, profit margin level, wages and salaries expenses, commissions earned and so on. These reports can

BSP
Bank Settlement Plan

IATA
International Air Transport Association

be generated daily, weekly, monthly, quarterly or other time period depending on their use and the needs of the enterprise. Most of these documents are the responsibility of the financial controller, bookkeeper or other accounts person.

Many tourism-based enterprises allow their customers or clients to maintain a credit account for the services or products purchased. For example, a travel agency may allow certain businesses to maintain an account that will be paid for within the agreed period (usually 30 days but may be as short as 7 days).

RECEIPTS

Receipts are issued in exchange for a payment. For example, a client paying for the services purchased (transport, entertainment, accommodation) will be issued a receipt. Most receipts are computer generated. Receipts are also received by enterprises for the supplies they purchase and have paid for.

Receipt
A document issued in exchange for a payment, detailing the nature of the transaction.

INVOICES

Invoices are received and sent on a daily basis. An invoice is a request for payment for the services or goods supplied and provides a detailed account of the actual goods or services bought by the business, date supplied, cost per unit and settlement details. With the introduction of GST, all businesses in Australia are now required to issue tax invoices for the supply of goods and services.

Invoice
A request for payment for the services or goods supplied.

These documents are usually forwarded to the enterprise's accounts department for processing. Examples include invoices for:

- food and beverage items (as required in an events and meetings venue)
- accommodation (booked for clients)
- transport arrangements
- services provided (e.g. access to entertainment venues).

TELEPHONE MESSAGE PADS

Many enterprises use pre-printed telephone message pads to record incoming telephone calls. Most messages we record are to be passed onto a colleague or management. A pre-printed message pad allows us to record all the relevant information by prompting us at each stage.

The pad is usually in duplicate. The top copy is passed onto the person for whom the message is; the duplicate copy stays in the message pad. By retaining a duplicate copy, if the original is lost then there is a copy to refer to. Recording of telephone messages is discussed in Chapter 4, 'Communicate on the telephone'.

POLICIES AND PROCEDURES

Policies and procedures are developed for internal use but may relate to work or job issues and staff behaviour in relation to customer service and how we perform certain aspects of our job.

A **policy** is a statement about the enterprise's position on an issue. For example, the enterprise may have a policy that states that theft by employees is a dismissible offence. It may have another policy that states that during an evacuation the priority of all staff is customer safety.

Policy
Statement about the organisation's position on an issue.

A **procedure** is a step-by-step guide to performing a task so that each task we perform (e.g. recording reservations, answering the telephone, recording payments) is performed in a specific way each time we undertake it. Procedures help make our job easier and ensure standards are consistently met.

Procedure
Step-by-step guide to performing a task.

MEMORANDUMS

Memo
Internal-use document used for communicating a brief message to a lot of people (staff) at once.

A **memorandum,** or memo, is an internal document used for communicating a brief message to a lot of people at once, such as changes to or introduction of a policy, notification of upcoming events or important decisions that have been made that may affect staff and/or customers. How memos are structured and processed is discussed in detail later in this chapter.

REPORTS

As we have seen, several reports relating to financial performance are produced on a regular basis. In addition to these, there are a number of other reports we may need to produce or read depending on the sector we work in and our specific job role.

Incident/accident reports

Accident report
A written record of injuries sustained by an employee during their working hours.

Incident report
A written record of an event ('incident') that may have implications for the employee or company afterwards.

An **incident report** or **accident report** is written when it is necessary to record the details of an incident or accident. For example, while working at a visitor information centre a colleague trips over torn carpet in the office and breaks their arm. An accident report is required to be completed so that the employee has written evidence of the injury and management has a record to show to their workers compensation insurance company.

An incident report usually relates to an event or occurrence that is unusual, but where no person is actually injured, for example a group member of a tour reports money stolen from their belongings to the tour leader who then writes a report.

The layout and design of a report depends on the requirements of the user (person who reads the report) and the enterprise itself.

AGENDA

Agenda
List of the points or topics to be discussed at a meeting.

An **agenda** is a list of the points or topics to be discussed at a meeting. An agenda is usually distributed before the commencement of the meeting to allow the attendees time to prepare for the meeting.

Most agendas follow a standard format. An example is shown in Figure 5.2.

MINUTES

Minutes
Record of a meeting.

The **minutes** are a record of a meeting, noting the date the meeting was held, who was in attendance and who wasn't (but was meant to be), what was discussed and by whom, decisions made, actions to be taken and anything else relevant to that particular meeting.

Minutes are distributed to those in attendance and anyone who may be affected by the information contained in the minutes. All minutes are filed after having been read and acted upon (for future reference).

---

file this

▶ The expression 'to minute something' means to formally record.

VOUCHERS

Many tourism-based enterprises issue vouchers in exchange for payment for travel-related goods and services. For example, a travel agent may issue a voucher to a client

FIGURE 5.2 *EXAMPLE OF AN AGENDA*

TRAVEL TRUNK PTY LTD
10 HAY ST, PERTH • TEL: 09 505 5055
for people on the move

AGENDA

Location:	The boardroom
Attendees:	Douglas, Alec, Melanie, Fiona, Trish, Mark
Chair:	Kathryn, Managing Director
Minutes:	Linda More
Date:	10 November 2001
Time:	3 pm

Items for discussion

1. Minutes of previous meeting
2. Domestic consultant trainees
3. New uniforms
4. New product development
5. Christmas planning
   - Rosters
   - Annual leave
6. Sales targets
7. Strategic planning for 2002
8. Other business

for accommodation booked. When the client arrives at the accommodation venue, they present their voucher as payment. The accommodation venue then invoices the travel agency, providing the original or a copy of the voucher as proof that the client actually stayed with them. An example is shown in Figure 5.3.

Many other tourism operators also sell vouchers, usually as a gift or a prize. For example, an accommodation venue may sell an accommodation voucher, which the purchaser can give to a friend, or it could be sold at a school fête. The voucher can

FIGURE 5.3 *EXAMPLE OF A VOUCHER*

TRAVEL TRUNK PTY LTD
10 HAY ST, PERTH • TEL: 09 505 5055
for people on the move

ACCOMMODATION VOUCHER

Supplier:	Diplomat All-Suite Hotel 14 Heathmont Road, Christchurch, New Zealand Tel: 03 355 5678	
Guest name:	Marcus	**No. of guests:** Four
Dates:	Two nights: Arrive 2 January 2002 Depart 4 January 2002	
Room type:	Two suites, city view	
Payment:	$390.00 per room	
Comments	Non-smoking rooms. Late arrival. Flight No. QF 345	

be issued for the use of almost any services provided by the accommodation venue. The voucher will list the services and goods the holder is entitled to and may or may not include the value. For example, a gift voucher may be for a night's accommodation, dinner in the restaurant or a package that includes room and breakfast. Gift vouchers are often purchased to give as a prize. They may also be used as a reward for loyal guests or for an outstanding employee.

A transport provider (for example, an airline or a coach company) may provide or sell a voucher for travel, to be used in a promotion. The voucher will list the services the holder is entitled to and may or may not include the value.

ITINERARIES

Itinerary
A detailed record of travel arrangements.

An **itinerary** is a detailed record of scheduled travel arrangements. Travel agents and tour operators are the most likely organisations to issue itineraries to their customers. An itinerary acts as confirmation of travel arrangements. An example is shown in Figure 5.4.

SUNDRY DOCUMENTS

All tourism-related enterprises would also stock a range of sundry documents, depending on the nature of the business. For example:

- brochures, pamphlets, promotional materials
- travel insurance information
- fee/tariff schedule
- visa requirements

FIGURE 5.4 *EXAMPLE OF AN ITINERARY*

TRAVEL TRUNK PTY LTD
10 HAY ST, PERTH • TEL: 09 505 5055
for people on the move

TRAVEL ITINERARY

Client name:	Marcus
No. of passengers:	Four
Travel details:	**Perth to Christchurch**
Departure date:	2 January 2002
Depart Perth:	14.30
Flight no.	QF 345
Arrive Christchurch:	20.45
	Christchurch to Perth
Departure date:	4 January 2002
Depart Christchurch:	15.50
Flight:	QF 346
Arrive Perth:	22.15
Accommodation details:	Diplomat All-Suite Hotel (separate voucher)
Comments:	You do not need to confirm your flight details with the airline. Please double check your time of departure and the departure terminal and give the airline a local contact number. Departure taxes are your responsibility. Check-in time is usually 2 hours before departure.

- travel tips
- luggage labels
- outgoing passengers cards
- reference materials (fare guides, travel books, maps, accommodation guides)
- sight-seeing guides
- guides to local wineries and other attractions
- day tour programs.

CORRESPONDENCE

Correspondence refers to written communication between the organisation and external entities (customers and suppliers, for example).

Incoming correspondence includes:

- requests for and confirmation of travel arrangements
- sales letters from other organisations
- requests for information
- letters of complaint
- job applications
- requests for payment.

Outgoing correspondence includes:

- confirmation of travel arrangements
- customer accounts
- responses to letters of complaint
- newsletters
- sales or promotional letters
- letters requesting payment of an account.

Correspondence
Written communication between the organisation and external entities.

Each of the documents discussed must be managed and processed in a way that is logical and complies with the organisation's procedures. How you physically process these documents is discussed later. First, we need to identify what equipment is available to us to help with processing documents.

check please

1. What are clerical and administrative tasks?

2. Explain the difference between internal-use and external-use documents.

3. Explain the use of minutes and agendas.

4. What is a voucher? Why do you think a voucher is issued?

5. Who are the most likely organisations to issue itineraries? What information does an itinerary contain?

6. Why is a telephone message pad in duplicate?

7. What is the difference between a receipt and an invoice?

8. What is 'correspondence'? With whom is a travel agent likely to correspond? An airline?

Types of office equipment

For all businesses to function effectively there are a number of pieces of equipment they must have, including:

- switchboard/telephone system
- facsimile machine
- photocopier
- computers (hardware and various software)
- printer(s)
- franking machine
- calculator
- filing cabinets
- paging system
- ink stamps
- sundry stationery items.

Even the smallest of operations today needs most of the above items. Whatever equipment is available in the enterprise, the idea is to help us do our job more effectively and efficiently. For most documents produced, we need to be able to create them, copy them, store them and retrieve them. The equipment available helps us do this.

But of course not every enterprise will have the latest, fastest, biggest, most recent version of each piece of equipment, so only a brief overview of their capabilities is provided. How we actually use each brand or style of equipment is usually learned on the job.

SWITCHBOARD

A switchboard is the piece of equipment that enables an enterprise to manage several telephone lines and multiple extensions. You may be familiar with the term PABX (private automatic branch exchange), which is an older style of switchboard. Smaller businesses may use a commander system, which is a less sophisticated telecommunications system suitable for smaller enterprises requiring only a few telephone extensions. Most systems are capable of:

- receiving several calls at once;
- making several calls at once;
- recording messages to extensions;
- interfacing with other software to record calls made and associated charges;
- placing calls on hold;
- transferring calls; and
- playing on-hold music or promotional messages.

Of course, most of these functions require some operator input. Telephone operations are discussed in Chapter 4.

FACSIMILE MACHINE

The word facsimile means an exact copy. A facsimile machine, or fax, reproduces written documents received from or sent to external locations by electronically scanning and transmitting the document via a telephone line. A fax allows you to send or receive the documents within minutes of transmission. The fax machine will process only one single-sided page at a time (although all modern machines allow you to load several pages at once) and you are usually restricted to a maximum A4 page size. A fax machine will not process stapled pages: fax machines work by feeding the printed image between smooth rollers and over a scanning mechanism and hence staples will jam the machine. An alternative to faxing a document is to send it by post.

Be aware, however, that the sender can easily alter faxes. False information or signatures can be added to the original document and faxed without the receiver knowing, so always verify with the author of the letter or document if in any doubt about the information being received.

file this

▶ Modern fax machines can also be used as a photocopier.

PHOTOCOPIER

A photocopier will produce an exact copy of a document. It enables us to reproduce documents without the need to retype or reprint them. The difference between a fax machine and a photocopier is that the photocopier produces copies only for the person using the machine; the document is not transmitted anywhere. Photocopiers have multiple capabilities, including:

- rapidly copying several one- or two-sided pages;
- sorting and collating documents being copied;
- stapling collated (photocopied) documents;
- reducing or increasing the size of the copied document;
- reproducing in colour or black and white; and
- producing overhead transparencies.

Photocopiers can achieve a high quality of reproduction in a relatively short time. Many of the documents we use need to be copied.

COMPUTER (HARDWARE AND VARIOUS SOFTWARE)

Today almost all organisations maintain some form of electronic automation in their operations, whether a travel agent, tour operator, accommodation venue, airline or other type of organisation.

The minimum requirements are usually a monitor (visual display unit (VDU)), a central processing unit (CPU) and a printer. Computers usually come fitted with a backup facility also, such as a floppy disk drive, zip drive, CD writer or magnetic tape.

Depending on the software applications installed and the nature of the operation, the computer enables us to:

- produce, save and store a range of internal-use and external-use documents, such as receipts, invoices, itineraries, memos, procedures and minutes;
- produce accurate and timely financial reports;

- maintain and generate reports relevant to the operational needs of the enterprise;
- access information and book transport, tours, accommodation, entertainment;
- access the Internet; and
- send and receive e-mail.

Using this technology requires training. And because of the variations and capabilities of the software available, it's not unusual to receive training on several systems, depending on the workplace.

Some of the more common applications include:

- word processing (for letters, memos, etc.)
- spreadsheets (for analysis or collation of financial information)
- desktop publishing (for producing newsletters, brochures, etc.)
- photo editing (for electronic reproduction of photographs)
- accounting packages (for the formal recording of revenues, expenses, etc.)
- payroll (for the efficient processing of salaries and wages)
- electronic interfaces to airline systems (e.g. Apollo, Sabre, Amadeus) or the Australian Tax Office.

PRINTER(S)

A computer system that can process all the above information and perform the necessary functions to manage clerical and administrative tasks is only really useful if the information can also be printed. Despite modern technology making our working lives easier, a hard copy (printout) of most of the information we need is still required.

The quality of the printed copy of the information will depend on the printer quality and our needs. For example, a copy of correspondence to a customer should be of a high quality.

Some types of printers include:

- dot matrix—low quality, cheaper recording/printing of internal records
- bubble/ink jet—good-quality print, although slower than laser printers
- laser printer—high quality, high speed, with no drying time
- combined printer/fax/photocopier/scanner—useful for smaller offices that do not have the space for all four pieces of equipment as separate units.

FRANKING MACHINE

A franking machine is a machine that allows you to stamp literally hundreds of envelopes quickly and efficiently by printing the correct amount of postage required and date on the envelope according to the envelope's weight and size.

For those enterprises that generate large quantities of correspondence to be sent by post, a franking machine is an excellent alternative to buying stamps at the post office and stamping each envelope individually.

The franking machine records the total of all stamps issued. At the end of the week or month or other agreed time, the amount of postage used is paid to the supplier along with a lease fee for the product.

CALCULATOR

A calculator is used frequently in almost any tourism-related enterprise to calculate the total of travel arrangements and amount of commissions, for example. Some computer systems have a calculator function, which eliminates the need to have a separate calculator.

BINDER

A binder is used to combine large documents. It allows us to hole-punch the entire document at once, then attach a binder to the document which holds the document together. An alternative to using a binding machine is to place large documents in a ring binder or other file.

The most likely use for binders is for the collation and storage of documents such as policies, procedures, operational guides and the like.

FILING CABINETS

Filing cabinets (and filing systems) are maintained for the storage of hard copies of both internal-use and external-use documents. Filing cabinets and storage facilities come in an array of sizes and colours, ranging from basic two-drawer cabinets to large compactus units. Filing systems are discussed later in the chapter.

PAGING SYSTEM/TWO-WAY RADIO

A paging system or two-way radio is used to maintain contact with staff within large organisations, such as airports, or with staff who don't work in one set location, such as coach drivers and tour leaders and porters in accommodation venues. The systems allow these staff to be readily located at all times while on duty and allow the staff to contact their supervisors when need be.

The 'control' panel remains in one location and may or may not be a function of the switchboard. When a staff member carrying a pager is required, a text message is sent to the pager number advising the pager holder of what is required of them. The two-way radio allows holders to be contacted similarly to a telephone call by the press of a button if the users are tuned into the same channel.

Those staff required to carry a pager or radio log their pager 'out' at the commencement of their shift and log it 'in' at the end of their shift. The reason a pager or radio is logged out and in is so that the enterprise is able to account for each individual pager and to regularly check when batteries are required.

INK STAMPS

A variety of ink stamps are used in many operations:

- time stamp—to record the time a document is processed;
- date stamp—to indicate the date a document was received or processed;
- 'faxed' stamp—stamping an item sent by fax as 'faxed'; and
- 'received' stamp—stamped on documents the day they are received. The date is written in the space provided to indicate the arrival date of the document.

Stamps are important tools for recording actions taken (e.g. sending a fax) or items received.

STATIONERY ITEMS

Finally, every office requires a supply of stationery items and sundry equipment. These are required to help staff process documents and manage the clerical functions.

These items include:

- staplers
- hole-punches
- clips (paper, bulldog)
- disks (for backing-up computer work)
- manila folders
- envelopes
- letterhead
- folders/binders (for filing items)
- answering machine
- desks and chairs
- pens, paper and pencils.

MANAGING EQUIPMENT MALFUNCTIONS

When considering what can go wrong with any equipment, a good rule of thumb is to assume that the greater the level of sophistication, the more that can go wrong!

Office equipment represents an enormous capital outlay for any business. As employees of the business and therefore users of the equipment, it is important to learn the correct way to use each piece of equipment, use it as it was intended to be used and report malfunctions immediately. Without a lot of the equipment most of us now take for granted, our job would be much harder, take longer to complete and often be quite tedious. Remember also that many of our customers also rely on the equipment we have and our ability to transmit the information to them.

For large and complex equipment—computers, facsimiles, photocopiers and franking machines—it is common for businesses to enter into maintenance and upgrade contracts with the supplier. The contract, for a fee, ensures that the equipment is regularly maintained, quickly replaced if broken and frequently updated as newer technology emerges (or as the business's needs change).

The maintenance contract for this equipment is voided if we attempt to fix the equipment in-house. Apart from fixing paper jams and replacing a cartridge, it is best to leave it to the experts.

If the equipment malfunctions or breaks down, we should:

- stop using the equipment;
- place a sign on it to say it is out of order; and
- report the problem to a supervisor.

Process a range of documents

Now that we are familiar with the types of documents we are likely to manage in our workplace and the equipment used, we need to understand how to process each document. Processing of documents may involve handling the document only once or handling it several times. The processing of documents sometimes requires us to create, collate, modify, save, store, bind, retrieve or distribute them, or to perform only one of these tasks.

Table 5.1 lists some of the documents discussed earlier and how to process each one using the equipment available.

TABLE 5.1 **Processing documents**

TYPE OF DOCUMENT	HOW TO PROCESS
Customer enquiry sheet	Completed while the customer is on the telephone or when you are face-to-face with the customer. On the enquiry sheet, record: • the customer's name and contact details • today's date • details of the enquiry. This information is often added to the customer's profile, when one is maintained, or the details of the subsequent booking are transferred to the profile.
Customer profile	Record details of the customer's bookings in here. The details are usually entered after the client has booked and paid for their travel arrangements or at the time of departure for accommodation venues. Remember to record all travel, tour and accommodation details, per trip or visit.
Financial control documentation	As indicated earlier, a finance department maintains much of the financial control documentation, with the exception of receipts or invoices addressed to us.
Receipts	Most enterprises use a standard receipt layout and, whether computer or manually generated, the receipt should include: • who the receipt is from (name of enterprise issuing the receipt) • name of person making the payment • what the payment is for • today's date • amount in figures and words • an authorised signature. The receipt is then given in person or sent to the customer.
Invoices	An invoice, like a receipt, is issued on a standard form. In Australia there is a legal obligation for enterprises to list the following details on an invoice if the company/person paying the invoice is to be able to claim the GST portion: • company name (providing the goods or services) and address • Australian Business Number (ABN) • the words 'Tax Invoice' • today's date • detail of the goods and services provided (e.g. quantity) • price of the goods or services • GST amount payable on the goods and services • total price of the goods and services. Invoices are then sent to the company/person who purchased the goods or services. Payment is forwarded to the accounts department for processing.
Telephone message pad	Record customer and colleagues' messages on the telephone message pad. Write clearly and legibly. Pass the original copy to the person for whom the message is. The second copy remains in the telephone message pad.
Policy manual	New policies should be read, signed as acknowledgement of having been read and then filed.

continues

TABLE 5.1 *continues*

TYPE OF DOCUMENT	HOW TO PROCESS
Procedures	Follow the same steps as for policies.
Memorandums	Memorandums are written using a standard format (an example is shown later in the chapter). After writing the memo, make the necessary number of copies and distribute them to those persons who are affected by the information contained in the memo. A copy of the memo is also filed.
Reports	Reports usually follow a standard format (discussed later in the chapter). Complete the report as soon after the incident as possible, following the standard format. Distribute the report to whoever is affected by, or needs to action, the information contained in it.
Minutes	Minutes are recorded by hand or tape recorder at meetings and later typed, usually following a standard layout. The minutes are copied and distributed to all staff in attendance at the meeting or to all staff who need to be aware of the information recorded in the minutes. A copy of the minutes is also filed.
Agenda	An agenda is usually typed and distributed to those required to attend the meeting. File a copy of the agenda after the meeting.
Vouchers	Vouchers are issued following a standard format and are only issued when the customer actually makes (and pays for) the travel arrangements covered by the voucher. A copy of the voucher is then issued to the customer and a copy retained by the enterprise (on the customer's file or in a voucher file).
Itineraries	Itineraries list details of a customer's travel arrangements and are produced following a standard format once all travel arrangements have been completed. A copy of the itinerary is issued to the customer and a copy often retained in the customer's file.
Incoming sales letters	Letters should be date stamped and passed on to the most relevant department to deal with the letter.
Requests for information	Depending on the organisational structure of the enterprise, requests for information may be passed on to someone who is responsible for sending information or to individual consultants. Date stamp the request and either pass the letter on or action it according to the procedure in the workplace.
Letters of complaint	These should be date stamped and passed onto the department head most suited to deal with the complaint (e.g. a complaint about poor service by a travel consultant is passed on to the consultant's supervisor).
Job applications	These should be date stamped and passed on to the human resources department or to the person in the organisation responsible for recruitment.
Requests for payments	Date stamp the request and pass on to the accounts department.
Customer accounts	Customers who have an account with the enterprise are usually sent an account monthly. The accounts department is responsible for generating the account.

continues

Purchase orders	These are orders for supplies needed by the enterprise. Either the purchasing officer, accounts department or department head will write the purchase order but we may need to send the order by fax or mail.
Responding to letters of complaint	The person who dealt with the complaint writes these. A copy is held on file with the letter of complaint (usually in a complaints file).
Sales and promotional letters	Most travel-related companies send letters promoting their services and facilities to other travel-related companies who may be able to promote these services to their customers. These promotional materials may arrive (or be sent) by mail or fax or even e-mail. Those arriving by mail need to be date stamped and distributed to those staff most likely to use the information.
Requests for payment from account holders	These are written by the accounts department but may be processed by the administration staff.
Newsletters	Many operations produce a newsletter to keep customers up to date with travel-related information. For example, the newsletter may include items about new staff, attractions or destinations/tours, reports from other customers who have visited certain destinations, or specials (for transport, accommodation, tours) among other things.

check please

9. How is a facsimile machine different from a photocopier?

10. What is a franking machine? What is it used for?

11. Explain how a paging system works.

12. How should equipment malfunctions be managed?

13. What is a maintenance contract? What benefit do you think they offer?

Writing correspondence

Many of the documents discussed above need to be written by us. Some are hand-written, others are produced on the computer.

Most businesses have standard formats for the layout and style of the documents they produce and here we learn just one of those standard formats and layouts for each type of document. And whether we are writing a formal letter and sending it by mail, confirming travel arrangements by fax or e-mail or writing an informal message and communicating it by memo, in any office environment there are a few 'guidelines' to keep in mind when writing these documents.

GUIDELINES FOR GOOD WRITING

Guidelines or generally accepted rules for writing help maintain consistency and improve the quality of what is written. The rules are not hard to remember, but they are essential for success when writing just about anything. Complicated writing is

paint a picture ▶ **Managing administrative tasks**

Sylvia arrived at work on Monday morning to find her desk littered with papers and several of her files on the floor. This was nothing unusual, as her office was always like this: files piled high in the corner, an overflowing 'to do' tray, and another pile of documents on her desk waiting to be filed. Whenever Sylvia needed to find something, she admitted it took a while. It was not unusual for her to find scrap bits of paper with notes on them belonging to a file long after a file had been archived!

On Friday, she had attended a meeting for which she was meant to distribute the agenda, but she had misplaced it. She was also required to distribute the minutes of the previous meeting, but had lost the original notes and wasn't able to do them. Feeling more than a little embarrassed, she resolved today to clear up the mess. Sylvia realised that in her position as a supervisor, she had to set a good example. She knew she was lousy at administrative tasks but the mess was out of control.

Poorly managed clerical and administrative tasks can lead to more than a little embarrassment. What do you think are the likely repercussions of Sylvia misplacing the notes for the minutes? Do you think it important that clerical and administrative tasks be completed in a timely manner? Why? What should Sylvia do in the future to ensure that she doesn't end up in the same embarrassing situation? Why should Sylvia set an example for others?

difficult for the sender and for the receiver. As we learned in Chapter 2, 'Work with colleagues and customers', the sender achieves effective communication when the receiver understands the message as intended. It may be helpful to keep in mind that our colleagues, supervisors and customers make assessments and a judgement about us based on how effective our writing is.

KEEP IT SIMPLE AND USE SIMPLE WORDS

To keep it simple means being concise or getting to the point. Write what is necessary to make the message easy to understand without unnecessary elaboration.

The use of simple words does not imply that our readers aren't as clever as us; it does mean that the message is likely to be easier to understand.

Not everyone who reads what we write will have the same level of understanding of all the words we use. If the reader doesn't understand what we are saying then effective communication has not taken place.

DON'T USE SLANG OR JARGON

Slang (colloquialisms and idioms) and jargon (industry-specific words) are inappropriate in most forms of communication because some people may take offence and others may simply not understand what is meant. Therefore avoid slang and jargon in all written correspondence.

Whatever the form of written communication it must convey the intended message in a way that is easily understood by the receiver. Imagine writing to a business seeking information about their products and in return you receive a letter that uses a lot of jargon, does not flow logically and never gets to the point? Think about the impression this has made on you. Would you go ahead and buy the products anyway?

Probably not. Your customers, colleagues and supervisors want and appreciate clarity when you communicate with them. They don't have time to wade through a lot of irrelevant, confusing and misleading information to get to the important and relevant details.

USE THE RIGHT TONE

The tone of what is said refers to how the information sounds. It expresses the feelings of the writer (or speaker). If you think you would take offence at receiving a document in the tone you have written, it's probable the receiver will also take offence. The tone should encourage the desired reaction from the receiver. For example, if we write a memo that requires certain action, the tone should encourage that action. If the tone of the memo is aggressive or offensive, it is unlikely to achieve the desired outcome. If in doubt, ask someone else to review what you have written before it is sent.

BE ACCURATE

Accuracy is another important feature of written communication. The information you convey may be relied upon at a future date. For example, we may advise a customer in a letter that all return flights to the UK during July are $1950.00. This may be true of one airline but is it true of all airlines? If our customers rely on this information to book their travel and find that this quote is for an airline they don't want to fly with, and which doesn't depart on the day they want to travel, then the customer has been misled.

Another example would be writing a report about an incident that occurred with a passenger. Management needs to be confident that we have accurately reported the details. It is not very helpful to remember half the information three days later or exaggerate the exact nature of the incident, especially if the customer sues our employer and we are expected to appear in court to verify what happened.

Before distributing your document check that all the information is correct.

BE LOGICAL

By this we mean check that what is written flows in a logical order. This may be chronological (i.e. in date or time order) or in order of the actions required. A logical flow of information makes writing and reading the document easier.

CHECK SPELLING AND GRAMMAR

An important component of any written communication is correct spelling and grammar. The English language is such that the same word can have a different spelling for a different meaning. If we are not sure if it is the right word to use, we can look the word up in a dictionary or find an alternative word to use in a thesaurus.

Grammar refers to the structure of our sentences—how we put the words together. We use punctuation in writing to help express our meaning. Punctuation provides the flow to a document. As a person reads our documents, they must know when to pause, how long the pause should be and when a thought ends. If the punctuation is poor it is difficult to understand the meaning of the sentence.

Most word processing packages have a spelling and grammar checker. While these are useful they are not entirely reliable. The main reason is that the word typed may in fact be spelt correctly but be the wrong word to use!

SENTENCE STRUCTURE

Short simple sentences are easier to understand than long complicated sentences. Long sentences, with several thoughts and ideas separated by commas, are more difficult to read and understand. Try to construct sentences with only one main thought.

PROOFREAD YOUR DOCUMENT

Before distributing any document, proofread it. To proofread it means to read the document and look for errors and correct them. We are looking for:

- clarity
- accuracy
- jargon and slang
- spelling and grammatical errors.

If we don't think it is clear it is not likely that the reader will. If we think it is inaccurate we are likely to mislead the reader. If we find jargon or slang used in the document we need to substitute more appropriate words. And if there are spelling and grammatical errors we need to correct them!

TYPES OF WRITTEN CORRESPONDENCE

Now that we understand the rules we can start to produce a range of correspondence.

Mostly we need to write:

- business letters
- memorandums
- reports
- messages
- itineraries.

BUSINESS LETTERS

Business letters are written forms of communication between businesses, between a business and an individual, and between individuals. The most common business letters we produce are:

- letters of confirmation
- responding to an enquiry
- responding to a complaint.

Business letters sent from our organisation and those received by our organisation from other businesses are usually printed on letterhead. Letterhead is pre-printed stationery with the company's logo and address details.

Business letter layout

Throughout the business community there is general uniformity in the layout of a business letter. Layout refers to the way in which information in the letter is presented on the page. Uniformity in layout is useful because it helps maintain consistency and maximise readability. It is helpful for producing and reading similar document types if information is located in the same place.

If in doubt, most word processing packages provide templates or examples of the most common layouts for us to use. Figure 5.5 shows one layout commonly used when writing business letters.

Parts of the letter

The letter in Figure 5.5 indicates the various parts that are standard for most letters we will write.

1. Organisation's name and address

All correspondence from the organisation is written on the business's letterhead, for example *Travel Trunk Pty Ltd*, which should include the organisation's name and address.

2. Inside address

An inside address, or the recipient's details, includes the name, title and address of the recipient of the letter.

3. Today's date

Always date your correspondence in a standard format. In Australia, the standard format is day, month, year, for example 9 November 2001.

FIGURE 5.5 *BUSINESS LETTER LAYOUT*

TRAVEL TRUNK PTY LTD *10 HAY ST, PERTH • TEL: 09 505 5055* *for people on the move*	**1. Organisation's name and address**

Mrs Angeline Marcus
Director
Marcus Consulting Pty Ltd
PO Box 290
CITY BEACH WA 6015

2. Inside address

12 October 2001

3. Today's date

Dear Mrs Marcus

4. Greeting

Please find enclosed your itinerary for travel to Christchurch and your accommodation voucher for the Diplomat All-Suite Hotel.

5. Body of the letter

Your Visa card has been debited $4580.00 for the flight. A receipt is enclosed. Please pay the hotel directly for your accommodation.

Thank you for choosing Travel Trunk Pty Ltd. We look forward to being of service to you again in the future.

Yours sincerely

6. Close

Melanie Morecomb

7. Signature

Melanie Morecomb
Senior travel consultant

8. Writer's name and title

Encl.

9. Enclosure

4. Greeting

A greeting or salutation is always included. Use the formal title of the recipient and precede it with 'Dear', for example 'Dear Mrs Reilly'. If the recipient's name is unknown then 'Dear Sir or Madam' is an acceptable salutation.

5. Body of the letter

Now type the body of the letter. The contents of business letters should flow logically. After the greeting:

- in the first paragraph, introduce the reason why you are writing;
- in the second (and third) paragraph explain the details; and
- in the final paragraph explain what action you will take or expect the reader to take.

6. Close

How you close your letter will depend on the greeting:

- If the letter is addressed to a specific individual, such as Mrs Reilly, then the close is 'Yours sincerely'.
- If the letter is not addressed to a specific person, for example Dear Sir or Madam, then the close is 'Yours faithfully'.

7. Signature

Always sign your correspondence.

8. Writer's name and title

Your name and full title is typed here. Alternatively, you can finish by writing:

Yours sincerely
Travel Trunk Pty Ltd

9. Enclosures

When we need to include items in addition to the letter, we type 'encl.' or 'att.' at the bottom. This alerts the reader to the fact that there should be attachments to this letter. In the example given, the enclosures included the gift voucher and the receipt. Do not use 'encl.' if no enclosures are included.

STANDARD LETTERS AND TEMPLATES

Standard letters
Used when the same information needs to be conveyed to several people.

Because many of the business letters we write contain essentially the same information and follow the same layout, to save time a **standard letter** can be developed and stored in the word processing software in the computer. A standard letter saves time because all the basic information required in the letter already exists; you need only to add the personal details of the person for whom the letter is intended and the information specific to this person.

Standard letters are used when the same information needs to be conveyed to several people. For example, a sales letter to be sent to 500 people does not need to be retyped 500 times. One letter is typed and can be personalised with the addition of each recipient's name and personal details. Of course, we could enter each person's name separately 500 times or use the mail merge function in the word processing package. An example of a standard letter is shown in Figure 5.6.

Template
A blueprint for text, graphics or layout, or a combination of all three.

A **template** is a blueprint for text (fonts, type sizes), graphics or layout, or a combination of all three. Many of the documents we produce contain a number of elements, or predefined styles, that remain essentially the same: letterhead, insertion of date,

FIGURE 5.6 *STANDARD LETTER*

TRAVEL TRUNK PTY LTD
10 HAY ST, PERTH • TEL: 09 505 5055
for people on the move

[*Type name and inside address here*]
[*Address*]
[*Address*]
[*Address*]

[*Date*]

Dear [*recipient's name*]

Thank you for choosing to book your travel arrangements with Travel Trunk Pty Ltd. Enclosed please find a copy of your itinerary. Your accommodation details are as follows.

Hotel name and address: [*insert*]

Date of arrival: [*insert*]
Date of departure: [*insert*]
Room type: [*insert*]
Room rate: [*insert*]

Your reservation has been guaranteed with your [*insert*] Card.

We wish you an enjoyable journey.

Yours sincerely

[*Insert sender's name here*]
[*Insert sender's title here*]

Encl.

---

insertion of inside address, salutation and the close, font and type size, and other attributes. These documents also follow the same layout each time they are produced. Instead of reproducing the same layout and elements each time, it is possible to set up a template that makes our job easier and quicker to perform, avoids repetition and routine in letter writing and maintains consistency in the way in which information is presented.

Templates can be designed and customised to best suit the users' needs. Most word processing packages include pre-designed templates but also allow us to modify these or create our own. Each of these has internal 'help' functions to guide us through their use.

Templates are not limited to business letters, however, and can be created for any other type of document we use frequently, such as those summarised earlier in Table 5.1.

An example of a business letter template is shown in Figure 5.7.

FIGURE 5.7 *BUSINESS LETTER TEMPLATE*

TRAVEL TRUNK PTY LTD
10 HAY ST, PERTH • TEL: 09 505 5055
for people on the move

[*Type name and inside address here*]
[*Address*]
[*Address*]
[*Address*]

[*Date*]

Dear [*recipient's name*]

[*Body of letter*]

[*Close*]

[*Writer's name*]
[*Writer's title*]

How it works

The template has the basic elements and layout already in place. When a template is opened on the computer, our input includes filling in the 'blank' spaces. For example, the template indicates where the date should be and how it should be written. We can also set up the template to insert today's date automatically.

We then fill in the rest of the information required as we would for any other business letter:

* Inside address
* Salutation
* Body of the letter
* Close
* Signature

Once the document is created using a template, it is saved according to the standard save and file procedures in our organisation. Whatever name we give our document and whichever file we save it to in the computer will not affect the original template structure. Thus, if we need to we can use the same template time and again.

MAIL MERGE

Almost all tourism organisations maintain records of their customers' names and addresses. This information is stored in the organisation's database in a standardised manner. It is useful to have this information for a number of reasons:

- It helps to keep track of and locate your customers.
- It facilitates the reservation process.
- It allows mail merge with standard letters.

Mail merge allows us to use our guest's details (name and address) to personalise standard letters. We can also use the mail merge function to print labels and envelopes.

Mail merge involves merging the standard documents we create with the database of names and addresses. The database contains the information needed to personalise each standard letter, which contains the information every recipient will receive. When we create a standard letter, we instruct the computer (program) where to insert the merge fields that will be used when we use the merge function. Thus, if we were to mail merge the standard document shown in Figure 5.6 it would now look like the document shown in Figure 5.8.

FIGURE 5.8 *MERGED STANDARD LETTER*

TRAVEL TRUNK PTY LTD
10 HAY ST, PERTH • TEL: 09 505 5055
for people on the move

Ms Andrea Hislop
46 Anaconda Drive
SNAKE BEND WA 6301

24 November 2001

Dear Ms Hislop

Thank you for choosing to book your travel arrangements with Travel Trunk Pty Ltd. Enclosed please find a copy of your itinerary. Your accommodation details are as follows.

Hotel name and address:	Chateau Fleur
	14 Swan Lake Drive
	Morgan
	South Australia 5609
Date of arrival:	23 March 2002
Date of departure:	26 March 2002
Room type:	Central Suite
Room rate:	$285 per night

Your reservation has been guaranteed with your American Express Card.

We wish you an enjoyable journey.

Yours sincerely

Melanie Morecomb

Melanie Morecomb
Senior travel consultant

Encl.

MEMORANDUMS

Memos are written when we need to communicate the same information to several people, usually at once. It is an internal-use document (for staff only), and more effective than trying to communicate the same information verbally.

Memos are used to convey information that affects the workplace. For example, we may need to write a memo about an upcoming event, a new or changed policy, changes to work procedures or a request for information or assistance.

To get the response you need from those who receive our memos, always show the same courtesy you would in any business correspondence.

Memo layout

In general, memos follow a standard layout as shown in Figure 5.9. From the example, we can see that the memo follows a less formal approach than a business letter; it does not have a salutation or a close; however, the addition of common courtesies, such as 'thank you for your assistance' or 'kind regards', does make the memo less officious. Memos are generally brief and to the point. We do not need to type our name at the bottom of the memo because it is entered at the top. However, the person who wrote it signs the memo.

Parts of the memo

Like a business letter, there are standard parts to a memo that help maintain consistency and aid readability. The parts are clearly indicated and explained on the sample shown in Figure 5.9.

When writing memos:

- Try to keep it to one page.
- The first paragraph should introduce the topic.
- The second paragraph should provide details of the topic.
- The final paragraph should state what action, if any, is required.

SIMPLE REPORT WRITING

Apart from the reports that are produced as a consequence of the daily activities undertaken by most tourism organisations, such as activity reports and financial reports, and that are mostly computer generated, you may need to write a report as a result of an accident or other incident, or in response to a request from management.

Many workplaces have standard report forms for us to use. This saves time and ensures information is not overlooked. We need to complete the blank spaces on the form in as much detail as possible.

If we need to write a simple report there are guidelines we should follow:

- Always type the report.
- Number the pages.
- Date the report.
- Introduce the report with a brief background of the event.
- Provide specific details of the incident or event including:
  - what happened
  - who was involved
  - when it happened
  - how it happened
  - where it happened
  - what action was taken.

FIGURE 5.9 *MEMO LAYOUT*

TRAVEL TRUNK PTY LTD
10 HAY ST, PERTH • TEL: 09 505 5055
for people on the move

MEMORANDUM

To:	All staff	**Type recipient's name(s) or position here**
From:	Kathryn Mallory Managing Director	**Type your name or position here**
Date:	29 October 2001	**Type today's date here**
Subject:	New office chairs	**Type the subject or topic here**

Type the body of the memo here

The new office chairs are due to arrive this Friday!

As there is likely to be congestion with the removal of the old chairs as the new ones arrive, I would appreciate everyone working cooperatively to facilitate the changeover to minimise disruption to our customers.

Would all staff please remove their old chair and store it outside ready for collection first thing Friday morning (9 am).

Once these old chairs have been removed (around 9.15 am), your new chair will be delivered.

Thank you for your cooperation.

Kathryn

Sign the memo at the bottom

- Make recommendations (to prevent the incident occurring again).
- Sign the report.

The report is then handed directly to the person who requested the report, or it may be accompanied by a memo explaining that a report has been written and why. Attach the report to the memo. A simple report layout is shown in Figure 5.10.

Always keep a copy of reports. They are frequently referred to later and can be used to refresh our memory when questioned about the incident later.

As you can see, the simple report shown in Figure 5.10 follows a similar layout and structure to a memorandum. However, it is likely to extend to several pages.

Finally, all reports should:

- be easy to read and understand;
- be written in a rational and objective manner;
- follow a logical sequence;
- be written in a concise and lively style;
- draw valid and logical conclusions; and
- be proofread.

FIGURE 5.10 *SIMPLE REPORT LAYOUT*

TRAVEL TRUNK PTY LTD
10 HAY ST, PERTH • TEL: 09 505 5055
for people on the move

INCIDENT REPORT

To:	Kathryn Mallory
	Managing Director
From:	Melanie Morecomb
	Senior travel consultant
Date:	3 August 2001

Introduce the report with a brief background of the event.

Provide specific details of the incident or event:
· What happened
· Who was involved
· When it happened
· How it happened
· Where it happened
· What action was taken

Make recommendations (to prevent the incident occurring again).

Sign the report.

HOW BUSINESS DOCUMENTS ARE SENT AND RECEIVED

Business documents may be sent or received by:

• Mail (post, courier or hand delivered)
• Fax
• E-mail

MAIL

Sending documents by mail simply requires that the correspondence be produced then placed in an envelope, and the envelope sealed, addressed and stamped. It can then be posted, or delivered by courier or by hand.

FACSIMILES

Sending documents by fax usually requires that the correspondence first be produced as described earlier and then faxed with a covering page, or for short, informal messages typed or handwritten directly onto a fax cover page. When this is the case, facsimiles are written in a standardised format and usually created from a template. A facsimile is usually a less formal form of communication than a business letter but contains many similar elements, only presented differently. An example is shown in Figure 5.11.

E-MAIL

Like a fax, an e-mail can be sent with attachments (being the formal documents) or, for short, informal messages, typed directly onto the e-mail cover page.

FIGURE 5.11 *FACSIMILE LAYOUT*

TRAVEL TRUNK PTY LTD
10 HAY ST, PERTH • TEL: 09 505 5055
for people on the move

FACSIMILE TRANSMISSION

To: _____	**Fax no:** _____
Attention: _____	**From:** _____
Date: _____	**Total pages:** _____

Message

Always remember, however, that like facsimiles other people may see e-mails, so we should not use this format for highly confidential communication unless we are certain that the receiver will be the sole recipient.

There are numerous examples of highly sensitive information that has leaked out through sloppy clerical procedures.

check please

14. List five rules to remember for successful writing.

15. Why are the rules important?

16. Why shouldn't we use slang or jargon when writing?

17. Name four types of correspondence you may be asked to write when working in a travel agency, airline or coach tour company.

18. What is letterhead? Why do you think businesses send out letters on letterhead?

19. What types of correspondence might you use a standard letter for?

20. What are the advantages of using a template?

21. When would you mail merge?

22. Why would you send staff a memo? List three examples of things you would write a memo about in a travel agency, visitor centre or attraction venue.

23. Why is it important to keep the tone of a memo polite?

24. What does each paragraph in a memo discuss?

25. Why might you need to know how to write a report when working as a tour guide?

Maintain storage and filing systems

Most businesses generate large quantities of printed and manual documentation, and whether the documentation is in current use (active) or theoretically finished with (inactive) it needs to be filed and stored.

Active documents (documents that relate to current events, ongoing events, current customers or reservations) are filed where they are readily accessible. **Inactive documents** (documents that have no immediate use) are filed in a central location where they are readily accessible but out of the way—a storage cupboard or similar facility.

Much of the documentation is kept for a number of years as reference material, for example internal memos, purchase orders and newsletters. Other documents, such as tax invoices and copies of customer accounts and payment method, are kept for legal reasons, for tax auditing purposes.

Some documents can be filed manually, such as in a filing cabinet, and some can be filed electronically, such as those records maintained on a computer.

Whatever the reason for keeping records, and however it is managed (manually or electronically), it is important that documents be filed and stored logically for both ease of reference and security.

WHAT IS FILING?

Filing is the process of arranging and storing documents according to a particular classification. Printed documents, such as itineraries, reports, memos, correspondence and customer accounts, are filed manually. This information can also be filed electronically, but a customer's itinerary, for example, produced on the computer may also be printed (hard copy) and filed manually. Details of a deposit received for a reservation are recorded in the computer and a receipt printed. A copy of the receipt is sent to the customer and another filed with the customer's profile.

Filing can be classified, or indexed, into five categories:

1. Alphabetically
2. Numerically
3. Geographically
4. By subject
5. Chronologically

ALPHABETICALLY

Documents filed alphabetically are filed according to the first, and subsequent, letter of the sender's or receiver's name, or according to the type of document, such as policies and procedures. For example, employee files are filed according to the employee's surname. Group reservation files may be filed first under 'groups' and then by group name. A letter requesting information may be held in a 'pending' file by customer name. Customer profiles are maintained alphabetically.

NUMERICALLY

Filing numerically means filing documents according to a number, such as an invoice number, account number, flight number or other numerical identifier, such as a procedure number. For example, procedures for managing a tour are allocated a procedure number and filed together numerically.

GEOGRAPHICALLY

Filing geographically means filing according to a location or designated area, for example Victoria, western region or southern district. This type of information can be useful for the sales and marketing department—it helps the department identify regions where the enterprise's customers (target markets) live.

BY SUBJECT

Some documents cannot be filed any other way except by their subject matter. Examples of files filed by subject include complaint letters (filed under 'complaints'), training (filed under 'training'), contracts for equipment maintenance, quotes, suppliers' lists and so on.

CHRONOLOGICALLY

Documents filed chronologically are filed in date or time order. For example, when a reservation has been entered into a computer it is stored by date (although it may also be filed by flight or tour number).

CLASSIFICATIONS WITHIN CLASSIFICATIONS

Many of the filing examples used above are filed in more than one way under a main heading. For example, a customer's booking may be filed under their name and also by departure date. Groups are often filed under 'groups' and then alphabetically (by group name) or numerically (by group code). Many other documents can be filed in this way.

MANUAL FILING

Despite predictions of a paperless office with increased computer technology, most offices maintain a paper-based filing system. There are several reasons for this (computer breakdown, for example) but for most businesses the reason is the need for a hard copy of all information that may be stored on the computer. For example, if a customer needs a copy of their itinerary it may be easier to photocopy it.

FILE PREPARATION

Before filing any documents, there are a number of tasks to complete:

- Collect all relevant documents.
- Inspect the quality of the documents.
- Cross-reference the files.
- Code the files.
- Sort the files.
- File the documents.

Collect relevant data

Before filing documents check that all details are included in the one file. For example, if filing a letter of confirmation for travel arrangements, with a deposit, check that there is a copy of the deposit slip, that the method and amount of payment are listed and that a copy of the confirmation letter is attached. If there is a query about the booking or deposit at any time, it will be easy to check all relevant details because they have been collected and filed together.

Inspect the quality of the paperwork

Paper is easily damaged and, over time, can deteriorate. Before filing documents check the quality of the items. Is the paper torn? Does it need to be photocopied and replaced? Is there an excess of staples and paper clips to be removed? Make sure that all the paperwork is straightened and neat before placing in the file.

Cross-reference files

Cross-referencing means linking one file, or information in a file, to another, relevant, file. For example, a group file filed under 'groups' (alphabetically) is cross-referenced with the reservations file (filed chronologically, by date).

Code files

To code a document means to give it a reference number or name that differentiates it from any other similar document. A code is often required because we may have more than one file with the same name. For example, Southern Pacific Tours make several group bookings each year and we may have several groups booked for the coming months. If we filed them all under 'Southern Pacific', we would be unable to identify information specific to each group. By allocating a code we have a distinctive identifier. For example, the code may be the group name (or abbreviation) and the arrival date, thus SouthPac2010 and SouthPac1012. The first Southern Pacific group is departing on 20 October and the second group is departing on 10 December.

Sort the files

Sorting simply requires us to put like files with like files. For example, we put customer profiles together, group files together and so on. Often the file storage facility for each of the different files is located in various areas, therefore instead of moving backwards and forwards between the various filing cabinets and locations we are able first to file all of one type of file, then the next and so on.

File the documents

Once we have everything together, cross-referenced, coded and sorted, we are now ready to file. Documents can be filed in a filing cabinet, A4 folders, index boxes or shelving, depending on the equipment and filing system used by the enterprise.

---

activity 5.1

▶ The table below lists a range of documents that need filing. On the right, indicate how you would file each document. For example, a reservation slip is filed chronologically (by date of arrival). Indicate which, if any, you would cross-reference and to which file you would cross-reference it.

DOCUMENT	FILE CLASSIFICATION
Fax requesting information on tours	
Memo about new staff uniforms	
Sales letter to be sent to all residents in a particular suburb	
A new policy about staff leave entitlements	
A variation to the emergency evacuation procedure	
Incident report	
E-mail requesting a booking	
Letter of complaint	
Letter to a customer confirming their booking	
A customer's itinerary	

Whatever system is used follow the established system (alphabetical, numerical, etc.) and place the documents in the correct location in the file. A misplaced or incorrectly filed document can create problems at a later stage.

ELECTRONIC FILING

Some information is filed and stored electronically. Information collated and filed onto a computer reduces the need for a lot of physical filing storage space. The storage medium is either the hard drive of the computer (the computer's 'memory') or one of the methods noted earlier (floppy disk, zip disk, etc.). What was previously stored in a three-drawer filing cabinet can now be stored on several diskettes, which are in turn filed.

When we need to retrieve and access the information stored on the disk it can be reloaded onto almost any computer operating the same system in which the information was originally saved.

Apart from its portability, the advantages of saving data to disk are:

- Reduced filing space
- Reduced filing time
- Easy access and document modification
- Readily traceable document changes

FILING DOCUMENTS ON DISK

Just as it is important to have an organised manual filing system, so it is important to maintain an organised electronic filing system. Like manual filing, documents must be first named and/or coded and then filed according to a logical classification. For example, to file documents electronically we may decide to create 'folders' into which we place each file. A folder name should clearly identify its contents, for example 'Memos', 'Complaints', 'Welcome letters' and so on and within these folders we then place the file. For example, we have just written a memo to all staff about the introduction of a new computer system. The memo is given a name and filed in the 'Memos' folder.

To organise electronic filing efficiently:

- Label files in an easily recognisable and logical manner. Depending on how recent the word processing package in use is, most file names can have in excess of 200 characters.
- File documents to folders.
- Always back up the files to disk. In other words, save the document on the computer hard drive and on a disk.
- Label and keep secure all disks (as we would our filing cabinets).
- Treat the disks with care. A broken or damaged disk may lose literally hundreds of hours of work and multiple documents.

RECORD MAINTENANCE

Once a document is filed it may need to be updated and maintained. For example, a manually maintained customer profile needs updating after each trip or visit by the customer. When files are handled in this way follow the procedures for file preparation, making sure that the files are always kept neat and clean and in an orderly fashion. At times we may need to access files and make changes to them (record utilisation) and on other occasions we may need to remove a file altogether (archiving).

RECORD UTILISATION AND TRANSMISSION

From time to time we need to access files in order to change or refer to their contents. This means we need physically to remove a paper-based file from its storage facility or retrieve an electronic file on the computer. For example, a group booking we processed needs to be changed (at the group's request). We need to remove the group file from the files, and retrieve the details in the computer, make the changes on the file and in the computer record, then re-file the group's file and save the change in the computer.

When we retrieve a document (such as a letter or memo) that is saved to disk (or the hard drive of a computer), then adjust it and close the file again, the computer remembers where to file it. The computer is also able to record automatically the date the file was last accessed and which computer terminal accessed the file.

When removing a file from the manual filing system it is important that there is a record of the movement. The record should indicate the date the file was removed, by whom and where it has gone. This helps keep track of files and reduces the likelihood of lost files. Also, if someone else needs to access the file they will know where to find it. Figure 5.12 shows an example of a file movement marker used for this purpose. The movement marker is placed in the filing cabinet in place of the original file. An alternative to this is a file movement book, which records essentially the same information but in a logbook.

ARCHIVING

Archiving is the practice of removing a file or record from everyday use and storing it in another location. The file is not disposed of but transferred to where it is still accessible, although not as easily. Documents are archived:

Archiving
The practice of removing a file or record from everyday use and storing it in another location.

* to make room (there is limited storage space in an office environment);
* because they are not used as often as they were; and
* because most records must be kept (by law) for a minimum of five years.

Archives may be located in a basement or cupboard or a storage facility away from the office. Wherever we archive documents the area must be dry and clean. A damp environment will cause deterioration of the documents: it will cause mould and mildew and potentially attract pests such as silverfish and moths.

Deciding when to archive a document is quite subjective. Most businesses archive when the filing cabinet is full! Others are quite methodical about their archiving—some documents are archived after three months and others at the end of the financial year, such as financial reports.

Archived documents need to be labelled clearly. They are stored usually in date order (the date on which they are archived or the period to which they relate).

FIGURE 5.12 *MOVEMENT MARKER*

File name:

Removed by:

Date:

Returned date:

26. What is the difference between active and inactive files? Give two examples of documents that may be regarded as active or inactive. When might documents become inactive? What do we then do with them?

27. Why is it so important to file correctly?

28. List the five different ways in which files can be arranged. Briefly explain each. What use do you think this is?

29. What would be the best way to file a complaint letter? A customer's itinerary?

30. What tasks need to be completed to prepare a document for filing?

31. Why would we cross-reference a file? Give an example of a file that may be cross-referenced.

32. What is the difference between manual and electronic filing?

33. Why should you always back up documents to disks?

34. Describe the advantages of using a movement marker when removing a document from a file.

35. What is archiving?

36. Where is the best place to store the archived documents? What conditions should archives be stored in? Why?

Deal with conflict situations

CHAPTER 6

LEARNING OUTCOMES

On completion of this chapter you will be able to:

- define conflict and explain the different types of conflict;
- identify the different causes of conflict;
- recognise potential conflict situations;
- resolve conflict situations;
- use a range of conflict resolution techniques;
- develop communication skills in conflict resolution;
- implement conflict resolution techniques; and
- respond to customer complaints.

This chapter complies with the Tourism Industry National Competency Standards, unit THHGCS03A, 'Deal With Conflict Situations'.

Handling conflict successfully is, for many of us, a difficult challenge. Indeed, many people avoid conflict altogether, preferring to ignore the situation or just give in to the other side rather than be confronted by it. While conflict has the potential to be negative, it can also be positive. We have a responsibility to manage conflict in our work environment. Our challenge is to turn conflict into positive opportunities for the organisation, colleagues and ourselves.

The concept of conflict being negative and something to be avoided is a fairly typical view and assumes that all conflict is harmful to the organisation. Certainly if conflict remains unresolved or is ineffectively resolved then it can be harmful; however, in any organisation conflict is generally inevitable. We therefore need to identify ways to turn it into something positive.

When handled appropriately, conflict can actually lead to improved working relationships and customer service, increased productivity and opportunities for us to develop our interpersonal skills.

The conflicts that present themselves on a daily basis in a tourism environment can leave us feeling exhausted and frustrated or challenged and relieved. The skills we develop to manage conflict will determine which outcome occurs.

In this chapter we aim to provide the skills and knowledge necessary to manage conflict to achieve a positive result every time.

---

paint a picture ▶ **Conflict with Colleagues**

Ismael and Gloria are both customer service officers, attending to the Giant Water Slide at Water World. When they go for a break Ismael starts arguing with Gloria, accusing her of jeopardising the safety of customers by allowing them to follow each other too quickly down the waterslide.

Gloria tells Ismael to mind his own business and what would he know, he was too busy talking to the girl in the red bikini anyway. Both Ismael and Gloria return to work feeling dissatisfied with this exchange and do not talk to each other again the rest of the day. How might this exchange have been better managed?

What is conflict?

Conflict
Any situation where there is disagreement between two or more individuals.

Conflict in the workplace is usually any situation where disagreement occurs between two or more individuals. The disagreement usually flows from a misunderstanding about expectations and needs. Conflict in the workplace can occur between colleagues, staff and customers and staff and management. What is important is that conflict must be identified before it can be resolved.

TYPES OF CONFLICT

Types of conflict
· Within ourself
· Between colleagues
· With a customer
· Between organisations
· Between customers

When we think of conflict, we usually only associate it with a disagreement between people. However, there are in fact several types of conflict for us to be aware of; these are discussed below.

CONFLICT WITHIN OURSELF

This type of conflict arises when we are 'in two minds' about something. For example, it could be as simple as having difficulty in prioritising the completion of two tasks.

The conflict can also be more serious and have ethical or legal implications that may impact on others, such as taking the credit for work we didn't do or not employing someone because of our biases. It may also be as a result of being given instructions with which we are uncomfortable.

CONFLICT BETWEEN US AND A COLLEAGUE

In the workplace, conflict between colleagues is a common occurrence. It is important to recognise that it exists and to learn how to manage it. Unresolved conflict between colleagues can be disruptive and potentially damaging to the standard of service delivered and the wellbeing of the establishment. On the other hand, if handled correctly differences of opinion can be used to produce better solutions to issues. Many of these conflicts are role related, while others are personality related (also referred to as the 'cause of conflict').

CONFLICT BETWEEN US AND A CUSTOMER

It seems hard to believe, but conflict often occurs between customers and staff. As a service industry, tourism is usually concerned with providing customers with the best possible service within its means. However, many organisations frequently find they have failed to meet the customer's expectation of service, thus creating an area of conflict.

CONFLICT BETWEEN ORGANISATIONS

Conflict between organisations arises because each organisation is striving to achieve its own goals (of profit, success, growth, market share) and this may sometimes be to the detriment of similar organisations. Perhaps a more appropriate term for this type of conflict is 'competition'.

This form of conflict (competition) is generally perceived as 'good' as it contributes to the wellbeing of the economy (and therefore will benefit our customers). This form of conflict sometimes leads to the development of better services and products or lower prices; however, it can also create an extremely negative view of the industry if not handled professionally.

CONFLICT BETWEEN CUSTOMERS

Occasionally customers will argue between themselves and we have to be very sensitive in dealing with these types of conflict. These may be due to the influence of drugs, alcohol or just emotion, and in all situations we must weigh up the wellbeing of all the people involved, including other customers and our staff. Throughout this chapter we will focus on conflict between us and our colleagues and us and our customers.

---

check please

1. What is conflict?
2. Identify the different types of conflict.

Causes of conflict

Now that we have identified the different types of conflict and that conflict is generally considered a form of misunderstanding, it is important that we identify the main causes of conflict arising in the workplace. These are:

- *Different expectations* Throughout this book we have talked about the customers' expectations of us and our organisation's products and services. Failing to meet the customers' expectations may lead to conflict.
- *Communication barriers* Conflict between colleagues as well as between us and customers may result from communication barriers. For example, language differences, poor verbal skills (i.e. an inability to express the proper meaning of information), poor communication due to poor systems or failure to follow procedure, poor listening skills, preconceived ideas, prejudices and a range of other factors may cause communication barriers.
- *Motivation factors* In Chapter 8, 'Promote and sell products and services', we talk about the factors that motivate us to do something. These factors vary between each of us and will influence how we respond to others. For example, if in the workplace we are motivated to do a good job and our colleague is not as motivated, this could lead to conflict if we believe they are not pulling their weight.
- *Cultural values* The many people we encounter in tourism come from a varied cultural pool. Our cultural influences lead us to behave and react in certain ways. For example, cultural values will influence work ethics, how we respond to people from other cultures and how we deal with authority. It is not surprising therefore that we all don't behave in the same way or react to the same event in the same way. As a result, we have conditions for potential conflict.
- *Personality* Personality refers to our individual characteristics. Even those of us from the same cultural background will experience conflict that may be personality related. Sometimes we just don't like someone. We may not even be able to pinpoint what it is about this person that we don't like. But this is a very real and frequent cause of conflict in the workplace and may relate to a colleague or a customer. Personality traits are not something we can do much about, but we can and should learn to live (and work) with others' 'irritating' ways. After all, no one is perfect, are they?
- *Safety and security issues* Where a person feels their safety or security is compromised (whether real or imagined) conflict may arise. Feelings of safety usually relate to a person's physical wellbeing or that of people close to them. Security may also relate to a person's state of mind. For example, if a colleague feels intimidated or insecure about their position in the workplace, conflict may arise as they may feel they can't fully undertake their duties.
- *Organisational structure* Organisational structure refers to how the services and facilities offered by an establishment are organised and grouped so that the establishment can conduct its business in a way that best meets its customers' needs and expectations. This grouping into a structure of departments allows for a better control of the services offered. Grouping into departments is also useful for staff. It helps them clearly identify their roles and responsibilities and allows them to see where they fit into the overall structure of the establishment. A potential cause of conflict with roles and responsibilities (organisational structure) lies in the fact that many people are unsure as to what their exact responsibilities are or, alternatively, feel that 'It's not my job' when confronted by a request that is usually performed by someone else. In tourism all requests are everyone's responsibility where the customer is concerned, even if it means that we take a request and refer it to a colleague for completion.

- *Organisational change* Conflict is sure to arise whenever change occurs in the workplace. The main reason for this is our general resistance to change: 'What's wrong with the way we do it now?' 'We've always done it this way . . .' etc. Most of us are resistant to change because it takes us out of our comfort zone and into siuations with which we feel uncomfortable, or forces us to deal with situations we would rather not face.

Of course there are numerous other potential causes of conflict, such as our (and others') attitude, stress levels, experience, training, frame of mind and skill level, to name a few. These will all potentially cause conflict and affect how we manage conflict with both our customers and our colleagues.

Causes of conflict
· Misunderstandings
· Different expectations
· Communication barriers
· Motivation factors
· Cultural values
· Personality
· Safety and security issues
· Organisational structure
· Organisational change

file this

▶ Conflict is a normal part of interaction between humans. Solutions to conflict can always be found if both parties are willing.

Identifying potential for conflict

Identifying potential for conflict is the necessary first step to managing it. How do we identify potential conflict? Think of it in context to the workplace. Because conflict is usually any disagreement between two or more people, in a tourism environment the most likely cause of conflict arises from differences in expectations. In other words, what are the expectations of our customers? Our colleagues? Our employer? How does our body language and what we say cause conflict?

CUSTOMER EXPECTATIONS

Our customers expect us to:

- be able to do our job;
- do our job efficiently;
- be professional in dealing with them;
- solve their problems.

If at any point we are unable to meet these expectations there is the potential for conflict.

COLLEAGUE EXPECTATIONS

Whether we consider it reasonable or not, colleagues have expectations of each other. These expectations extend beyond our immediate work group to include colleagues in other departments. For example, if we recommend to a customer that they book one of our tours in preference to another, because we have experienced that particular tour and believe it to be excellent, we expect that the tour will live up to the expectation we have created in our customer's mind. If the tour turns out to be a poor experience for the customer because of the staff, there is potential for conflict between us and the tour staff (we will be reluctant to recommend the tour again) and potentially between us and the customer as their expectations have not been met.

Colleagues also expect us to:

- have similar work-related goals;
- do our job well;
- pull our weight (do our fair share of the work);
- be reliable;
- meet customers' expectations;
- meet the expectations of the organisation.

If we (or a colleague) are unable to meet all of these expectations then there is the potential for conflict to arise.

ENTERPRISE EXPECTATIONS

The organisation we work for tries very hard to establish and maintain standards of service in order to attract and retain its targeted market. The organisation relies on its staff to meet the expectations it has created in its customers thus reducing the likelihood of conflict between the organisation and its customers. The organisation also expects us to:

- have good interpersonal skills;
- meet customer expectations;
- be motivated (to do our job well, following established procedures);
- be reliable and consistent in performing our tasks;
- be professional (in our attitude and presentation).

Already we are able to identify a number of events that may lead to conflict. If we don't live up to all the expectations listed there may be conflict. Having an awareness and understanding of these expectations will help us take action quickly, diplomatically and professionally to prevent a major incident.

BODY LANGUAGE

As discussed in Chapter 2 customers and colleagues communicate thoughts and feelings using body language (in addition to the spoken word). Identifying potential conflict through body language presents an opportunity for us to address the problem before it escalates. Some of the body language signals we may encounter include:

- Someone tapping their finger or feet (impatience)
- A frown or a snarl (anger)
- Arms crossed (defensive)
- Poor eye contact (not listening to us)
- Aggressive action like finger pointing or arm waving
- Shrugging the shoulders (not interested)
- Shaking of the head, eyes closed (they do not agree with what we are saying)

While there are many more examples, it is important to remember that body language signals are not universal. In other words, cultural factors may influence the message being sent via body language, therefore body language signals should not be considered in isolation. We need to *listen* to what the other person is *saying* as well as indicating. Their arms may be crossed because they are cold, they may be pointing at something unrelated to us, they may be tapping their feet to a tune they can hear, or they may be shrugging their shoulders because they cannot understand us.

THE SPOKEN WORD

What a person is saying and how they are saying it can clearly indicate potential (or actual) conflict. For example:

- The pitch of their voice may be rising.
- The rate (speed) of their speech may increase or slow down.
- The tone of their voice may be sarcastic or condescending ('Perhaps I should speak with your supervisor who *would* understand what I'm saying?').
- They may be accusing us of something ('*You're* the one who messed this up, *you* fix it').
- They may be telling us how to behave ('Perhaps you should get a better attitude').

activity 6.1

▶ A customer is standing at a flight check-in desk late at night. He is obviously tired and grumpy and it is clear he is anxious to check in because his flight is due to leave soon. He is tapping his fingers and looking around. The customer service attendant cannot find the reservation, the phone is ringing and several other customers keep staring at this untidy and impatient person. Finally the customer becomes quite angry and begins yelling at the staff, complaining of their incompetence.

In small groups, discuss how you should handle this situation. When you have found a solution that you think will satisfy this customer, you may like to role-play the scenario and determine how effectively you managed the situation.

However we handle it, we should not ignore conflict and hope it goes away! While we may feel uncomfortable, the customer may feel even worse! Customers rely upon us to solve their problems and address their concerns. It is important not to take conflict as a personal affront, but rather look on it as an opportunity to improve communication between people. Once this hurdle is overcome, customers will often return to us to help them in the future because we have demonstrated that we can!

check please

3. Discuss five causes of conflict. Having identified causes of conflict, how do you think you might avoid conflict arising?

4. Why is it important to manage conflict in the workplace?

5. In what ways can conflict be positive for the workplace?

6. What value is there in understanding the expectations of others in relation to managing conflict?

7. How can body language and the way in which a customer speaks help you identify potential conflict?

Resolving conflict situations

Each of us will approach conflict differently. Some of us will be good at handling it, others will shy away from it; some of us will become aggressive when confronted by it, while others will take the opportunity to learn from it. We each have a preferred way of managing conflict, therefore it's as important to be aware of conflict management styles as it is to identify potential causes.

FINDING A SOLUTION

Finding a solution to conflict is not necessarily an easy task. It frequently requires us to explore areas we would rather avoid. Pretending conflict doesn't exist, hoping it will go away or ignoring the problem altogether will escalate the problem in the long run. Our goal should be to resolve the conflict quickly and satisfactorily.

Conflict outcomes
· Lose-lose
· Win-lose
· Win-win

Our response to conflict in the workplace will also determine whether the outcome is constructive or destructive. An important goal of conflict management therefore should be to achieve resolution that satisfies *all* parties. Because the outcome is so important, we will look at the possible outcomes of conflict before moving onto the actual techniques that can be used to resolve conflict.

LOSE–LOSE OUTCOME

This outcome results in everyone being unhappy and dissatisfied. Everyone walks away feeling resentful and frustrated. For example, a customer complains about the length of time that it took for a staff member to acknowledge them. The staff member replies that 'we are very busy and I'll get to you when I can'. Who wins here? Nobody. The customer certainly lost and the staff member resents the customer for the negative feedback.

WIN–LOSE OUTCOME

In this situation one party loses and the other party wins, usually at the expense of the other party. For example, a customer said that they lost some jewellery on a coach tour and claims someone stole it. If it then turns up in a vacuum cleaner, it is very easy to tell the customer that they were wrong. In this situation the customer goes away feeling embarrassed and is not likely to return. We have won the argument but lost the customer.

A win–lose situation can have a positive outcome if the person in the wrong can acknowledge this. However, getting someone to understand, in a non-threatening or non-accusatory way, that they were wrong requires exceptional interpersonal skills.

WIN–WIN OUTCOME

Certainly the preferred outcome in most conflicts, win–win reflects the desire to resolve the conflict to the satisfaction of all parties. To do so, however, requires collaboration between the parties and consideration of all underlying influences that caused the conflict in the first place.

To achieve a win–win situation, we must be willing to:

1. respect and acknowledge that everyone has different expectations and perceptions, and has a right to complain if these aren't met;
2. verbalise what we want—if we cannot do this, the outcome will be win–lose because we merely gave in to another's point of view (they won, we lost);
3. identify and practise appropriate conflict resolution techniques.

▶ A customer with a broken leg boards a Qantas flight from Melbourne to Perth and has specifically asked her travel agent to request extra leg room to accommodate the cast on her leg. When she obtains her seat allocation, however, she finds herself placed in a normal seat with insufficient leg room. When she complains, the Cabin Manager realises that the customer's travel agent has failed to notify the airline about the extra room required. As there are no seats available either in the exit row or at the front of the economy class cabin (where more leg space is usually available), the Cabin Manager decides to upgrade the passenger to Business Class, thus making the customer happy. The customer is thus aware that the fault was not with the airline, yet airline staff have taken action to acknowledge the customer's concern and have made appropriate arrangements to assist her.

RESPONSIBILITY FOR RESOLVING CONFLICT

Responsibility for resolving conflict usually rests with those directly involved. However, other factors may influence who is responsible for resolving some types of conflict.

OUR POSITION IN THE WORKPLACE

Depending on our position and level of responsibility, we may or may not be expected, or allowed, to resolve all conflict situations. For example, if the conflict is about locating a customer's lost luggage we can take responsibility for finding it. The customer needs to feel that whoever they deal with in the organisation has the authority to solve simple problems like finding their lost luggage.

If, on the other hand, a customer is extremely aggressive and demanding something of us that we do not have the authority to grant, such as paying for lost items, we need to call in our supervisor or manager. Some customers may only be satisfied when dealing with a higher authority anyway. If this is the case give the customer what they want: call the supervisor.

THE PEOPLE INVOLVED

The example above deals specifically with a customer; however, conflict may sometimes be with a colleague. Most organisations have in place a procedure for conflict resolution (a grievance procedure which usually requires us to attempt to resolve a conflict with a colleague before following formal procedure). For example, if we are unhappy with a colleague's work performance and feel it is affecting our own performance, we should approach the colleague first to voice our concerns. If the colleague is non-receptive or dismissive of our concerns, we may then feel it appropriate to follow the formal procedure and involve more senior staff.

NATURE OF THE CONFLICT

Some conflict, by its very nature, requires intervention by others. For example, any incident that results in potential or actual safety or security breaches requires the involvement of management. An example might be two customers fighting in a bar, or a customer complaining about theft from their belongings. Because both these incidents may require police involvement, it is appropriate to include management in resolving the conflict.

It is important that we involve our supervisor whenever we do not feel totally comfortable or in control of a conflict situation. Losing control of a situation will almost certainly guarantee a lose–lose outcome.

check please

8. Why is a win–lose outcome not acceptable in conflict situations?

9. To get to win–win, three things must happen. What are they? Why are they so important to the outcome?

10. How does your position affect your ability to manage conflict situations?

11. When would it be appropriate to ask for your supervisor's intervention in a conflict?

Conflict resolution techniques

The possible outcomes resulting from conflict have been highlighted in the previous section. Clearly a win–win situation is the most preferred and most of the time this is what we will achieve. But to get to win–win, we need to be aware of the resolution techniques that work and the ones that don't. The following demonstrates what is required to achieve a certain result and when it is and is not appropriate for these techniques to be used.

Of the many conflict resolution techniques available the ones used will depend on the factors discussed earlier (the nature of the conflict, the people involved and our position in the workplace). Remember, we are trying to achieve a win–win outcome, but not all approaches to conflict resolution result in win–win.

COMPROMISING

This technique attempts to find a 'middle' ground between the conflicting parties. The idea is that both parties achieve a few 'wins' and both parties make a few sacrifices. Of course, it is hoped that the 'wins' and the sacrifices counter-balance each other so that the final outcome is win–win, but this rarely occurs. Most of the time the outcome is lose–lose because both parties have had to give in.

Compromising
When each party involved in a conflict is required to concede something they value to resolve the conflict.

The technique of **compromising** usually requires the input of a third party or 'mediator'. This allows both parties the opportunity to express their viewpoint without being overpowered by the other. Assertiveness skills and cooperation are required to both express our point of view and consider the other view.

The disadvantage of this technique is that sometimes the solution is only partially acceptable to both parties. While the conflict may appear to have been settled, this technique leaves itself open to simmering conflict that may occur again.

Compromising is usually used between conflicting colleagues, although it may be used in a conflict with a customer. For example, if two colleagues can't work together, and both insist they are 'right' (and the other wrong), the solution may be to have them rostered on different shifts. This way, no one loses their job or feels that they have to leave. However, the new rosters may not suit; the two parties still have a conflict and the other 'loser' may be the organisation.

Using the technique of compromising with a customer may be appropriate when, for example, a customer is demanding their travel agent provide a total refund of their holiday because the tap dripped in one of their hotel rooms all night. It is not likely that the travel agent will want to give a total refund; however, they may seek some compensation from the hotel on the customer's behalf. This way the travel agent has demonstrated a willingness to assist but not given in to the customer.

ACCOMMODATING

Accommodating, or smoothing things over, involves playing down the real issues at hand (the reason for the conflict). It also plays up the similarities between the parties and focuses on these to achieve a resolution. The recognition of common interests serves to establish a peaceful co-existence long enough to develop a genuine resolution.

This conflict technique can work and achieve win–win only if the conflict is addressed early. If the conflict has been allowed to 'fester' then this technique is less effective as it has a tendency to force a submissive approach where one of the parties needs to put the other person's needs before their own. The other disadvantage is that accommodating potentially leads to one party taking advantage of the other, thus resulting in a win–lose or lose–lose outcome.

Accommodating is frequently used when managing some forms of conflict with a customer. For example, a customer is checked into a hotel room that they insist is not what they booked. They say that they explicitly remember requesting a room with a view and a spa bath. Even though we remember taking this booking and that these things were *not* requested when offered, we agree to move the customer immediately. There is no point arguing with this customer.

Accommodating
Plays down the differences and plays up the similarities between the conflicting parties in the hope of 'smoothing' things over.

COMPETING

A **competing** conflict resolution technique frequently means that there is a clear-cut winner and loser. This may be from force, authority, domination or superior skill.

The competition may be about who is right and who is wrong or who did what better, for example. It may be about supervisor and subordinate roles ('I'm the boss so you have to do what I say'). It frequently requires the intervention of a third party to impose a solution (you win, you lose) or recommend a compromise. It is rare that both parties are right (at least in the eyes of the other). If a competing technique is used, it's only going to be effective if the conflict is over something trivial in the first place (who sold the most souvenirs!). If it is over a (perceived) major issue ('I'm the most efficient worker here and I'm really upset with the rest of them slacking off') then this technique won't work. It is clear to see that this technique mostly results in win–lose outcomes.

The only time that this may be appropriate when customers are involved is when immediate action needs to be taken. For example, if there is a large, rowdy and drunken group of people creating a disturbance, other customers may be at risk. If another customer complains about the group's behaviour and they are concerned for their family's welfare, immediate action must be taken to ensure the wellbeing of others. The action we take must be diplomatic as well as assertive to ensure that we don't make the matter worse by offending the rowdy group.

Competing
This technique results in victory for one through force, authority, domination or superior skill.

AVOIDING

Avoiding
One or both of the parties ignore the conflict issues in the hope that they will go away.

Avoiding frequently results in a lose–lose situation. This is an extreme case of not dealing with the problem at all. For example, if the customer who complained about the rowdy group saw that we did nothing to allay their concerns, they would feel we had failed in our duty to protect them and their family. The organisation has probably lost a customer. Neither party got what they wanted.

Needless to say, this is a poor technique to use in a tourism environment. Whether we feel a customer's complaint is reasonable or not, some form of resolution must be sought.

Avoiding is extremely ineffective, essentially because the conflict is brushed aside or 'swept under the carpet' in the hope that it will go away. The conflict will not be resolved (the rowdy group may eventually leave but the poor image left with the complaining customer is still there).

If the conflict issues remain unresolved, there is the potential for them to 'simmer' and grow and eventually manifest as an even bigger problem at a later stage.

Sometimes temporary avoidance is appropriate if the timing to address the problem is not right (in the middle of a busy service period) or if the conflicting parties need time to think about the issue and 'cool off'. Remember, however, that temporary avoidance is just that—temporary. Be sure to tackle the conflict as soon as possible before it gets out of hand.

COLLABORATION

Collaboration
The most effective and direct technique for achieving win-win conflict resolution. It uses problem-solving techniques to resolve the issues of each of the conflicting parties.

Collaboration is the most effective and direct approach to getting to win–win. It is a positive approach that involves recognition by all that something is wrong and needs to be resolved. Only through collaboration can both parties constructively present their point of view and have all of their expectations met.

Collaboration works through the stages of a problem: that is, by isolating and agreeing what the problem is, gathering and evaluating all the relevant information, then identifying possible solutions and agreeing on the most appropriate solution.

Collaboration takes time, well-developed interpersonal skills and problem-solving skills. But, whether colleague or customer related, it is well worth the effort and the most effective means by which everyone is satisfied.

As demonstrated, there are several techniques for managing conflict. Being aware of each gives us the opportunity to avoid the pitfalls and take advantage of the benefits (and correct application) of each.

check please

12. Why does the technique of compromising frequently end up with a lose–lose outcome? Give an example of when it may be appropriate to use this technique.

13. What is the usual outcome of an accommodating technique? Is it appropriate to use this technique to resolve conflict between colleagues? Why? Why not?

14. When is using a competing technique appropriate for conflict resolution? Why?

15. If the avoiding technique results in lose–lose, what benefit is there in knowing it exists? When might 'avoiding' be appropriate?

16. Why is the collaborating technique the most preferred for getting to win–win? Explain briefly how it works.

Communication skills in conflict resolution

Whichever conflict resolution technique is used, to be effective requires excellent communication skills. We will need to be able to express ourselves clearly, assertively and diplomatically. Here we take a brief look at these skills to help understand their application in the conflict resolution process.

INTERPERSONAL SKILLS

Interpersonal skills are those skills relating to how we interact with other people. Everyone has interpersonal skills: what varies is how well developed these skills are and how we use them in a daily context. Success in conflict resolution requires highly developed interpersonal skills, which means we are able to:

Interpersonal skills
Those skills relating to how we interact with other people.

- communicate thoughts and ideas clearly;
- communicate using appropriate words and gestures;
- demonstrate effective listening skills;
- display empathy and sympathy;
- display understanding;
- be assertive;
- demonstrate integrity;
- act appropriately for the situation;
- be attuned to others' needs and wants.

Good interpersonal skills take time to develop and increase the likelihood of success in resolving conflict. It means that we need to think about what we say before we say it, consider how the other person may feel about our words and actions and be open to others' ideas and views.

ASSERTIVENESS VERSUS AGGRESSIVENESS

Assertiveness is the ability to express our own concerns and needs in a direct and honest manner tactfully and with concern for the other person's feelings. Assertive people have high self-esteem, respect for others' viewpoints and clear and strong values that they are able to clearly express.

Assertiveness
The ability to express thoughts and feelings with regard to the other person's point of view confidently. Assertiveness is demonstrated both verbally and non-verbally.

In a communication context, assertiveness is demonstrated both verbally and non-verbally. That is, what we say and how we say it is supported by our body language. What an assertive person communicates is a clear explanation of their views and needs without feeling guilty or selfish yet with due consideration for the other person's needs and views. The assertive person is flexible, constructive in their feedback and confident in their opinion. Their body language is likely to be open and they take responsibility for how they feel. For example, 'I feel frustrated when I am unable to assist you with the problems I think you sometimes have communicating with customers'. In this example, the assertive person is not accusing or blaming the other person, but letting them know how they feel in response to the actions of the other.

By contrast, an **aggressive** person is likely to impose their point of view forcefully on another, fail to respect the other person's views, ideas and opinions and be not only dominating but also demanding. The aggressive person puts their own wants

Aggressiveness
Forcefully imposing our views and ideas without regard for the other person.

and needs before others'. Their body language will reflect their aggression too. They may stare (or glare) a lot, and they may be inclined to poke their finger and invade others' personal body space. During conflict, aggressive people are likely to 'accuse' their opponent of causing them to feel the way they do, for example '*You* make me very angry when . . .'

A **passive** person's behaviour is fairly submissive. This person is likely to be 'eager to please' and reluctant to 'make waves'. This person often lacks the ability to express their opinion confidently and usually defers to the other person. The passive person is likely to cast their eyes down and have slumped shoulders during conflict situations and agree to just about everything, for example 'You're right, it is my fault . . .'

In a conflict situation, assertiveness is a more desirable attribute (and communication technique) than either passiveness or aggressiveness. However, it is useful to be aware of all three styles as this helps us to manage the situation more effectively when dealing with each type. It is also useful to help us identify traits *we* may demonstrate during conflict that may hinder the resolution process.

DIPLOMACY

Diplomacy is the ability to manage personal relations tactfully and intelligently. In other words, we use our assertiveness to express our ideas and opinions, yet show sympathy, respect and **empathy** for others (by placing ourselves 'in their shoes') when they are expressing their views, and demonstrate understanding through listening (which allows us to ask relevant questions) and positive body language.

Demonstrating tact is possibly the key to maintaining effective diplomatic relations during a conflict. Tact is the ability to say and do the right thing at the right time. We all like to feel that we are being listened to and that our 'version' or complaint is taken seriously and duly considered. If this does not happen ('You're not listening to what I'm saying . . .') the conflict resolution process can be frustrated and will stall. The end result will be a lose–lose situation.

As shown above, our communication skills are vitally important in conflict resolution. We need to think about what is being said, think about the impact of our words on the other person, think about our body language and think about solving the problem. Don't think about who is right and who is wrong!

Passiveness
Submissive behaviour that demonstrates a willingness to allow others to dominate and impose their viewpoints without consideration for our own.

Diplomacy
The ability to manage personal relations tactfully and intelligently.

Empathy
Putting ourselves in the position of the other person, to better understand their point of view.

check please

17. From the list of interpersonal skills, what does 'display empathy and sympathy' mean?

18. Why is it important to be attuned to others' needs and wants?

19. Explain the difference between assertiveness, aggressiveness and passiveness. During which conflict resolution technique might we be aggressive? Passive?

20. Why is diplomacy important when resolving a conflict with a customer?

Implementing conflict resolution techniques

We now have the knowledge and understanding of conflict resolution techniques. We also have the knowledge that allows us to communicate effectively in conflict resolution situations. What we now need is the skill to effect conflict resolution. Any of the techniques can be used but different outcomes for the same problem may result. Whichever technique we choose, there are five steps in the implementation process:

1. Collect and discuss the facts.
2. Clarify our position.
3. Identify alternative solutions.
4. Agree on a solution to the problem.
5. Implement the decision.

Remember, both parties need to acknowledge that there is a conflict in order to resolve it! This may seem obvious, but frequently one or both sides pretend there isn't a conflict (avoidance) so that they don't need to confront the problem. Alternatively, one person may think that they don't have a problem but the other person obviously does. Getting both sides to recognise what has happened and that there is a conflict is the first step. (After all, it takes two to tango!) Once this is achieved we need to decide whether a mediator is needed or if we are able to resolve the conflict between ourselves. This is possible only as long as both parties respect the implementation process.

1. COLLECT AND DISCUSS THE FACTS

Now that both parties have acknowledged that there is a conflict, there is a need to collect and present the facts. This means initiating an open and honest line of communication. It means allowing first one person to state their side then the other to state theirs, without interruption, judgement or accusation.

Using phrases that begin 'I believe . . .', 'I feel . . .' or 'My understanding is . . .' are far more effective (and assertive) than saying 'You did this . . .' or 'You make me feel . . .' or 'It's your fault because . . .' which are aggressive and unhelpful.

Deliver the facts without embellishment and without unnecessary dramatic effects. For example:

> *Jill*: 'Jenny, there is a procedure in place for depositing customers' valuables in the safety deposit box. For security reasons it should always be followed. Is there any reason why you may not be following procedure?'
>
> *Jenny*: 'Well, I usually follow procedure. But it gets so busy at reception sometimes and when I'm on my own . . .'

So, we have established that Jenny usually follows procedure, but not when it is busy. We now need to find out why.

2. CLARIFY AND EMPATHISE

This is our opportunity to respond and question the other person. We can only do this if we have actively listened to the facts as they were presented. When the other person has stated their side of the conflict, we can ask questions to clarify what we don't understand. At this point, we should try to put ourselves in their shoes. How would we feel if we were that person? Are we being unreasonable or unfair? Are they being unreasonable or unfair?

> *Jill*: 'You are saying that it gets so busy on reception that sometimes it's hard to follow all procedures to the letter?'
> *Jenny*: 'Well, yes.'
> *Jill*: 'Yes, I know it can get busy, so the problem isn't that you don't know the procedure but that sometimes you're too busy to follow procedure?'
> *Jenny*: 'That's right. I don't think you fully appreciate how hard it is when I'm out there on my own with no support during the busy periods.'

3. ALTERNATIVE SOLUTIONS

Once all the facts are clearly stated, it helps to summarise the problem to ensure we both have the same understanding of the issues. How does each person feel about the facts? For example, if the conflict is a work-related issue, we need to make sure we are both talking about the same procedure or policy.

> *Jill*: 'So, the real issue here is that there are times when you need additional help on reception? Is that right?'
> *Jenny*: 'Basically, yes. There are times when I'm on my own and some procedures can't be followed correctly because there are other, more important things to do at the time.'
> *Jill*: 'How do you think we could deal with this problem?'
> *Jenny*: 'Well, we can either change some of the procedures to reduce the time it takes to do them, or we can get an additional staff member to cover the busy periods, because that's when most of the problems arise.'

4. AGREE ON A SOLUTION TO THE PROBLEM

Now we have a few alternative solutions it's time to solve the problem. We do this by evaluating each alternative solution in turn until we find one choice that is going to deliver the most acceptable outcome to all parties; that is, one that is going to meet the needs of all. We need to consider what the advantages and disadvantages of each solution are. Is one solution the best solution? Does a compromise need to be agreed to? Is one person right, the other wrong? Is a win–win solution achievable or does someone have to lose?

Given a limited knowledge of Jill and Jenny's conflict it's possible that all solutions may work. However, it is probable that one solution is better than the other.

> *Jill*: 'Most of the problems arise when you're on your own and the busiest times are when staff take their lunch; what about if we reschedule lunch breaks so that they don't conflict with those busy periods? Unfortunately it's not likely that management will agree to give us another staff member just to cover the busy lunch period. And procedures for the safety deposit box are there to ensure the safe keeping of the customers' valuables, so I don't think it's possible to adjust the procedure. Unless you have an idea for adjusting the procedure without compromising security?'
> *Jenny*: 'Afraid not. And you're right about not getting another staff member. But I do think the idea about moving lunch breaks is workable.'

This solution was achieved by appropriate conflict resolution technique (collaboration) and effective communication skills. Both parties were able to walk away feeling satisfied.

5. IMPLEMENT THE DECISION

Now that a solution has been found it is important to implement it (change the lunch times so that Jenny has help on reception during the busy times) and later we will need to evaluate its success (is Jenny now able to follow established procedures?).

Failure to implement the decision will compound the problem and it will be even more difficult to resolve later.

Before implementing the decision, however, we need to consider whether or not we have the authority to implement it, or whether the decision has to be presented to a 'higher authority' for approval. Sometimes this can stall the process, but generally including management in the solving of the problem and implementation stages makes it easier to implement the decision. (Remember, many people are resistant to change but may accept it more readily when it comes from higher up.)

The successful ingredients of this particular conflict resolution were that each person listened to the other, the problem was clarified, and neither party's needs or values were compromised.

check please

21. Why is it important for both parties to the conflict to acknowledge there is a conflict?

22. What is likely to happen if you skip any of the steps to conflict resolution?

23. Why are alternative solutions necessary?

24. What would be the consequence of failure to implement the decision?

activity 6.2

▶ Until recently, you and a colleague have enjoyed a good working relationship. Since the colleague was promoted to supervisor, you feel that the relationship has deteriorated. She always expects you to work late, and asks you to do things no one else wants to do and takes credit for things you did. You have avoided confronting her until now but feel it's time to let her know how you feel.

Working with two other people, role-play the above scenario with the third person observing how each of you deal with the conflict resolution process. At the end of the role-play, the third person is to provide feedback on your technique, communication skills and outcome. That is, note which technique was used, whether or not the five steps to conflict resolution were observed and the communication styles used.

Respond to customer complaints

We learned earlier that customers have expectations of us and our ability to perform our job. Customers expect us to be professional, meet their needs and solve their problems. If we are unable to meet any of these expectations the customer may complain.

We say 'may' complain, because not every customer that has a problem will complain. It is not uncommon for customers to choose not to complain when something goes wrong. Instead they leave the organisation feeling disappointed and frustrated and, rather than confront the issue, tell several of their friends and colleagues about the experience and vow never to return. We never get a chance to find out why we have lost a customer, or get the opportunity to fix the problem.

Complaints need to be viewed as opportunities for us to:

- create a positive impression;
- retain the customers' business;
- improve the processes that caused the problem in the first place.

CUSTOMER EXPECTATIONS AND COMPLAINTS

The expectations of our customers will vary depending on their needs and wants. For example, some customers will be satisfied with a particular standard of service, while others will not be. Some customers will understand that a flat tyre on the tour bus is 'one of those things', while for others it will ruin their whole trip. Some customers may seem impossible to please or rude and ungrateful, while others will be exceedingly appreciative of our help and concern.

Because of this variability of customers' expectations, all customer complaints must be:

- handled sensitively, courteously and respectfully;
- taken seriously;
- immediately acted upon;
- followed up.

HOW CUSTOMERS EXPRESS THEIR COMPLAINTS

Customers will complain in a number of ways:

- immediately the problem arises
- after they have left
- to another part of the organisation
- aggressively or pleasantly.

Most complaints are directed at the most visible or nearest representative of the organisation. This is because the customer service staff represents the 'face' of the organisation and accordingly is perceived as the solver of all problems. Whether the complaint is about the audio connection on the plane, the uncomfortableness of the coach seat or the porter who dropped their bags, complaints are usually made to the first staff member in view!

Sometimes people prefer to complain to someone other than the one who caused the problem (avoiding direct confrontation). This is also why so many complaints are not made to the establishment but friends and colleagues get to hear all about it.

IMMEDIATELY THE PROBLEM ARISES

For most simple problems customers will advise of their unhappiness immediately the problem arises. For example, if a Tourist Information Bureau has no local maps in their brochure rack, some people may simply ask the staff member to find some. For another person this may be a more serious matter, especially if they have had problems all through their visit to the area. They may ask to see the senior manager of the bureau and complain that the bureau has failed in its duty to assist tourists.

Either way, the customer complains immediately and the organisation thus has the opportunity to fix the problem immediately, thereby ensuring that the rest of the customer's experience meets their expectations.

AFTER THEY HAVE LEFT

Complaining after leaving is a useful way of avoiding confrontation. For many people it is also a useful way to express their disappointment about something while not considering it fatal to their relationship with the organisation.

For example, a couple may have had a bad experience with collecting some duty-free goods. The staff took too long to process the purchase and as the couple had to meet others in the departure lounge they left as soon as they had received their goods. It was only after arriving home that they decided they were really not happy with the outcome, as the time delay meant they had had less time with their friends. In this case, they would probably write a letter or send an e-mail to convey their unhappiness with the level of service.

However customers communicate their concern after departure, the organisation should use this opportunity to investigate the complaint and thank the customer for bringing it to their attention.

TO ANOTHER PART OF THE ORGANISATION

As we have already seen, many customers prefer to complain to someone other than those who caused the problem. If there was a problem with the food, why would the customer not tell the waiter? Why wait until later to mention it? If there is a problem with the standard of cleanliness in the cabin on board ship, why tell the activities coordinator and blame them?

Apart from wanting to avoid direct confrontation with the person who can actually fix the problem, the customer has often formed a comfortable relationship with other staff. They may have handled other queries for the customer and handled them satisfactorily, and this rapport may not exist with other staff. It may also be that the customer is not actually looking for a resolution but simply wants the problem acknowledged and an apology.

AGGRESSIVELY OR PLEASANTLY

A seemingly minor problem ('I didn't get my free ticket wallet') may be conveyed aggressively or pleasantly. Similarly, a major incident ('I slipped on the steps up to the plane and hurt myself') may be conveyed aggressively or pleasantly. Whether we think the problem is minor or major is irrelevant. And whether we think the attitude and behaviour of the customer is rude or aggressive or inappropriate is also irrelevant. However, an aggressive and rude complaint can sometimes get in the way of solving the problem. We are left wondering why this person is being so rude instead of thinking clearly about what the problem is and how we can fix it.

What the customer really wants (and expects) is for us to take them seriously, fix the problem promptly and respond courteously.

If the customer is being rude and aggressive in a public area, try to calm the customer down and remove them to a more private area. For example: 'Ms Frederick, I can appreciate that you are upset and I am sorry that this happened. If you would like to take a seat over here we can talk about how we can fix this for you.'

It is very difficult for someone to continue being aggressive when we are calm, pleasant and concerned. Because of our immediate attention and concern, it is likely that the customer will be willing to sit and talk more quietly about their problem. Once we have gained some control over the situation, we will be able to implement a complaint handling strategy.

COMPLAINT HANDLING STRATEGY

Whatever the complaint is about, it should be managed within a standard framework that will ensure no steps in the process are omitted. Whether the complaint is the result of a simple error (by us or a colleague) or a more serious event, we should focus on a solution that satisfies the customer.

Most of us will develop our own style for handling complaints, but we should not ignore any of the steps that ensure successful outcomes. The complaint handling strategy follows these steps:

1. Listen to the customer and acknowledge the problem.
2. Express concern and empathise.
3. Take responsibility for resolving the complaint.
4. Indicate what action will be taken.
5. Take action to resolve the complaint.
6. Follow up to ensure customer satisfaction.

LISTEN AND ACKNOWLEDGE

People make complaints about all sorts of things. Some of these things are easy to fix (a misspelt name on an itinerary, for example), while others are complicated (the customer has told us that they believe someone has opened their luggage). Some complaints may seem petty and unimportant, while others will require immediate action and incur a cost to the organisation.

Always allow the customer time to explain the problem, without interruption, and then acknowledge the problem. It is important to find out the exact nature of the problem and all the related details.

Take the problem seriously. Ignoring it won't make it go away but will compound it.

DON'T TAKE IT PERSONALLY

It's not uncommon for customers to blame us for their problem even when it has nothing directly to do with us. We are the 'face' of the establishment, and as far as the customer is concerned their problem *is* our problem. Don't get upset or defensive when the customer is accusing us of sabotaging their romantic weekend away. Remain calm, attentive and focused.

CONCERN AND EMPATHY

Our concern must be sincere and appropriate to the complaint. For example, if a customer tells us that their itinerary has not yet been sent with the correct spelling, they don't expect us to behave as though it's the end of the world. They just want us to fix it. Now. If a customer has told us their luggage has been tampered with, we need to express concern for their wellbeing and empathise with their discomfort.

TAKE RESPONSIBILITY

Even though we didn't cause the problem, we must take responsibility for it occurring. This means that we immediately and sincerely apologise on behalf of the organisation for the customer's unhappiness. We shouldn't blame someone or something for the complaint. It is appropriate to let the customer know that we take responsibility for the issue, even if there is nothing we can do to fix the problem except refer the matter on to our supervisor. (It should be noted that we are not accepting responsibility in the legal sense, but we are saying that we are sorry that the customer has experienced an inconvenience which we will endeavour to fix.)

INDICATE WHAT ACTION WILL BE TAKEN

The action we take will naturally depend on the nature of the incident.

Fix it ourself

Whether we can fix a problem ourselves or not will depend on the extent of our authority in the organisation. If the problem is simple, let the customer know we will fix it immediately. Where legal or financial concerns are involved, it is common to refer the matter on to our supervisor.

If we constantly receive complaints of a similar nature, for example customers constantly having spelling mistakes in their correspondence or experiencing difficulty with a third party provider (for example, hotel or coach company), then this too may need to be referred to our supervisor.

Refer the problem on

The complaint about luggage that has been interfered with may need to be referred to a supervisor. There may be legal repercussions that need further consideration. Let the customer know that a senior manager will contact them.

TAKE ACTION

Now that we have indicated what we are going to do, we should do it! If we need to call our supervisor, call the supervisor. If we need to contact another part of the organisation, call them.

If we say 'I'll look into that for you', the customer is not likely to feel very confident. The customer wants us to act now, not later.

FOLLOW UP

A complaint doesn't go away just because we have listened, empathised and apologised. Most complaints need to be followed up. This means that we need to make sure that what we said would be done has been done. Even if someone else is going to fix the problem the customer expects us to follow up.

Call the other departments and check that they have done what was asked of them for the customer. Ask the supervisor how the complaint was resolved.

In many cases it is also appropriate to follow up with the customer. For example, we may call the customer and ask if everything is now OK. This gives them an opportunity to express satisfaction (or dissatisfaction) with how the complaint was handled.

Record the incident

Some complaints need more than a quick call to the customer to make sure the problem has been resolved. The nature of the complaint, and the policy in our organisation, may mean that we document the incident. Incidents that result in a customer sustaining an injury or loss need to be recorded. The complaint about the misspelt name doesn't need to be recorded unless it is a common occurrence and our supervisor needs to be advised.

Incident reports

Most organisations will have in place an incident report form. Even if our workplace doesn't have a standard form the following information needs to be recorded:

- Name and address of customer
- Date of the incident
- Nature of the incident
- How the incident occurred (exact and specific details)
- Witnesses to the incident
- Action taken
- Organisation representative

This information may be required later, particularly if legal action results. The report should include, when relevant, conversations, diagrams and results of the subsequent investigation. Although this may appear unnecessary at the time, these notes may be used in a court of law, or for an insurance claim.

Reports should be completed as soon as possible after the complaint was made. The next day may be too late as relevant details may be forgotten.

TURNING COMPLAINTS INTO AN OPPORTUNITY

While it's easy to conclude that all complaints create a bad impression (negative 'moment of truth'), this doesn't have to be the final outcome. We said earlier that complaints are an opportunity for the organisation to improve the way it does things. This is only true if we take the complaint seriously and handle the complaint properly.

By following the complaint handling strategy, being aware that each of our customers is different, developing our interpersonal skills and managing conflict with win–win in mind, complaints will give the organisation the opportunity to:

- reassure the customer that it is a professional operation and has a high standard of customer service;
- convince the customer that they are important to the organisation;
- persuade the customer to return;
- highlight the ability of its staff;
- create positive moments of truth.

check please

25. Why do you think some customers do not even bother to complain?
26. What opportunities arise for the organisation from a complaint?
27. Why do you think some customers are more likely to complain to another department than to the department that caused the problem?
28. The complaint handling strategy follows six steps. Why should each of the steps be followed when resolving customer complaints?
29. Why should you take responsibility for a problem when you weren't the one who caused it?
30. What sorts of complaints are you likely to be able to fix yourself?
31. Why is the follow-up stage important in complaint handling?
32. Under what circumstances would we need to complete an incident report?

Follow health, safety and security procedures

LEARNING OUTCOMES

On completion of this chapter, you will be able to:

* explain the role of the National Occupational Health and Safety Commission and the states' and territories' responsibilities for health and safety in the workplace;

* describe the objectives of occupational health and safety (OHS) legislation;

* describe the obligations of employers in relation to employees and third parties as defined in the OHS legislation;

* describe employee responsibilities for OHS in the workplace;

* explain the importance of developing OHS enterprise policies and procedures;

* explain a range of ways an enterprise can meet its OHS responsibilities;

* explain 'hazard management' in the workplace;

* describe the legal requirements of first aid in the workplace;

* describe the legal obligation of employers to maintain records of workplace injuries and 'near-miss' reports;

* list potential emergency situations in the workplace and describe the action to take in the event of an emergency or potential emergency;

* explain the key security issues in a tourism enterprise; and

* describe the insurance requirements of an enterprise to meet its legal and moral obligations including workers' compensation and public liability.

This chapter complies with the Tourism Industry National Competency Standards, unit THHCOR03A, 'Follow Health, Safety and Security Procedures'.

According to the National Occupational Health and Safety Commission, one in 12 workers suffer a work-related injury or illness each year in Australia, with a total cost to the Australian economy of an estimated $27 billion.

Some industries, by their very nature, are more dangerous, or have the potential to be a greater health risk, than other industries. Irrespective of the industry, however, employers are required by law to provide as safe an environment as possible for employees and others.

Accordingly, occupational health and safety (OHS) legislation exists as a framework for the prevention of work-related injuries and specifies the rights and obligations of the parties bound by the relevant Act in each state ('The Act'). In this chapter we will look at the responsibilities of both the individual and the employer for OHS in the workplace.

The final area of discussion in this chapter is security. Providing security in a tourism establishment is the broad task of protecting both people—customers and employees—and assets—cash, valuables and property. Each enterprise is different and will therefore have different needs but all will have many security factors and issues in common.

Role of the NOHSC

The National Occupational Health and Safety Commission (NOHSC) is a statutory body with government, employer and employee representatives. The Commonwealth government established it in 1985 to develop, facilitate and implement a national OHS strategy. It comprises members of the Australian Council of Trade Unions (ACTU) and the Australian Chamber of Commerce and Industry (ACCI), as well as the Commonwealth, state and territory governments.

The main aim of any OHS strategy is the reduction of workplace injuries. The NOHSC coordinates national efforts to achieve this through the development of strategies focusing on prevention; it also ensures standards and codes of practice are evolved where needed.

A range of publications and services (including Internet access), including a library, is available to assist organisations and individuals reduce the incidence and severity of injury and disease in the workplace.

STATE AND TERRITORY AUTHORITIES

Each state and territory has responsibility for making laws about and enforcing OHS but works in conjunction with the NOHSC, which is empowered under the *Occupational Health and Safety Act 1985* to enforce OHS legislation. In most states the working title is WorkCover Authority.

The Authority is therefore responsible for protecting the health and safety of employees and the public, and for facilitating compliance with the Act and achieving state and national OHS strategic goals.

file this

▶ Most state and territory WorkCover authorities provide a range of free publications and a representative who will speak to groups on safety issues.

Objectives of occupational health and safety legislation

All employees in Australia are protected by the respective state or territory OHS legislation irrespective of the workplace, except where a separate Act applies to employees of the Commonwealth government and those working in the mining industry.

An employee may be fulltime or part-time, a casual worker or apprentice, contractor or subcontractor. A workplace can be a retail travel outlet, cruise liner, train or coach, aircraft, hotel or restaurant. It can also be any other place of work in any industry.

Legislation has as its main objectives the reduction of work-related accidents, the elimination of risks to health and safety at work, the protection of persons at work against risks to health and safety, and the provision for involvement of employees in the identification and management of health and safety issues.

CODES OF PRACTICE

To help private enterprises and industry in general meet their obligations under respective state or territory legislation, codes of practice have been put in place. A **code of practice** is a guide to conduct, not a legal regulation. Codes of practice provide for a number of options and give practical guidance for employers and individuals to meet OHS standards.

Code of practice
A practical and flexible guide for meeting OHS standards in the workplace.

A code of practice exists not necessarily for specific industries but for general functions. For example, manual handling, first aid in the workplace and noise all have specific codes of practice that operate in conjunction with the relevant OHS legislation.

file this

▶ Occupational health and safety—it's everyone's responsibility.

Health and safety responsibilities in the workplace

In the workplace it is the employer who has the main responsibility for OHS, although all employees are required to assist employers fulfil this responsibility.

EMPLOYER OBLIGATIONS

Employers have a duty of care to both their employees and the general public. A duty of care is the responsibility one person has for another, in the eyes of the law, for that person's health and safety.

Duty of care
The responsibility one person has for another, in the eyes of the law, for that person's health and safety.

Although there do exist some differences between OHS legislation in each state and territory, the general legal obligations mean employers are responsible for:

- maintaining equipment used by staff, training for use of the equipment and ensuring safe systems of work;
- ensuring that the ways of storage, handling and use of hazardous substances are safe;
- ensuring that the way work is done is safe and does not affect employees' health;
- providing employees with adequate information, instruction and training needed to perform their job safely (where necessary, in languages other than English);
- monitoring the health of employees;
- involving employees and/or worker representatives in health and safety initiatives in the workplace; and
- monitoring, recording and evaluating the workplace and incidents.

(Adapted from Worksafe Australia, *Keeping Work Safe*, AGPS 1997. Commonwealth of Australia copyright. Reproduced by permission.)

quick thinker

▶ In the workplace we use signs to indicate that a danger or risk exists: Slippery Floor, Chemical Hazard. What others are you familiar with?

EMPLOYEE DUTIES

Employees have a duty of care for the safety of their colleagues and the public. While at work, employees are expected to perform their duties competently and:

- take reasonable care for their own health and safety and that of anyone else who may be affected;
- cooperate with employers to comply with the requirements imposed by or under the Act;
- report breaches of safety and potential risks;
- work and behave in ways that are safe; and
- follow instructions and rules imposed by the employer (that are legal).

Developing policies and procedures for OHS

It is hard to imagine any workplace without potential hazards. Because legislation is non-industry specific, individual enterprises can develop their own policies and procedures—that comply with the legislation—to suit their needs.

In a tourism workplace, all sections and departments and work functions pose potential threats and hazards. The employer is responsible for eliminating or minimising hazards, and can achieve this with relevant, realistic, timely and effective OHS policies and procedures.

'Policy' and 'procedure' are two key terms that are sometimes confused; however, they are two essential tools that contribute to maintaining a safe work environment.

A policy is the position an organisation takes on an issue. It can also be a rule or regulation, but is most often a position or course of action, as illustrated in Figure 7.1.

An organisation's policy should form part of its overall goals to achieve OHS in the workplace. It should state the organisation's intention to provide a safe work environment and acknowledge its legal obligations. Specific policies are designed to deal with controlling specific hazards. Policies may also include issues such as returning to work after an accident, rehabilitation, counselling options, safety guidelines and minimum standards for specific functions.

A procedure is how to carry out a task or duty, for example what specific action to take in the event of an emergency. A general procedure is illustrated in Figure 7.2. Specific procedures should provide clear directions or instructions for performing a task or responding to an event in a step-by-step manner for every stage. Each procedure must be simple and easy to follow, state who has responsibility for its completion and be communicated to all employees affected. All tourism-based enterprises—tour operators, attraction venues, transport companies, etc.—have in place individual policies and procedures that comply with legislation and protect the well-being of employees and visitors (the public) and meet their individual needs.

It is important that policies and procedures are complied with. One way organisations test the effectiveness of their procedures is to have a 'drill'. A drill is a trial run, for example a fire drill. This is conducted to ensure that the procedure in place (to evacuate everyone safely and efficiently from the building in the event of a fire) is effective.

FIGURE 7.1 *A COMPANY OCCUPATIONAL HEALTH AND SAFETY POLICY*

TRAVEL TRUNK PTY LTD
10 HAY ST, PERTH • TEL: 09 505 5055
for people on the move

The company recognises and accepts its obligation to take all practical action to ensure the health and safety of its employees. All company people have a legal and moral obligation to ensure that nothing is done to make ineffective any company policies, procedures or systems of work.

Each employee is encouraged to contribute to the OHS strategies as an individual, as a representative of their work group or as a member of the OHS committee.

Managers are responsible at all times to ensure that all persons under their control work in a safe manner and in a safe environment. All workplace operations are to be monitored to identify potential hazards and prevent accidents.

In the event an accident does occur, it must be fully investigated and appropriate recommendations made and action taken to avoid recurrence.

Date:

Authorised Signatory:

FIGURE 7.2 *HOTEL EMERGENCY PROCEDURES*

STANDARD
FIRE ORDERS

1 **ASSIST ANY PERSON IN IMMEDIATE DANGER ONLY IF SAFE TO DO SO**

2 **CLOSE THE DOOR**

3 **CALL THE FIRE BRIGADE ON** **OOO**

4 **ATTACK FIRE IF SAFE TO DO SO** ⚠

5 **EVACUATE TO ASSEMBLY AREA** ✓

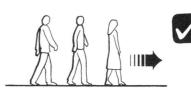

6 **REMAIN AT ASSEMBLY AREA AND ENSURE EVERYBODY IS ACCOUNTED FOR**

SOURCE: Reproduced with the kind permission of the Metropolitan Fire and Emergency Services Board, Melbourne.

TYPES OF PROCEDURES

The most common examples of written health and safety procedures include:

- Emergency evacuation (fire, bomb threat)
- Manual handling (pushing, carrying, holding, lifting)
- Reporting and recording incidents, injuries, illness
- Use, maintenance and cleaning of equipment
- Security breaches (which may also potentially cause harm)
- Protective personal clothing requirements
- Use of chemicals

file this

▶ Policies and procedures can only be useful to us if we are familiar with them.

Meeting OHS requirements

Effective management of OHS issues is facilitated by the commitment, consultation and cooperation of everyone in the workplace. Although the legal obligation is structured to allow for flexibility to meet individual needs, there exist options that assist compliance.

The combined efforts and involvement of all encourage participative resolution to OHS concerns.

WORKPLACE OHS OFFICER

Under OHS guidelines a requirement exists for the appointment of a person to act as the OHS representative (officer) for each organisation. This role is usually carried out in addition to that person's main role within the organisation and the officer acts as the employer's representative when health and safety issues arise.

The person taking the role may be the only OHS representative in the workplace or may work in conjunction with other nominated representatives.

DESIGNATED WORK GROUPS

OHS legislation sets out the responsibilities for employees and provides for their contribution and participation in ensuring a safe work environment. This can be achieved through **designated work groups** (DWGs); however, not all states and territories have this facility in place.

A DWG can be either made up of representatives from a specified section or department within an enterprise (drivers, tour guides, reservations), or a group that represents the collective interests of all employees—depending on the number of employees.

The DWGs are formed by nominating a colleague, or several colleagues for large departments, to act as the representative(s) on OHS issues affecting their specific work area. The group liaises with management and the OHS officer to resolve OHS issues, within the legislation, to ensure a safe and healthy work environment.

Designated work group (DWG)
A group made up of representatives from a specified section or department of an enterprise, or a group representing the collective interests of all employees, that liaises with management and the OHS officers on OHS issues.

Employees may ask employers to establish a DWG or the employer may initiate one. The key feature of a DWG is representation of the department or section by an employee who is familiar with the potential hazards in their area. Although not required under legislation, if employees request a DWG then an employer is legally obliged to facilitate its establishment and ongoing success (assuming it is a provision in that state's or territory's legislation).

file this

▶ All employees should know whom to contact in the event of an accident.

HEALTH AND SAFETY COMMITTEES

A health and safety committee is an additional way of achieving OHS goals. A committee does not replace the OHS officer, nor does it replace policy and procedure; however, it will contribute to the design and enforcement of these tools.

A committee works in a consultative manner that involves both employees and employers (and often industry representative bodies) with the primary objectives of achieving safety in the workplace and to aid all parties to meet their legal obligations. It usually comprises representatives from each level and department within the organisation (such as the DWGs) to ensure a balanced and objective representation of all concerned.

If committees are formed, usually half the members are employees (because of their first-hand experience and knowledge of systems and procedures in the workplace). Management representation is equally as important because of their access to relevant organisational policy and strategy and their role in the decision-making process. In some instances a committee is given the authority to stop a process or task in the workplace if a risk or potential hazard is identified.

INSPECTORS

WorkCover inspectors are appointed under the Occupational Health and Safety Act and have the authority to visit most work sites.

WorkCover inspectors visit the workplace in response to a complaint about safety or as part of a strategy that focuses on specific hazards or an industry. They have right of entry at any time as required or requested. It is an offence to refuse access or to obstruct an inspector.

Inspectors not only inspect a workplace, they also investigate any incident of serious injury or fatality. They can also take photographs and samples, seize property, examine and copy documents, conduct interviews and enquiries and seek assistance from technical experts, interpreters or others to assist in their duties.

INS AND PNS—SERVING NOTICES

The power conferred on an inspector is necessary to ensure healthy and safe environments in which to work. During an inspection an inspector may determine that a situation is dangerous or there is the potential for it to be dangerous, or may witness a breach of the law. These situations cannot be dealt with next week or next month. The danger is immediate so action must be taken immediately.

An inspector has the authority to issue an Improvement Notice, Prohibition Notice or written directions for immediate action to be taken to ensure the safety of the workers.

An **Improvement Notice** (IN) is a written directive requiring a person or organisation to fix a breach of the law. A time limit is set in which to comply.

A **Prohibition Notice** (PN) directs an individual or organisation to stop an activity that is, or has the potential to be, a risk. That risk must be removed before the activity can recommence.

An employer can appeal if they consider the IN or PN, or any other action taken by the inspector, unjust. This can result in the original decision being upheld, the appeal upheld or the original decision altered.

Where a prosecution is brought under the Act by a WorkCover authority or authorised inspector, it will be brought before a court, which can impose either a financial penalty, a jail sentence or both if the prosecution is successful.

Improvement Notice
A written directive requiring a person or organisation to fix a breach of the law.

Prohibition Notice
A direction to an individual or organisation to stop an activity that is, or has the potential to be, a risk.

activity 7.1

▶ Each of the ways presented in which an organisation can meet its OHS requirements is an overview only. In small groups, research and present to the class one of the following—OHS officers, DWGs, committees—in detail, as the legislation applies in your state or territory.

check please

1. What is the role of the NOHSC and the role of the authority in your state or territory that administers OHS legislation?

2. What purpose does a code of practice serve? How may it assist an organisation to meet its OHS obligations? Which ones have relevance to the tourism industry?

3. Explain, in your own words, an employer's 'duty of care' to employees and third parties.

4. Give an example, in a tourism environment, of how you can meet your employee responsibilities under OHS legislation.

Hazard management

Hazard management is the identification of hazards in the workplace that pose a potential threat and the implementation of steps to eliminate those hazards.

To be able to provide a healthy and safe environment, an employer must have a process to:

- identify hazards in the workplace;
- assess the associated risks that may result from hazards; and
- control the risks.

This is the basis of all prevention activities in the workplace.

Source: Worksafe Australia, 'Organising health and safety training for your workplace', Jennifer Gibb, Worksafe Australia, National Occupational Health & Safety Commission, AGPS, 1996. Commonwealth of Australia copyright. Reproduced with permission.

HAZARDS IN THE WORKPLACE

Hazards are anything that can potentially cause harm to anyone working in the organisation or the public. Hazards may be identified through inspections of the work area, monitoring of reported incidents and keeping up to date with OHS issues.

A **risk** is the likelihood that a potential hazard will result in injury or disease. The risk must also be measured in terms of the extent of injury that may result, for example permanent or total disability.

Risk control, an employer obligation, means eliminating or reducing the likelihood of injury that could result from exposure to the hazard. An example is the introduction of seatbelts on many touring coaches.

TYPES OF HAZARDS

Hazards vary depending on the industry and the enterprise but may be classified as follows.

PHYSICAL HAZARDS

Physical hazards are those that impact on the body through noise and vibration, ultraviolet radiation and heat and cold. Physical hazards also arise as a result of the workload, equipment in use, lack of training and pressures of time. The result is fatigue and lack of concentration, which can result in injury.

Noise, one of the most widespread hazards facing Australian workers, can cause **industrial deafness**. However, in many tourism-based enterprises (hospitality venues, entertainment venues, aircraft, etc.) it is more likely to cause other accidents as a result of an employee not being able to hear a warning because of the level of noise. A good example would be on board an aircraft or a train.

The workplace can be surprisingly noisy, resulting in people having to shout over the noise created by machinery, such as in a laundry or large industrial kitchen, or created by music and people, such as in a nightclub.

file this

▶ Hearing damage caused by noise hazards can be reduced by using ear plugs. Be alert to other potential hazards at the same time.

Vibration, the rapid motion of an object, may impact on the body if a worker is exposed for great lengths of time. The extent of the impact is affected by the frequency of the vibration. For example, vibration occurs in a moving vehicle, which can cause motion sickness, in an industrial laundry and while operating any electrically powered tools.

Vibration can be felt through the floor so it is not necessary to be actually using or touching the vibrating equipment.

file this

▶ Turn off any equipment that causes vibration hazards when not needed.

Heat and cold hazards more commonly exist when working outdoors. However, they can impact on people indoors as well. Working in the ski fields of Thredbo, for instance, can have an impact on people such as lift operators.

Conversely, working in the centre of Australia creates a different set of hazards, ranging from temperature-related hazards to dangerous wildlife such as snakes.

Working in hot conditions can induce **heat stress**. This occurs when more heat is being absorbed into the body than can be dispersed through perspiration.

Heat stress
This occurs as a result of working in hot conditions. Heat stress begins when the body absorbs more heat than can be dispersed by perspiration.

file this

▶ Control room temperature and provide good ventilation to prevent heat hazards.

Cold stress, on the other hand, can begin when the body temperature falls below 18°C. Hypothermia (adverse reduction of body temperature) can start when the body temperature falls below 10°C.

file this

▶ Appropriate protective clothing is the only defence when working in cold work areas.

file this

▶ The temperature, humidity and flow of air in the workplace will affect the comfort of workers.

Cold stress
This occurs as a result of exposure to very cold working conditions. Cold stress can begin when the body temperature falls below 18°C.

Ultraviolet radiation is another hazard that can affect some tourism professionals, the most common source being the sun. Those most at risk include outdoor workers—recreation/sports professionals, gardeners, waiters and anyone else required to work outdoors on a regular basis.

UV radiation
Hazard resulting from
exposure to ultraviolet
radiation, the most
common source being the
sun.

Ultraviolet radiation can affect the skin (sunburn) and eyes and can cause long-term (permanent) damage. Over-exposure in hot conditions can also lead to heat stress. Wearing protective clothing can prevent this. The provision of such clothing is usually the employer's responsibility.

file this

▶ For protection against UV radiation use wide-brimmed hats, broad spectrum sunscreens (30+), sunglasses and cool, loose-fitting clothing.

CHEMICAL HAZARDS

Many chemicals are used in various tourism sectors; how we handle, use and store chemicals is what creates the hazard. Chemicals become dangerous from use and misuse as a result of:

- Spillage
- Handling
- Leakage
- Inhalation
- Consumption
- Storage

Types of chemicals

The nature of a chemical dictates how it can affect us if mishandled. The reason we store so many different chemicals is because each has its own use and effectiveness. Chemicals may be classified as:

- poisonous or toxic: absorbed by the body—ammonia;
- corrosive: can burn the skin—solvents, acids, bleaches;
- irritants: can inflame the skin—detergents, degreasers, cleaning agents, sanitisers; and
- explosive or flammable: can also be any of the above—fuel, gas.

One of the most common mistakes made when using chemicals is the failure to read the instructions for use and dilution quantities. Another common hazard in chemical handling is the failure to use protective clothing—this includes facemasks and gloves.

Chemicals in the workplace—a checklist

The varieties and strengths of chemicals used in tourism operations will depend on the needs of the users. Users of chemicals are most likely to be cleaners, engineers, food service staff, kitchen staff and laundry staff, among others. Because of the high risk factor associated with chemicals, the following checklist will help identify the necessity for each chemical in use:

- Is it the right product for the job? Is it suitable for cleaning bathrooms, cleaning floors, sanitising benches, washing dishes?
- Use—have the users been trained?
- Access—who has access? Should access be restricted?

- Storage—is it stored correctly? Consider room temperature, ventilation, accessibility, container.
- Quantity—will it deteriorate over time? Is there a risk storing this much?
- Personal protective clothing—who is responsible for providing this? Is it being used correctly?
- Is its use monitored?
- What emergency procedures exist in the event of an accident?
- What is the enterprise policy on safety standards? Is everyone aware of the policy?

activity 7.2

▶ Make a list of all the chemicals in your home. Note their location, storage container, storage access, use, frequency of use and potential danger. Is it the right chemical for the job? What risk exists with each chemical? What action should be taken in the event of an emergency?

MANUAL HANDLING

Manual handling is the physical manoeuvring of items. Many jobs require the worker to stand for hours at a time, or to bend, lift, sit, push, pull or perform repetitive tasks. Injuries can occur as a result of these manual handling tasks—lifting boxes and luggage, making beds, reaching up or bending over, cleaning the floors, pushing trolleys, chopping food and moving heavy equipment.

Manual handling injuries are often related to poor ergonomic design. Ergonomics is concerned with the design aspects of work processes and equipment and their relationship to the human body. The less in line the bodily movements are in relation to the work process, the more likely a manual handling injury may result.

Ergonomic injuries also often occur because of lack of training in the task to be performed. Many tasks seem straightforward or simple to complete, such as typing at the computer or driving a coach, but by their very nature injury can occur.

The reduction of manual handling injuries in the workplace requires the cooperation of the employee and the employer in developing systems and procedures that guard against injury. This is achieved in part by the ergonomics of workplace design but also by training employees in risk identification, lifting techniques and correct posture, and by reducing the frequency of performing repetitive tasks.

Before manually handling any object:

- Assess the risk.
- Do you need assistance?
- Position your body correctly (it is not enough simply to bend at the knees).
- Assess the shape of any item you are going to lift—will this cause a lifting problem?
- Ensure you have a clear path to your destination.
- Ensure there is a clear place for the object to be put.
- Is a trolley available to move heavy, awkward items?
- Adopt the right posture.

PSYCHOLOGICAL HAZARDS

Psychological hazards are those that impact on our mental wellbeing. Probably the most common outcome is stress. Because of the restructure of the workplace and the simplification of many tasks as a result of advances in technology and work process design, many people are doing more work, with greater responsibilities, than before.

In tourism, some of the changes that have contributed to psychological hazards include:

- reduced staffing levels, placing greater stress on remaining staff;
- enterprise agreements that allow for 12-hour shifts; and
- pressure for increased productivity—cleaning more rooms, serving more customers.

Each individual reacts differently to these changes; however, the most common result is employee fatigue (a physical hazard) from increased productivity expectations and other work-related pressures. This in turn reduces alertness and increases stress, which can cause anxiety, depression and more serious psychological disorders.

GENERAL HAZARDS

There are numerous other hazards that exist and all employees must take an active role in identifying and eliminating them. Be alert to:

- poor storage
- torn carpet
- fire hazards
- safety signs
- instructions for use
- unguarded machinery
- obstructions
- sharp edges, slippery floors and spillages
- equipment, utensils, tools with safety guards
- faulty or damaged equipment
- appropriate protective clothing
- electrical appliances that are faulty or have frayed cords
- poor maintenance
- poor lighting.

▶ Brendan and Margaret White were enjoying a week-long holiday after a busy Christmas period in their gift shop. They had travelled by car to the region and were staying in the Weary Traveller Motel, which they had booked for the last two days of their trip. On arrival at the motel they were greeted by friendly and helpful staff who were enthusiastic and knowledgeable about the region and confidently informed the Whites about what they could see and do while staying in the area.

When Brendan and Margaret turned to leave reception, Margaret tripped on torn carpet and, although she didn't fall, everyone who saw her realised that she could have been injured. Judy, the receptionist, was quickly at her side to reassure her. 'Sorry about that, Mrs White. We've been trying to have that fixed for months now. You might want to watch out for that the next time you come into reception.'

Not feeling very reassured or confident, Margaret nodded and headed to her room with her husband. On looking around their room, they quickly realised that torn carpet wasn't the only problem this motel had; the television electrical cord was frayed and the chair in the corner of the room had torn fabric. On closer inspection they could see also that the back leg on the chair was damaged. In the bathroom, the porcelain washbowl was cracked and the shower rose leaked. Feeling by now a little cynical, Margaret and Brendan looked for the fire escape plan usually posted on the back of motel doors. There wasn't one.

If you were the Whites, what action would you take in this situation? List the hazards that they have encountered. What responsibility does the motel have for the safety of their guests? How could an actual accident be avoided?

First aid in the workplace

Legislation requires employers to provide adequate facilities for the welfare of employees; therefore the employer is obliged to make available facilities for the administration of first aid. In some instances this may extend to the appointment of an industrial nurse or other suitably qualified person. It is not only employees who may require first aid and prevention is preferred.

Preventive measures include:

- personal protective clothing
- following OHS procedures
- reporting faults
- correct lifting techniques
- cleaning spillages
- correct storage.

Under OHS legislation, employers are also required to maintain records relating to the health and safety of their employees. In some instances—for example, where an employee has an infectious disease or a fatality occurs in the workplace—the employer is required to report the incident to WorkCover.

First aid is defined as the application of emergency care, in the first instance, to an injury. Sometimes this may be a temporary measure before removal to hospital or attendance by a doctor, but it is certainly intended to aid and give relief to the injured person, and to ensure that no further danger exists to that person. In some cases the application of first aid can save a person's life.

To administer first aid a person must be suitably qualified. This is not to say you cannot offer assistance if you do not hold a current first aid certificate, but many procedures should only be performed by a qualified attendant.

The most common injuries and accidents in tourism environments requiring attention include:

- burns and scalds: oil, water, fat (in commercial kitchens, for example);
- cuts and abrasions: knives, sharp edges, glass (in restaurants, for example);
- falls: slipping on floor, tripping (at attractions, or on public transport such as a plane, for example);
- electrical shock (while operating cleaning equipment, for example);
- strains and sprains (in almost any work environment); and
- machine injuries (in theme parks while operating rides, for example).

Other incidents may include, but are not limited to, heart attacks, epileptic seizures and drug-related issues such as overdose and needle-stick injuries.

Legislation also requires suitably located first aid kits. To determine what is appropriate for a workplace, we identify those areas where injury is most likely to occur, assess the potential risk—that is, likelihood of an injury occurring—and evaluate what first aid facilities are required to administer treatment.

The needs of a retail travel outlet will be different from those of an airport, airline and theme park, which are also different from those of a large hotel, small café and conference centre. Wherever we work, it is important to know the location of first aid facilities and the contents of kits, who is qualified to administer first aid and emergency contact numbers.

file this

▶ First aid helps save lives. Check that your qualification is up to date.

check please

5. What is meant by the terms 'hazard management' and 'risk control'?
6. Of what relevance to tourism is an understanding of chemical hazards? What will you now do differently when using chemicals?
7. What are the likely injuries that can occur as a result of poor manual handling? What will you do in the future to ensure you do not suffer from a manual handling injury?
8. What legal requirement is there to provide first aid in the workplace? Refer to the applicable legislation.

Reporting and recording injuries

Almost everything we have discussed so far has focused on prevention of injury in the workplace. The fact remains that, even if we put in place preventive measures and comply completely with legislation, accidents will still happen.

While procedures should exist for what to do when someone is first injured (administer first aid, call an ambulance), what happens after the event is also important.

A written report should be submitted to the employer for every injury, accident and 'near miss' in the workplace. A near miss is an incident whereby an injury almost or could have occurred. For example, a customer trips over torn carpet in your premises—they are not injured but could have been. The torn carpet will need to be replaced to ensure that an accident doesn't actually happen. Minor accidents, which may or may not result in injury, can point to a risk that should be eliminated.

file this

▶ A 'near miss' is an accident waiting to happen.

Legislation compels employers to notify WorkCover of serious incidents in the workplace and to keep a record of near misses. This allows identification of the cause of the incident, which in turn contributes to the development of strategies to prevent further occurrence.

The use of standardised reporting forms can ensure all details are recorded accurately and in a timely manner. The WorkCover Authority will require this information and any other written reports, such as witness accounts, and if workers' compensation is claimed. It is also a useful tool for risk management.

Risk management is the identification of incidents that may or do occur as a result of the same risk and putting into place procedures to prevent further injury. The reports and records we keep on accidents and near misses assist in identifying why and how accidents occurred which in turn enables management to implement decisions that prevent them recurring.

Risk management
Identification of incidents that may occur as a result of the same risk and putting in place procedures to prevent further injury.

COST OF ACCIDENTS

Most people think only of medical costs when discussing accidents, but what about the other costs? Accidents have a four-fold impact on the workplace. The first is the human cost. The person, or persons, may have received a lifetime injury, which not only causes considerable physical pain but also emotional pain. The injury can potentially affect that person's capacity to work, support a family or their ability to return to the life they had prior to the injury.

Cost of accidents
· human cost
· social cost
· financial cost
· psychological cost

The second is the social cost. This refers to the reaction and subsequent frame of mind of the injured person's colleagues, and the impact on their family and friends.

The third cost of accidents is financial. Associated with all accidents is the cost of medical care, rehabilitation, legal advice, compensation and labour. Revenue may be lost, staff may leave, production may decline and a range of other factors may affect the financial position of the organisation.

Finally, among other things, the organisation must commence assessment of how the accident occurred; restructure processes and work practices to ensure it doesn't occur again; deal with associated legal proceedings and investigations; manage the reactions of the other employees; and review procedures and policies.

Emergencies and potential emergency situations

An emergency can be any act or event that has the potential to harm people or property.

There is the potential for an emergency in all tourism operations. The size and type of the enterprise, the skills of its employees and the procedures in place to deal with an emergency will all contribute to minimising the risk.

TYPES OF EMERGENCIES

The primary objective of an emergency procedure for any organisation is the safety of everyone. How successful this objective is is often dependent on how people respond to the emergency.

Types of emergency include:

- fire or explosion
- gas leak
- ventilation system contamination
- bomb threat or explosion
- structural fault or damage
- natural disaster (e.g. cyclone, flood)
- civil disorder.

It may not always be necessary to initiate a partial or full evacuation for every emergency and there may be times when it is more appropriate to remain in the building. However, if directed by an emergency services member to evacuate then it is necessary to do so.

There is no 'most likely' scenario for any of the above emergencies. There are, however, 'less likely' scenarios depending on the location of the enterprise. For example, although history tells us that any of the above emergencies can occur in Australia—earthquake in Newcastle, cyclone in Darwin, bomb explosion in Sydney and so on—we know that Melbourne, Sydney and Adelaide are unlikely to have a cyclone, and that gas leaks are unlikely if the building doesn't use gas!

FIRE

Before any business can commence trading (and remain open), local building ordinances and legislation require specific measures to be adopted for the prevention of fire. An inspection by the fire service will be carried out to ensure compliance with the regulations. Compliance will include:

- establishing emergency procedures, including practice drills and training all staff on fire and emergency evacuation procedures;
- installing fire fighting and emergency systems and equipment, including:
  - fire-resistant doors;
  - smoke detection and suppression systems;
  - sprinkler systems;
  - escape shutes;
  - fire blankets;
  - fire alarm and warning systems;

- fire hoses; and
- fire extinguishers;
- training staff in the use of fire extinguishing equipment, identification of class of fires and how to extinguish each class of fire;
- allocation of wardens to take control during an emergency;
- ensuring adequate means of escape; and
- displaying emergency procedures throughout the premises.

Causes of fire

Fire can start at any time, anywhere. Customers have a role to play to the same extent as employees, through their actions, in the prevention of fire. Although it is more likely a fire will originate in a non-public area—for example, kitchen, storeroom, electrical housing—customers need to feel confident that all measures are taken to ensure their safety.

Most fires in tourism-based operations occur as a result of:

- faulty or misused electrical or mechanical equipment;
- carelessness by smokers;
- hot oil and fats in the kitchen;
- poorly stored and handled chemicals; or
- human actions (i.e. deliberately lit).

Characteristics of fire

All fires have three characteristics in common. They require:

- fuel (source);
- means of ignition (heat); and
- oxygen.

Many fires begin from one source, such as wood, but because of the presence of other sources, such as oil, a fire may develop into more than one class.

Classes of fire

Fires are classified by the type of fuel the fire needs to burn. The different types of fuel dictate how we extinguish the fire. The classes of fire, description and appropriate extinguishers are detailed in Figure 7.3.

Fire prevention

Because fire prevention is everyone's responsibility, what we do as individuals to maintain fire safety in the workplace can make the difference between a tragedy and a successful outcome.

What can we do as employees?

- Familiarise ourselves with evacuation procedures.
- Familiarise ourselves with fire fighting equipment and its location in the building.
- Report electrical faults and any other potential fire hazards.
- Don't store combustibles unnecessarily or carelessly.
- Consider the consequences of how and where we extinguish a cigarette or empty an ashtray.
- Handle fats, oils and chemicals correctly.

FIGURE 7.3

PORTABLE FIRE EXTINGUISHERS
Suitability for different kinds of small fires

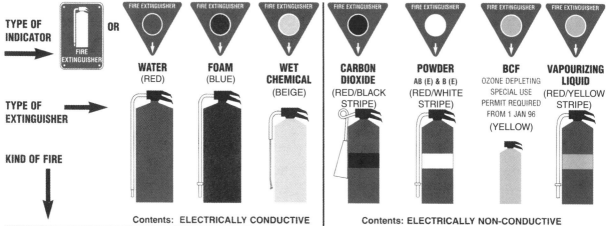

KIND OF FIRE	WATER (RED)	FOAM (BLUE)	WET CHEMICAL (BEIGE)	CARBON DIOXIDE (RED/BLACK STRIPE)	POWDER AB (E)	POWDER B (E)	BCF (YELLOW)	VAPOURIZING LIQUID (RED/YELLOW STRIPE)
	Contents: ELECTRICALLY CONDUCTIVE			Contents: ELECTRICALLY NON-CONDUCTIVE				
WOOD, PAPER, TEXTILES RUBBISH, ETC	YES MOST SUITABLE	YES	YES	YES	YES	NO	YES	YES
FLAMMABLE LIQUIDS	NO	YES MOST SUITABLE	NO	YES	YES	YES	YES	YES
LIVE ELECTRICAL EQUIPMENT	NO	NO	NO	YES	YES	YES	YES	YES
COOKING OILS AND FATS	NO	YES	YES MOST SUITABLE	YES	NO	YES	NO	NO

Type of indicator: FIRE EXTINGUISHER OR FIRE EXTINGUISHER

BCF: OZONE DEPLETING SPECIAL USE PERMIT REQUIRED FROM 1 JAN 96

PRECAUTIONS: For special Hazards such as water miscible flammable liquids and reactive metals - expert advice should be sought

Rooms and confined spaces should be ventilated before re-entry after fire

• Switch off power or fuel before attacking fire appliance / equipment

• In all cases call the Fire Brigade on **000**

THIS BROCHURE IS REPRODUCED WITH PERMISSION OF THE COMMONWEALTH FIRE BOARD

---

activity 7.3

▶ Walk around your college or place of work and make a note of all the systems and measures in place for fire prevention.

Are the extinguishers easily accessible? Is it easy to identify which extinguisher is for which class of fire? When were the extinguishers last checked (serviced)? Are evacuation instructions signposted? Do you know how to raise the alarm if you discover a fire? How prepared do you think your college or organisation is to handle a fire emergency effectively?

Fire wardens

Not every organisation will have designated fire wardens. Fire wardens generally investigate situations, initiate evacuation procedures, fight the fire if safe to do so, and assist emergency services personnel with identifying the type of fire and its location, and advise of any other potential dangers.

Because human safety is the first priority in an emergency evacuation, fire wardens usually have the authority to take control of the situation to ensure that relevant information is passed on, everyone is accounted for and the evacuation is conducted efficiently and safely.

Bear in mind, however, that fire wardens are not the only ones responsible for fire safety.

Rights and wrongs in an emergency

It is unlikely that a fire warden will be the person to discover a fire or other emergency. It may be any employee or even a customer. But whoever discovers the fire should resist the temptation to shout 'Fire'—the outcome is usually panic!

If you witness an emergency

Figure 7.2 on page 158 provides a six-point general procedure in the event of a fire.

The following is a comprehensive procedure for employees in the event of almost any type of emergency:

1. Stop, think, act.
2. Assist anyone in immediate danger if safe to do so.
3. If the emergency is a fire, isolate the fire by closing doors.
4. Raise the alarm—contact the switchboard and the head fire warden and tell them:
   (a) the exact location of the emergency;
   (b) what it involves;
   (c) your name and department.
5. Break the glass on a Red Break Glass Alarm (if it is a fire) or call the fire brigade on 000.
6. Attempt to extinguish the fire if safe to do so.
7. Stay calm—customers depend on us because we know the building better than they do. Assist with evacuation through designated escape routes.
8. Then report to designated assembly point and await instructions from management, fire warden or emergency services personnel.

   Do not:

- Endanger your own or another's life.
- Use the lifts under any circumstances.
- Attempt to retrieve personal belongings or other items of value in the building.
- Ignore directions given by a fire warden or emergency services personnel.
- Panic.
- Enter a closed room if the door or door handle is warm.

activity 7.4

▶ As a class exercise, in conjunction with your course coordinator/director of education and local fire authority (and any other affected parties), arrange an evacuation of the building. In the group, designate fire wardens, a time keeper and observers. Carry out the evacuation in accordance with established procedure.

After the exercise the fire wardens are to report on the level of cooperation received and how well they believe they carried out their duties. The observers are to report on how successfully they believe the evacuation was performed and how it could be improved. Timing may be one of these issues. No specific time can be given as each situation and premises will be different.

A final point to remember is that death in most fires is not caused by the flames but by the smoke. Because smoke rises, fresher, cleaner air is along the floor. If necessary, crawl.

SMOKING

It has been a long-established and well-documented fact that smoking harms us all. Not only is it the largest preventable cause of death in Australia for smokers, but passive smoking (the breathing in of another's tobacco smoke) can also cause harm to non-smokers. Passive smoke in the workplace is a health risk, and has already been the subject of several legal claims by employees against employers.

For many, it is hard to imagine that in a country that supports freedom of choice, what they do by choice may soon be illegal in all enclosed public places. In Australia, legislation has been introduced in a number of states and territories (Western Australia, Victoria, South Australia, New South Wales, Australian Capital Territory) preventing smoking in food service areas. Not every state and territory at this stage plans to follow suit. Most businesses cite a potential loss of business and profits for their reluctance to embrace non-smoking areas in their venues.

The duty of care imposed on every employer to safeguard the health of employees and the public means they have a responsibility to ensure that no one is exposed to passive smoke. In Australia, several complainants have received compensation for discomfort or disease caused by environmental tobacco smoke, which can lead to emphysema, irritation of the eyes or the triggering of an asthma attack, among other things (Victorian Smoking and Health Program, Going Smoke Free).

Many workplaces, travel agents, conference venues, tourist attractions, government buildings, hospitals, offices, shopping centres and retail outlets, airlines and public transport, cinemas and even some sporting venues are already smoke free. Many workplaces in the hospitality industry, however, are not smoke free. In response to a perceived concern by the public, many hotels, motels and other commercial providers of accommodation have introduced smoke-free rooms and floors, and several restaurants (in states where smoking is not banned in food service areas) have allocated smoke-free dining areas. However, because the industry is not entirely smoke free, every day we are exposed, voluntarily or otherwise, to passive smoke, and so are our customers. In a safe working environment we should not be exposed to passive smoking.

file this

▶ Many tourism enterprises have smoke-free areas available in response to demand by the public.

The purpose of the legislation, however, is not to deny the rights of the smoker, but to protect the rights of everyone. No smoking in all enclosed environments throughout Australia is inevitable. The challenge for the tourism industry and its various sectors is how to adapt.

Another risk factor associated with smoking in enclosed environments is the potential for fire. In many tourism environments the dangers are extensive. Careless disposal of cigarettes can cause an outbreak of fire in a guest room, public area or employee-only area. Indeed, falling asleep with a burning cigarette has been linked to several fires in private homes and commercial premises. Imagine the consequences of a carelessly discarded cigarette in a national forest!

check please

9. Of what value are evacuation drills?

10. What potential hazards exist in a theme park? On a coach? In a travel agency? In a commercial kitchen? What 'class' do they fall into?

11. 'The best thing to happen to the tourism industry is the introduction of laws preventing smoking.' Present a case for or against this statement.

Security in tourism

Providing security in a tourism environment is the broad task of protecting:

- people
  - customers
  - employees
- assets
  - cash
  - valuables
- property.

How each of these security areas is protected is a policy issue for individual enterprises. Industry can provide standard guidelines but because of the uniqueness of each establishment, policy and procedure will be designed to meet individual needs.

SECURITY ISSUES

When we think about the physical size of many tourism operations and the extent of activities that take place, the issue of protecting the two primary players—people and assets—becomes a major responsibility.

Major security considerations include:

- emergency evacuations—bomb threat, fire
- theft (money, vehicles, goods)
- security staffing
- suspicious people
- control of access to certain areas
- disturbances
- financial control and record keeping.

DEVELOPING A SECURITY SYSTEM

Any security system should have prevention as its primary objective—although not all potential crime is preventable. The involvement of staff in identifying potential security issues and developing procedures is encouraged because it is a member of staff who will most likely be the first to spot the problem, implement and follow the procedures and finally report the incident.

A well-planned and effective security system will include:

- written procedures;
- staff training in prevention and procedure in the event of a security breach or emergency situation;
- regular review of existing systems;
- clearly defined lines of authority in the event of a security breach; and
- reporting systems/evaluation after an event.

file this

▶ Security measures are for everyone's protection.

BOMB THREAT PROCEDURES

In Australia we are less likely to believe that a bomb threat will be carried out than we are to believe that a fire may start. The reality is that many tourism-based enterprises (and other organisations) do receive bomb threats, which must be taken seriously, more often than serious fires occur.

A standard procedure for dealing with bomb threats follows three steps.

1. RECEIVING THE THREAT

It is generally believed that actual bombers are quite specific with detail when they make a bomb threat. However, having received a bomb threat, attempt to gain as much information about the threat as possible—type of bomb, location, time due to explode, caller's name, reason for planting a bomb. Listen carefully to the voice and follow instructions. Do not disregard the threat and do not hang up on the caller. Report immediately to management that the threat has been received and alert the police and fire departments.

2. THE SEARCH

This may be a partial or complete search of the premises. It is necessary to be systematic and thorough—look in places where the public have ready access first. Search from the floor to the ceiling. If a suspicious package or bomb is found, do not touch it but report immediately to the head warden or person in charge.

3. THE EVACUATION

The decision to evacuate may be taken immediately upon receiving a threat or after it has been determined a bomb actually exists. The evacuation must be orderly and follow the same principles as for a fire evacuation.

THEFT

Theft and pilferage can occur in every department of an organisation. Theft by employees is an expensive cost incurred by almost every establishment, although much of it is preventable.

Most establishments have a policy dealing with employees who are caught stealing. What many don't have are effective prevention procedures. A prevention procedure sets out how each asset—money, tickets, attractions, displays, food, beverages, linen, utensils, equipment, furnishings—is to be accounted for, by whom, how and when. The types of measures used include stock requisition and transfer forms, stock auditing and ordering controls, access restrictions, accounting systems and many others.

Another security issue is theft by someone other than an employee. Robbery can include theft by customers of items in their hotel rooms or from a public area, or a hold-up with the sole intention of obtaining money or goods. This latter type of theft potentially poses a far more serious risk to personal safety.

ROBBERY PREVENTION STRATEGY

In developing a strategy for the prevention of robbery, and a strategy in the event a robbery does occur, the primary focus must be on human safety. Financial losses can be made up, but human life cannot be replaced.

A robbery prevention strategy should, as a minimum, include:

- a written, detailed description of all valuable property;
- an alarm system;
- effective lighting and other security aids, for example closed-circuit television monitors;
- staff training;
- a standard procedure for the recovery of property removed by customers from the enterprise;
- a procedure for transfer of money around the enterprise;
- a standard procedure for staff to observe in the event of a robbery; and
- a reporting and accountability procedure after a robbery.

file this

▶ If a hold-up does occur, always cooperate. Do not enter into a discussion or argument and do not refuse to give the perpetrator what they want.

Because a follow-up report must be completed, and the police become involved, it will be useful to retain as much information about the episode as possible—what the perpetrator looked like (full description), time of day, what you were doing at the time, were there witnesses, how the offenders escaped and any other relevant information.

SECURITY STAFFING

The size and design of a particular establishment, its services and facilities, and its location and available resources will determine the need for and use of security staff. While it is an effective strategy for staff to be aware of potential security issues, there may be valid reasons for specialist security staff. Options include:

- In-house security department
- Contract services
- Security company patrols

Before the decision can be made, the following must be considered:

- likely effectiveness;
- training;
- expertise;
- financial resources available; and
- physical demands.

It is more likely that a physical presence (crowd controllers, security guards) will be required where large numbers of people gather, such as at tourist attractions, airports, entertainment complexes and sporting venues.

SUSPICIOUS PEOPLE

Most organisations have public access irrespective of whether the person is a customer or not. Most people have a legitimate reason for being in a public access area; a few do not. It is the few who do not with whom we are concerned.

A **suspicious person** can be an employee or customer or other person. As staff go about their normal duties they are in a position to observe others—does that person need assistance? Should they be in this area? Are they acting strangely?

WHAT TO DO ABOUT SUSPICIOUS PEOPLE

Of course some people may simply be lost, waiting for someone or just looking around, but if you feel someone genuinely looks suspicious:

- alert your supervisor;
- only approach and offer assistance if you feel comfortable doing so;
- don't just ignore them—watch them carefully; and
- be observant of their actions, clothing, manner, where they go and what they do.

ACCESS CONTROL

Restricting access is concerned with security and safety. Access control deals with restricting access to the enterprise's entrances, especially those that lead to public areas during specified hours and employee-only areas.

The main tools of access control are keys, locks, monitoring systems and physical barriers. From an internal control perspective, access control can be managed with the use of procedures that give or deny access to specific employees.

Restricting access to certain areas helps reduce the incidence of theft and, as a safety measure, can prevent accidents. For example, a customer may be placed in danger if permitted in non-customer areas—not only is there an issue of stock security, but one also of OHS.

All staff should be familiar with those areas that are restricted (such as store-rooms), who has access, access procedures and breach procedures.

GUEST ROOM SECURITY

In accommodation venues the security of guests and their valuables is the responsibility of the venue irrespective of the location of the guest (when on the premises). That is, if a guest is not on the premises but has their personal belongings in the room, they have a right to assume that the belongings are safe. When a guest is in the venue, they have a right to assume that they too are personally safe.

This safety can be assisted in a number of ways:

- advice to guests of security options for their valuables;

Suspicious person
Anyone who gives the impression that something might be wrong. It can be the way a person looks or behaves. Suspicious people often look nervous or out of place, and try to avoid eye contact or conversation with staff.

- good lighting in all public access areas;
- strict key control procedures;
- locks, latches, chains;
- in-room safe;
- peepholes in room doors;
- telephone and emergency numbers directory in room;
- emergency procedure (posted in room—required by law); and
- restriction of information about guests.

Legislation exists in each state and territory which covers liability for hoteliers ('innkeepers') with regard to their guests and their guests' property.

SAFETY DEPOSIT BOXES

Safety deposit systems in accommodation venues range from the installation of an in-room safe to a security room requiring double key access—one key held by the guest and one by a staff member, usually in the front office—to simply leaving valuables at reception for safe keeping. Whatever the system, the safety of the guests' personal valuables is the object and access should be limited.

Innkeepers legislation severely limits the liability in the event of theft of guests' personal property when in a guest room. However, if the innkeeper accepts property for safe keeping, this liability may be far greater. Irrespective of liability, it is prudent to have in place procedures that minimise any risk to guests' valuables.

An in-room safe puts the onus of protecting valuables on the guest. The guest is able to access their valuables at their convenience and is able to select their own code for the safe.

The most common system used when securing guests' valuables with the front desk requires the guest to sign a form that limits the venue's responsibility and indicates what is actually in the safety deposit box. The form is dated and signed.

For security reasons it is preferable that safety deposit transactions not be completed in a public area.

LUGGAGE STORAGE

In addition to the facilities described above, many tourism-based enterprises provide facilities for the safe storage of luggage and personal belongings of the customer. Airports, coach and train terminals and even many attractions provide a luggage storage facility for both the customer's convenience and security reasons. For example, enterprises that have open access to items of value that may be easily slipped into a bag often require visitors to place their luggage or handbag in storage before giving access to the venue to the customer.

LUGGAGE SCANNING

Yet another security measure is the scanning of personal items and hand luggage at airports. The purpose of this is the detection of items that may be considered dangerous on an aircraft, such as weapons and aerosol cans.

KEYS AND LOCKS

Keys and locks ensure customer privacy, safety and security. They also protect the assets of the operation. Strict control of issuing keys, and procedures for the changing of locks, are important crime prevention tools.

The introduction of computer-generated plastic keycards with a magnetic strip for guest room access in accommodation venues has contributed to a reduction in theft from guest rooms, and reduced the cost of replacing locks and lost or stolen keys. However, even these are not entirely crime-proof as there is still room for human error; they are also expensive to install.

Most enterprises have in place a checklist for securing the premises out of operating times. A patrol of the premises is usually conducted during which all doors and gates are checked to ensure they are locked. As each door and lock is checked or secured it is marked off the checklist.

As a means of protecting people and assets a few simple measures can be put in place. The following are procedures that can be followed in hotels or any enterprise that provides accommodation:

- When guests register don't say the room number out loud.
- When returning to the venue, guests will usually ask for their key by room number. Ask guests their name, to check against registration, before issuing the room key.
- Don't stamp room numbers on keys.
- Don't identify the venue on the key tag.
- Change locks if keys are misplaced or stolen.
- Never issue a master key to a guest.
- Lock all spare keys in a cupboard and restrict access to the cupboard.
- Introduce a system for signing out and signing in keys issued to staff (key register).
- At checkout, ask the guest for the key.

OTHER SECURITY MEASURES

Security issues can appear in the most unlikely places. We need to be alert to this and put in place security measures accordingly, such as:

- checking the signature on credit cards against the signature on the voucher/docket;
- issuing identity cards with a picture to staff;
- conducting regular physical checks of the premises; and
- screening tradespeople before giving access to restricted areas.

DISTURBANCES

Distrubances
Any event or occurrence that interrupts the normal activities within an organisation.

A **disturbance** is usually any event or occurrence that interrupts the normal activities within an organisation. It may be a brief, non-offence encounter or it may pose a serious health, safety and security risk. Some likely disturbances include:

- unruly behaviour in a publicly accessible area (that affects customers or staff);
- an attempt to break into a customer's room or car;
- an attempt to break into the premises;
- intoxicated people;
- loud arguments;
- violence (e.g. a fight);
- emergencies;
- accidents; and
- vandalism.

Many disturbances are not foreseeable and are beyond our initial control. Some can be prevented if we are observant and alert to potential problems (e.g. intoxicated or suspicious people). Some instances may require the involvement of police or other emergency services people. When in doubt, alert your supervisor.

FINANCIAL CONTROL AND RECORD KEEPING

Large sums of cash can pass through tourism operations every day. Equally valuable are credit cards, vouchers and cheques. All money is handled several times within the operation before it reaches a bank; therefore control procedures must exist for the handling of all transactions, stock movement, payroll, banking and cashiering.

To verify the integrity of the accounting process we need to implement audit procedures, staff accountability, receipting and invoicing, reconciliation and recording procedures. For example, money issued as a float should be signed out and in for each shift. A **float** is a 'starting bank' for the day's trade for each register. Floats are usually kept in the venue's safe, with very restricted access, and issued at a set time, and later returned with the day's takings. All floats should be counted by the receiving department, with a witness, before signing out. Conversely, they should be counted back in on return.

Float
A set amount of money issued as a 'starting bank' to enable financial transactions.

Without these systems in place we are not able to account for all transactions and theft is very likely. All organisations are required by law to maintain true and accurate accounting of all transactions for taxation purposes and other reasons. Standard forms and procedures are used to justify every transaction and to protect the employee. If procedures don't exist, the integrity of record keeping cannot be maintained.

The accounts department is responsible for maintaining the final accountability of all monies. They control credits and debits, payroll and issue of floats and finalise all banking transactions. Depending on the size of an operation, the transfer of money between the operation and the bank can be in person or by an armoured vehicle. There should be no set pattern for money transfers as this leaves both the person and the asset vulnerable.

---

activity 7.5

▶ In small groups, write a procedure to deal with one of the following:

- receiving a bomb threat
- armed robbery
- suspicious people
- disturbances
- safety deposit box.

To test the effectiveness of the procedure role-play each procedure/scenario in class. The other members of the class can observe and offer feedback on the level of success of the procedure.

Insurance requirements

Insurance is a way of protecting the interests of a business if anything goes wrong, including fire, theft, injury or damage. Insurance takes the form of a policy, which is a contract between the insurer and the policy holder, whereby the insurer guarantees to compensate, financially or otherwise, the other party should something ever happen to the insured item.

Insurance can be bought for almost every contingency arising out of the day-to-day running of a tourism-based business. Some insurance policies are required by law, while others are taken out because of the item's replacement value. Either way, all tourism operators hope they never need their insurance.

As a minimum, all tourism enterprises should have the following insurance policies:

1. Liability insurance:
   (a) Employees—covered under workers' compensation, which is a compulsory insurance scheme that protects employees in the event of an accident.
   (b) Public liability—also compulsory and will cover the public in the event of an accident on the insured premises as a result of negligence by the owner or an employee.
   (c) Personal insurance—a good idea for the self-employed. Proprietors of small organisations need to protect themselves in the event of sickness or an accident, which may otherwise result in the loss of the business or profits.
2. Property insurance:
   This insurance covers buildings and property, such as fixtures and fittings, cash, plate glass, equipment and plant, against damage and theft.
3. Fire insurance:
   Fire insurance includes cover for the premises, equipment, fixtures and fittings, furniture, utensils and so on. Some individual items may be of great value, in which case separate, additional cover can be taken out.
4. Loss of profits:
   If a business is forced to close as a result of fire, accident, damage or any other reason, there will obviously be loss of profits until it can reopen again. This insurance will protect against such loss.

Insurance can be bought for many other situations also, such as riot or civil commotion, flood, for articles located in more than one place or even for damage caused from aircraft and items falling from aircraft! The nature of the business and even the location will dictate the insurance required.

file this

▶ If it can be stolen, broken, injured, burned or lost, insure it.

WORKERS' COMPENSATION INSURANCE

Workers' compensation is an insurance scheme to which all employers must contribute on behalf of their employees. This insurance is protection for the employer and employee in the event of an injury in the workplace. State and territory WorkCover authorities manage the scheme, although employers may choose any number of insurance companies for their policy.

Accident compensation legislation makes provision for the rights of employees who have sustained an injury in the workplace. These rights include rehabilitation, return to work programs and adequate and just compensation. The definition of injury in the Act is any physical or mental injury and includes aggravation of a pre-existing injury or disease, industrial deafness and any disease contracted in the course of the worker's employment.

The amount of compensation awarded, and the period over which payments are made, can depend on the extent of the injury, the ability to return to work, availability of other suitable employment, income at the time of the injury, number of dependants and a range of other qualifying factors.

IF AN INJURY OCCURS

The procedure may vary slightly between states and territories. The basic steps to follow if an injury occurs are:

- Report immediately to your supervisor or OHS representative.
- If medical help was required a WorkCover claim form must be completed and passed to your employer. Your employer is responsible for forwarding this to WorkCover.
- If your claim is accepted you are entitled to reasonable medical and treatment costs. If you are unable to return to work immediately you may be entitled to weekly benefits (a medical certificate will be required).

WorkCover aims to help injured workers return to work as soon as possible. That is not to say that an injured worker will be required to perform at the same level as before the injury, but it is believed that returning to work—if only on a part-time basis and/or performing a different role—can aid recovery.

question point

1. Providing security in a tourism environment is the broad task of protecting people and assets. Explain how this can be achieved.
2. What is the difference between a disturbance and a suspicious person?
3. As an individual, what role can you play in meeting the security needs of your customers? What should you do if you witness a security breach by a colleague?
4. Financial controls exist for the protection of monetary assets. List three procedures that aid this control.
5. Insurance is required for the protection of an organisation's interests. Briefly describe the four primary policies an enterprise should hold to protect their interests. Give examples of each.
6. WorkCover aims to help injured workers return to work as soon as possible after an accident. Why would they do this? What other services does WorkCover provide?
7. Distinguish between a policy and a procedure. In the workplace, what are the benefits of these tools?
8. Explain the right of entry an OHS inspector has and the action they can take if a breach of legislation exists in the workplace.
9. What is the difference between an IN and a PN? Under what circumstances would an inspector issue either of these notices?
10. What is an organisation's legal obligation in the reporting of accidents and injuries? What use can these records serve?

Promote and sell products and services

LEARNING OUTCOMES

On completion of this chapter you will be able to:

- identify the attributes of a successful salesperson;
- describe the principles of successful selling;
- develop selling techniques;
- describe promotional tools and their uses;
- identify the skills needed to promote products and services;
- distinguish between service, product and price differentiation; and
- state the relevant legislation that regulates the sale of goods and services.

This chapter complies with the Tourism Industry National Competency Standards, unit THHGCS02A , 'Promote Products and Services to Customers'.

Most tourism professionals are in the business of selling. Whether it is a holiday, a hire car, a hotel room, a restaurant meal, an admission ticket or a souvenir, our customers come to us so we can assist with their buying decisions. To be able to do this, we need the knowledge and skills to provide them with the advice and information required to purchase tourism products, both goods and services. Our role is not simply to provide service in a friendly, efficient manner, but to help our customers decide which products or services they would prefer by highlighting the features and by creating a desire to purchase through our descriptions.

Do we provide this higher standard of service only because it is expected of us? Because it is part of our job description? Or are we using all of our selling and interpersonal skills and attributes to give the best possible service?

Well, it's all of the above actually. We help customers make choices about what they want by adopting and using all these skills.

Attributes of a successful salesperson

Selling in tourism is not necessarily a 'hard sell'—we are not forcing customers to make a buying decision they are not interested in. Through our knowledge and skill, we present all the options available so our customers can make informed choices that suit their wants, needs and expectations.

And all successful salespeople have a range of attributes that contribute to the customer's experiences of the products and services they buy from us. These attributes are:

- a strong desire to satisfy customer expectation;
- highly developed interpersonal skills;
- excellent product knowledge;
- self-confidence;
- positive attitude;
- selling skills;
- enthusiasm; and
- motivation to sell.

We can all develop the necessary attributes to be a successful salesperson. Throughout this chapter we will provide knowledge about the skills required to help us in this important role.

Principles of successful selling

The principles of successful selling include:

- product knowledge
- capturing their attention
- maintaining their interest
- creating a desire
- recognising buying signals
- closing the sale
- after-sales service.

DEVELOPING PRODUCT KNOWLEDGE

The better we know the product the easier it is to sell. We have confidence in what we are doing and we are better able to describe the features of the product. Developing our product knowledge is the first important step to successful selling.

Product knowledge is an essential tool for the tourism professional to help us do our job and to ensure we don't misrepresent products or services offered by our organisation. Having an excellent knowledge of our product will give us a competitive edge. But how well do we know the products and services offered by our particular enterprise, our competitors or those available in the immediate environs?

For example, many tourism organisations are involved in selling holidays in various destinations around Australia (domestic and inbound markets) or around the world (international and outbound markets). Hence, an essential element for anyone involved in the selling of holidays is product knowledge of the destinations they sell.

The best way to gain such knowledge is to actually visit the destination. Often, airlines or product providers will join together to offer a free trip for travel agents to sample the products. These are referred to as **familiarisation trips**, which sound like a lot of fun but which are more to do with developing product knowledge and a familiarity with the destination—a serious learning experience and educational tool for tourism salespeople.

> **Familiarisation trips**
> Free trips offered by airlines or other tourism providers to travel agents to sample the products offered by those companies.

If you are currently working in the tourism industry, choose a destination and take the mini-test on p. 188. If you aren't yet working in the industry, think about where you went on your last holiday and imagine you are the travel sales consultant selling the product. If you can answer a customer query without hesitation, or have the general knowledge, tick 'Yes'. If you need to find out the answer, tick 'No'. Compare your 'Yes' responses to your 'No' responses. In six months, take the test again. This should show you how much progress you've made towards becoming a tourism professional and therefore of even greater value to your organisation.

RESEARCH

So how do we find all this information? Research skills are a set of techniques to help us locate information and to process it so that we can use the relevant data to assist us to build our knowledge and make informed decisions.

First we need to identify (i.e. list) the aims of the research, noting the exact information we require. We can then list possible sources for this information (brochures, magazines, newspapers, annual reports, the Internet, books, other organisations, industry associations, colleagues and so on) and start to sift through these, giving priority to those we think will be of most use.

Research can be as simple or as complex as we like—it all depends on how much we want to know!

Formal research

Formal research involves systematically gathering and analysing information from primary and secondary sources relating to a product or service or even the industry in general. Primary source information is information collected through interviewing (one-on-one or group sessions) or questionnaires (e.g. a survey) and secondary source information is information gathered from data that is already published.

> **Formal research**
> Systematic collection and analysis of data from primary and secondary sources.

While this may seem a little tedious, formal research can assist us in getting a job in the first place. For example, at the interview stage of recruitment, it is useful

Destination product/service knowledge	Yes	No
(a) Accommodation		
How many hotels were there at the destination?	❏	❏
How many rooms does each have?	❏	❏
What range of other accommodation is available?	❏	❏
Have they been classified according to standard/quality?	❏	❏
What facilities are available for children?	❏	❏
(b) Transport/travel logistics		
What airlines fly there?	❏	❏
What other modes of travel are available?	❏	❏
What is the standard of local public transport?	❏	❏
What range of special fare offers is available?	❏	❏
Could you recommend a suitable timetable for travel?	❏	❏
Do travellers need a passport or visa?	❏	❏
(c) General information		
What will the weather be like at this time of the year?	❏	❏
What and where are the main tourist attractions?	❏	❏
Are public toilets available and suitable for disabled travellers?	❏	❏
How far to the beach/shopping centre/theatre/train station?	❏	❏
What's on at the movies and where is the nearest cinema?	❏	❏
What's on at the theatre and where is the nearest theatre?	❏	❏
Directions to main railway terminal or airport?	❏	❏
Where can travellers buy personal goods?	❏	❏

Whew! This is only the beginning. Our product and service knowledge is only limited by our personal experiences and ability to research the information.

to know something about the organisation where we are seeking employment. A little research will provide the information we need. (Refer to Chapter 9.)

Informal research

Informal research
Collection of information from secondary sources.

Informal research is not as structured or as time consuming as formal research. It involves the collection of information from sources that have already been formally researched with regard to their products and services (secondary sources). This could include reading a brochure or a travel guide on various destinations.

Other forms of informal research include:

- Attending orientation and training sessions
- Talking with colleagues
- Reading the staff handbook
- Reading general media articles
- Visiting competitors
- Personal observation

It takes time to develop a high level of product knowledge and there is a lot to know. It is important that we take time to familiarise ourselves with all aspects of the products and services available in the organisation we work in. We should ask questions if we are not sure, as we never know when a customer may ask us the same question. The higher the level of product knowledge the greater our confidence and the higher the level of service we can offer our customers.

Internet

The **World Wide Web** (WWW) can give us a 'virtual' tour of many tourist destinations and information on many tourism organisations. By accessing their website, we can find information relating to the location, major attractions, services, facilities and prices of many destinations. Many also have an option on their site that allows anybody to book a holiday directly via the Web using e-mail.

World Wide Web (WWW)
Global network of Internet websites.

check please

1. Of what value is product knowledge?
2. What is a familiarisation trip and how does it help us develop product knowledge?
3. Distinguish between formal and informal research.
4. Apart from developing product and services knowledge, how else might formal research help you?

CAPTURING THEIR ATTENTION

When selling any product or service directly to a customer we usually have a captive audience. This means that the customer has sought out our products and services. This is particularly true once the customer is in front of us. The customer needs many things when using tourism products and services (transport, accommodation, tours, food, beverages) and they require information about each of these services and products.

However, we need to *capture* the customer's interest and create a desire for the many products and services options available from us (as opposed to our competitors). The customer needs to believe that we are offering them the best possible options. The customer needs to believe that we are interested in their specific needs and we can demonstrate this by being enthusiastic, courteous and knowledgeable.

MAINTAINING THEIR INTEREST

Once we have captured the customer's interest we need to hold it. The customer will soon lose interest if we lose interest. Looking the customer in the eye (if face-to-face) or keeping a pleasant tone in our voice if talking over the phone are just two ways we can maintain the customer's interest. Questioning the customer to find out what they really want and responding appropriately will help maintain their interest.

By using enthusiasm and telling the potential customer what we have to offer, we are able to maintain the customer's interest. If a customer telephones an organisation and has to work hard to get information, they will probably not be interested in booking any of the services or products on offer. If they then call another organisation that displays interest and is helpful, this is where they are likely to book.

CREATING A DESIRE

As we discuss later in suggestive selling techniques, we need to create a desire so that the customer feels they want the product and its extra services. Offering views, side trips, car hire and swimming pool facilities can create a desire in the customer just by the power of suggestion. If a view of the sea was never mentioned then the customer may never have known they wanted it.

RECOGNISING BUYING SIGNALS

Customers help make selling easy by giving us unintentional buying signals. These signals are an indication that they want us to give them more information and expand on their options. For example, a customer may say 'I can't decide if I want to go to Bali or Fiji'. The implication is that they want a beach island experience but are unsure about how to work out the difference or what really appeals. It is clear that they need or want help deciding. At this point a good travel consultant would suggest a particular destination, pointing out the main features and benefits that they know to be suitable to the customer from previous discussions or experiences with similar clients.

It is important to allow the customer to become involved in the decision-making process by making statements like 'There are a number of good-value package tours available to Bali depending on when you wish to travel and how much time you have to spare'. The use of brochures or other visual aids ('visual' selling can be very powerful) can also assist with the decision to buy. Furthermore, this is a good opportunity to suggest 'add-ons' or extra product features that will add value and create a feeling of satisfaction in the customer.

Another signal can be cost. For example, a customer wants to book a night in a hotel for a special occasion. They indicate that 'It's very expensive'. Because it is a special occasion, we know that they will probably book somewhere else if they don't book with us. At this point we offer alternatives and highlight all the benefits of our products or packages, emphasising the 'special occasion'. For example, 'Mrs Frederick, as it's your anniversary, the Romance Package at the Renaissance Hotel would be ideal. It includes the executive suite with ocean views, champagne on arrival, dinner for two in the privacy of your room, and valet parking, for $285 per person. Or, if you prefer, we can offer you the Deluxe Package, which includes breakfast but not dinner, for $40 less per person.' Although we have 'downsold', we have probably made a sale.

Positive buying signals include frequent agreement with the salesperson—'Yes, that's correct'—or specific questions about price or product features. Other examples of buying signals include:

- 'What else have you got?'
- 'What can you recommend?'
- 'I'm not sure . . .'
- 'Will it be safe?'
- 'But what is the weather like at this time of year?'

A good travel consultant will ask what type of experience the customer is seeking on their holiday or trip and then tailor a program for them.

If we are working face-to-face with a customer, non-verbal buying signals include:

- staying close to us and not walking away;
- open body language;

- eye contact that indicates interest; and
- bringing out their wallet.

CLOSING THE SALE

To close the sale means to have the customer make a purchase. The buying signals should provide us with the clue to when and how to actually close the sale—a verbal commitment from the customer to purchase. A number of techniques can be used to close a sale, including:

- The trial close—a question to test whether the customer is ready to buy, such as 'Shall I make a reservation for that flight?'
- The assumptive close—a positive statement that assumes the customer is ready to purchase, such as 'Well, Miss Williams, I will book that tour departing Melbourne on Tuesday, 5th June.' The salesperson takes the initiative and controls the situation.
- The summary close—offer the customer a range of choices or options, based on discussion and buying signals, and by choosing one, the customer makes a positive decision to buy. Keep the options to a minimum; do not introduce new or unnecessary options.
- Eliminate concern close—the salesperson gives a little ground based on what the concern is: 'Once I have resolved that issue I will make the reservation.' The salesperson may also offer a discount or a special offer if the arrangements can be made by a certain time or date: 'Well, if we book today I believe we can get a further 5% discount.'

There are a few hints to remember when attempting to close a sale:

- We should always expect to make the sale and be confident in our approach, otherwise the customer will suspect we lack credibility.
- We should stay focused on the subject at hand and the details of the sale.
- We should not be too pushy or put undue pressure on the customer. We should allow them to become part of the decision-making process.
- We should create a win–win situation—meet the customer's needs and expectations but balance the input of your time and effort with profitability on each sale.
- If we cannot close the sale, we should always remain friendly and courteous as the customer may well reconsider at some time in the future.

AFTER-SALES SERVICE

After-sales service is a technique used to determine the customer's satisfaction with their buying decision and to offer additional service. Not all organisations offer an after-sales service and not all products and services require it.

However, where appropriate, the sales transaction should include an after-sales follow-up, which will help build goodwill with customers and enhance our professional reputation and that of our organisation.

Most customers will require reassurance that they have made the right decision, particularly in regard to travel arrangements. We must also ensure that any promises or obligations we have given are followed through. With travel arrangements this is normally done with a letter of confirmation and a detailed itinerary. It is also helpful to phone the customer after they return from their holiday to check that their expectations were met.

By building up trust and goodwill we are investing in repeat business, not only from our own satisfied customers but also from those other potential customers that come through word-of-mouth.

CUSTOMER FEEDBACK

Tourism organisations gain feedback from customers in a number of ways: surveys and questionnaires; complaints; compliments; and observation. The main purpose of this feedback is not only to determine customer satisfaction, but also to find out what else we can do for the customer—in other words, continuous improvement opportunities.

Customer feedback is a useful tool that helps us evaluate our products, services and promotional activities. It helps us identify customer preferences and provides us with ideas from which we can formulate strategies to enhance our products and services to improve sales.

Not all feedback is positive, nor should we expect it to be. We need to recognise that we will probably never be perfect and that things do go wrong occasionally. How we respond to feedback, however, will often determine whether or not a customer will return; indeed, many organisations use complaints as an opportunity to show a customer how good they can be by the way they address the complaint.

Statistically speaking, in accommodation venues only between 1% and 3% of guests complete guest questionnaires. Furthermore, statistics show that when a customer is unhappy with a product or service they usually tell between eight and 14 other people about their dissatisfaction. When they are happy, they tell between six and eight others. Therefore we have to work a lot harder to make up for the negatives.

Accepting and acting on guest feedback is a major factor in determining our success and the success of the organisation, so we need to welcome and encourage it, using our selling skills to win the customer back again.

Successful selling is an important part of our working life in the tourism industry. The better we become, the more enjoyable our workday, so why not enjoy?

Develop selling techniques

There are a variety of 'techniques' that can be used, in conjunction with the principles of selling, to help customers decide what they want to buy:

- Suggestive selling
- Upselling
- Downselling
- Personal selling
- Add-ons or extras

SUGGESTIVE SELLING

Suggestive selling
Selling by suggesting alternatives and describing special features.

Suggestive selling is the selling of products or services by suggesting alternatives in a way that creates desire. To create a desire we need to describe the item to create a mental picture or advise the buyer of the features available. For example, Mrs Hobbs calls enquiring about a family holiday. The family wants to travel to an island in the Whitsundays and has two toddlers under four. We can suggest one resort that

5. How can product knowledge assist you in meeting customer expectations?

6. In the organisation where you work, who are the most likely sources of product information and why?

7. When is selling considered successful? Do you agree? Why? Why not? Are there times when selling is considered unsuccessful? Give examples.

8. The principles of successful selling tell us that we need to capture the customer's attention. What does this mean and how can we do it?

9. Once we have captured the customer's attention, we need to hold it. How do we do this?

10. What are 'buying signals'? How do buying signals help us to sell products and services?

11. What does 'closing the sale' mean? Why is it important to know how to close the sale?

12. How do after-sales service and customer feedback help the customer and the organisation?

activity 8.2

▶ With a friend, role-play selling products and services available at your place of work or that you have a good knowledge of. You may have to research some of the information first. If necessary, work from a script to help get you started. When you feel more confident, try selling some of the following:

- a cruise holiday;
- a better standard of room than requested;
- a day trip; and
- an ecotour to a customer who has said they 'only want to lie on the beach'.

we know has availability but no special facilities for children. Alternatively, we suggest another resort that does have children's facilities including a child-minding service. Mrs Hobbs's original intention was to book whatever was available on the dates requested; she hadn't considered a child-minding service until we mentioned it. By describing the resorts features we have potentially increased revenue and assisted Mrs Hobbs's decision in a way that will contribute to a more enjoyable stay.

Suggestive selling doesn't force a customer into a sale but offers them alternatives they may not have thought of before. For example, Mrs Bolt calls to book two interconnecting rooms at the Château Fleur for the weekend and Adrienne, the reservations clerk, offers her a family suite with two bedrooms and a lounge area. It is more expensive than the two interconnecting rooms but offers the advantage of a central lounge, a sitting area and a small kitchenette. Mrs Bolt is happy as the children now have somewhere to play and she has the option of preparing meals herself.

DEVELOPING SUGGESTIVE SELLING SKILLS

The ability to sell is not usually a skill we are born with. It is a skill that can be learned and, as with every other skill we learn in tourism, our competency is limited only by our attitude. Selling is not just something that other people do—we do it every day without realising it. We sell ideas to our parents, friends, teachers and lecturers ('Well, Mr Smith, I actually need to go to my Aunt's funeral this Monday so I won't be able to do the test as hoped!').

Selling is successful when another person accepts our idea or product as worthwhile and useful, and when the idea or product can be shown to benefit prospective users. So let's look upon selling positively. We can view selling as the opportunity to provide better service and as an integral part of our role as tourism professionals.

paint a picture ▶ **Suggestive selling skills: exceeding customer expectations**

Kellyann works in a retail travel agency. After nine months of hard work and dedication, she is very pleased to be promoted to a senior travel consultant's position.

She is dedicated, enthusiastic and positive in attitude. She seems to make friends easily as she has a confident, outgoing personality. It is not unusual for Kellyann to make follow-up phone calls to prospective clients who have visited the agency for information, who work nearby or whom she meets at various industry functions or through her own social networks. She is meticulous in keeping a database on current and prospective clients.

Until now, Kellyann has not been responsible for booking international tours. But her supervisor heard her discussing various options with a customer which not only included an around-the-world air ticket and various accommodation packages but also a hire car, a cruise tour around the Caribbean and a travel insurance policy. She was also able to provide advice on weather conditions, health warnings, foreign currency transactions and passport and visa documentation.

Kellyann is renowned for travelling widely and taking the opportunity to make many familiarisation trips offered to travel agents by the airlines, hotel companies and tour wholesalers. She has a broad knowledge of many of the most popular destinations; she knows the hotels and resorts; she knows about most of the main attractions. She also has a great memory for names and a good network of local contacts in these overseas destinations. If anyone in her travel agency needs to find out something, they ask Kellyann.

However, Kellyann can't succeed without the cooperation of her supervisor and other colleagues. Everyone contributes to the end result and Kellyann enjoys working as part of a team.

What sort of an impression do you think Kellyann makes on her customers and colleagues? How do you think Kellyann got to know so much?

In the 'paint a picture' above what Kellyann has been doing is selling more products and services by utilising her product knowledge and interpersonal skills. She achieves this through employing suggestive selling techniques. An example of suggestive selling is the technique employed by fast-food outlets such as McDonald's. Having placed our order, we are then asked if we would like 'fries/a drink/apple pie/nuggets with that?'. This is not forcing us to buy things we don't want, but suggesting options that we may not have considered or even been aware were available. By suggesting options and then describing the features of those options, we are providing a valuable service to our customers and fulfilling an important function for our employer—selling their products and services. Another reason Kellyann is so successful is her positive attitude and because she uses the principles of successful selling to help her customers.

UPSELLING

Upselling is a technique regularly used by sales consultants in the tourism industry to sell any number of products and services (flights, accommodation, tours). The consultant starts at the lowest priced item and then sells up to the next level and then the next, until the customer chooses the level and price of product or service they require based on the features described and the perceived value. For example, Mrs Armitage calls requesting a hotel room in Sydney for her wedding anniversary. We already know that this is a special occasion, so we can use this information to upsell the accommodation. For example: 'Mrs Armitage, there is a standard room available for $120.00 but for only an extra $50.00 we can offer you a deluxe room with a king-size bed, spa bath and an ocean view. There is also an executive suite available at the same hotel for only $220.00 which has a king-size bed, separate living room and a spa bath with ocean view.'

Mrs Armitage can now make a decision based on the information provided. To help her make the decision, it may be necessary to offer more information or simply ask 'Which room would you like me to book for you?'.

Upselling
Selling technique that starts at the lowest priced product or service and moves up through the price and quality levels.

DOWNSELLING

Downselling is when we start at the most expensive item and work down to the lowest price until the customer chooses the products or services they require. This would mean beginning with the executive suite and then working down to the deluxe room and then the standard room. For example, when Mrs Armitage says she is looking for a hotel room for her and her husband for their anniversary, we can say: 'Mrs Armitage, at the Park Haven there is a lovely executive suite available, which has a king-size bed, separate living room and a spa bath, for $220.00. They also have available a deluxe room, with a king-size bed and spa bath for $170.00 and their standard rooms are available for $120.00.'

Downselling
Selling technique that begins by suggesting the highest priced item and works down through the price and quality levels.

PERSONAL SELLING

Using **personal selling** techniques or the questioning method is presenting the customer with all the options available to them along with the benefits and attributes and asking the potential customer what, if anything, they specifically require from the product or service. Personal selling takes the form of an oral presentation usually face-to-face. However, the presentation can take place over the telephone in the form of a sales call.

Personal selling
Oral presentation made to a customer for the purpose of selling products and services.

QUESTIONING TECHNIQUES AND PERSONAL SELLING

The phrases and sentences we use contribute to the success of selling. When we are selling products and services we ask our potential customers questions to help us determine which products to offer them and which technique to use. We can use open-ended questions or closed questions depending on the response we want.

Open-ended questions are those that make it difficult to answer 'yes' or 'no'. The questioning technique requires using open-ended questions which assume that the customer is going to purchase and usually begin with *why, which, how, what* and *who*. For example, 'Which tour do you prefer, the fairy penguin tour or the Healesville sanctuary tour?'

Closed questions are those that make it easy for the customer to say 'no' or to make other non-buying decisions. Closed questions usually begin with 'would' (e.g. 'Would you like to book a holiday?'). 'Would . . .' can be an open question if a choice is offered (e.g. 'Would you like to book the beach holiday or the ski holiday?').

The open-ended question assumes that the customer is going to make a booking, whereas the closed question gives the customer the opportunity to say 'no' to making any purchasing decision.

In Table 8.1, consider the two questioning techniques to sell products and services and the potential responses.

TABLE 8.1 **Question structure for personal selling**

QUESTION	POTENTIAL RESPONSE
1a. 'Would you like to take a trip somewhere?'	Yes or No
1b. 'What type of holiday are you dreaming about?'	Assumes will want to buy a holiday
2a. 'Would you like me to book that for you?'	Yes or No
2b. 'Which date would you like me to book for you?'	Assumes will book
3a. 'Would you like travel insurance?'	Yes or No
3b. 'Which travel insurance policy would you prefer?'	Assumes will need travel insurance
4a. 'Would you like a hire car?'	Yes or No
4b. 'Which hire car firm do you normally use?'	Assumes will hire a car
5a. 'Would you like to visit a theme park?'	Yes or No
5b. 'Which theme parks would you prefer to visit?'	Assumes will visit a theme park
6a. 'Would you like me to book a flight for you?'	Yes or No
6b. 'Which flight would you prefer me to book for you?'	Assumes will book

ADD-ONS OR EXTRAS

Add-ons and extras
A selling technique used to persuade a potential customer to buy additional products and services.

Extras or **add-ons** (sometimes referred to as cross-selling) are what we can attach to the product to make it more desirable and to promote the use of other products and services. In other words, add-ons and extras are products sold that are supplementary to the main product or service the customer has bought.

A very common example is adding breakfast to the cost of the room to ensure that the customer has breakfast, thereby increasing revenue. For example, a corporate hotel rate could be $150.00 for a room but if breakfast is included as part of a package then the rate may be increased to $165.00. This is perceived as good value by the customer as breakfast in the hotel's restaurant would normally be $22.50. By including breakfast in the room rate, the customer saves money and the restaurant is guaranteed of having customers for breakfast.

When a travel agent sells a holiday they may suggest the customer purchase add-ons or extras such as:

- Travel insurance
- Pre-booked day tours
- Tickets for the theatre or a sporting event
- Special meal plans
- Airport transfers
- Car hire
- Bike hire
- Bus or rail pass

An airline reservations clerk may suggest:

- Arranging accommodation
- Car hire
- Travel insurance

These can provide added value to the customer by stimulating feelings of satisfaction like 'peace of mind', 'time saving', 'reliability' and 'sense of security'. We use suggestive selling techniques to sell add-ons and extras. And although the customer pays for these items, we have created a desire, offered them a choice and generated more revenue for the organisation.

activity 8.3

▶ Look at the following examples and determine which selling techniques you would use to offer better service to the customer. What products or services would you recommend and why?
- Couple spending the weekend interstate
- Family staying overnight in a hotel
- Businessman away from home at Christmas

check please

13. Explain how suggestive selling works.
14. Explain the difference between upselling and downselling? When do you think it appropriate to use each of the techniques? Give an example.
15. Extras and add-ons are used for what purpose? Give an example of each.
16. What is the difference between open-ended and closed questions? Which type of questioning technique is preferred? Why?

Promotional tools and their uses

Promotional tools are the ways in which organisations promote their products and services. All businesses that have a product or service to sell need to carry out promotional activities and use a variety of strategies to achieve the organisation's promotional focus, which is generally in line with their overall goal: normally to make a profit.

Promotional tools
The ways in which an organisation promotes its products and services.

The promotional focus may vary. For example, the organisation may want to promote one aspect of the business or the whole business, or a new product or service. The overall goal of the activity is usually product or service awareness and increased customer satisfaction, leading to greater profit.

The difficulty in promoting tourism-based enterprises lies mainly in the nature of the product. Tourism is primarily a service-based industry and it therefore relies heavily on the promotion of an *image*, or its range of services, rather than a tangible product.

Because of this image it is important for organisations to establish standards in the level of service they provide. This in turn can provide an organisation with the opportunity to focus on the staff that provide the services, as the tangible aspect of the product.

Of course, once a customer arrives at their destination many features and products they use are in fact tangible—products that can be touched and seen. But they are not tangible products in the sense that the customer can take the products away with them. They can only *use* the products while at their destination or during their travel, for example a seat on a plane or a hotel room, where they are really only renting a space for a certain time period. There is less potential for consistency and more variability in these products than in the provision of a tangible product.

What is fundamental to the success of a tourism business is attracting potential customers to the products and services offered in the first place. Which brings us back to the image created by an organisation or destination and the selling of an intangible service.

We have already stressed that all staff play a role in promoting the product, but there are other tools that can be used to attract potential customers.

PROMOTIONAL MATERIALS

Promotional materials are printed or electronic information about the products or services, such as brochures, leaflets or website information. Promotional materials are usually used in conjunction with other marketing tools (e.g. advertising, public relations), although some smaller establishments may limit their marketing activities to the production of promotional materials only. Examples of promotional materials include:

- Brochures
- Leaflets/Flyers
- Menus and wine lists
- Sales letters
- In-house displays
- Posters
- Business cards

These materials are designed to present the business or establishment and the products and services offered in the best light and create an expectation in the customer. For example, a well-designed brochure, menu or business card can influence the customer's perceptions of the product and in turn their purchasing decisions.

PROMOTIONAL ACTIVITIES

A service provider, such as a travel consultant, doesn't always sell just by diligently extolling the virtues of a product. In order to increase sales, attract more customers and provide better products and services, many organisations undertake **promotional activities**, for example, using holiday trips as prizes in competitions, or having a display booth at a travel show or a shopping centre.

A promotional activity may be used to increase an organisation's exposure in the market place, create a positive image, introduce a new product, sell excess stock or increase sales revenue.

Whatever the reason for the promotion, it requires us to be knowledgeable about its features and provide what has been promised in the promotion. Our contribution to the promotional activity is the use of suggestive selling skills to achieve its objective.

Promotional activities
Activities undertaken by an organisation to increase exposure in the market place.

ADVERTISING

Advertising is any paid-for space or air time in the mass media to promote a product or service. The organisation is attempting to 'sell' to the targeted market via:

Advertising
Any paid-for space or air time in the mass media for the promotion of a production service.

- Daily newspapers
- Local newspapers
- Selected specialised magazines
- Trade magazines
- Selected radio stations
- Television
- Outdoor displays (e.g. billboards)
- Internet sites

Advertising communicates information about the product or more commonly about a 'brand' of product. The primary objective of advertising is usually to create an awareness of the product. It is also designed to influence potential customers to buy and to help portray a positive image of the company in the potential customer's mind. Because of the high cost of advertising, companies are very selective about when and where they advertise.

RADIO/TELEVISION

Most businesses that use radio or television advertise selectively because of the high cost. Advertising undertaken by tourism-based organisations is usually to create an awareness of the product or services offered, then to persuade potential customers to buy its products and services rather than those of a rival company.

MAGAZINES/NEWSPAPERS

Organisations advertise in magazines where the specific target market can potentially be reached. For example, corporate clients are reached through business and in-flight magazines, often with an offer of bonus points in the airline loyalty program. For example, a stay at any Hyatt hotel or resort in August may attract an additional 1000 bonus points. Business papers are also a good place to reach corporate clients.

Leisure guests are targeted in travel magazines or auto club magazines, often with special rates offered if the advertisement is mentioned.

PUBLIC RELATIONS

Public relations involve a range of activities designed to portray the organisation in a positive light through generating 'publicity'. **Publicity** usually implies gaining a mention on the radio, on television or in the newspaper for free or minimal cost. For

Public relations
Activities designed to portray the organisation in a positive light through publicity.

example, when an organisation introduces a new product or service, a promotional event (or events) may be arranged to promote the product to those people most likely to use the product. The media will be invited in the hope that they write about the product or service. An example of this may be the introduction of a new loyalty program by an accommodation venue. The loyalty program is targeted at those guests who frequently need accommodation in a particular area. There are several ways this new product can be promoted.

LAUNCH PARTY

A launch party is a special event or party specifically designed to 'launch' a new product or service. The purpose of the party is to introduce and create an awareness of the product or service. A tour operator may invite all clients on its mailing list as well as the local media. At the party, the product is 'launched' to inform the invited guests about the benefits of the new product. The media are frequently given a promotional pack containing information about the product. While the party will cost money to host, the benefits gained by attracting potential new customers and the free publicity generated often outweigh this expense.

MEDIA RELEASE

To coincide with the launch of a new product or to announce an event of importance within the organisation, a media or press release may be sent to all the relevant journalists and commentators in the various print and electronic media outlets.

A **media release** should be an informative, newsworthy article, usually written by the sales or marketing manager, to promote the new service or product. The style in which it is written needs to meet the exact requirements of the media in which publication or announcement is sought. It is written in a way that allows it to be inserted into the print or electronic media with minimal changes.

Because the establishment writes the release, the information is controlled. It usually includes a quote from an authoritative figure (e.g. the general manager) and is always positive.

Its purpose is to gain publicity or 'free advertising' for the new product.

SALES CALLS

Sales calls, also referred to as **personal selling**, are face-to-face (or over the phone) promotional activities between sales representatives and potential customers. They are designed to inform people in targeted markets of the organisation or its products and influence them to buy. Sales calls launching a new product are specifically designed to communicate details of the new product to existing and potential customers.

Because of the intangibility of services, as discussed earlier, sales calls are an important promotional activity for many tourism organisations. They provide an opportunity for the potential customer to put a 'face' to the service (which can influence the decision to buy) and allow the sale to be tailored to meet the individual customer's needs.

MAIL OUT

A **mail out** is the term used to describe a sales letter (usually standardised) sent to a large number of existing or potential customers on the organisation's mailing list. Included with the letter may be a selection of brochures or other promotional

---

Publicity
Free communication to the public about the organisation (or its products or services) via the media.

Media release
A newsworthy article written to promote a new service or product.

Sales calls
'Face-to-face' or 'by phone' promotional activity.

Mail out
A sales letter sent to a large number of existing or potential customers on a mailing list.

materials. It is a relatively inexpensive (compared with advertising), although an impersonal, way (compared with personal selling) to promote a service or product.

The mail out may be designed to inform customers or to advise them about the features of a product or service or simply to keep customers up to date with what is happening within the organisation.

Mail outs are often used during the low season. Special discounted rates are offered to encourage customers to use the organisation's products and services when business is traditionally slow. For example, accommodation venues will discount rates over the Christmas and January period when corporate trade is usually slower, to encourage more leisure business and increase occupancy. Snowfield resorts reduce their rates during the off peak (summer) season to encourage customers at this time. They also promote other activities during this time, such as hiking and bushwalking.

LOYALTY PROGRAMS

Many organisations, particularly airlines and accommodation venues that belong to a chain, offer **loyalty programs** to regular customers to encourage repeat usage. Members of the loyalty program are frequently offered additional benefits not enjoyed by other customers, such as express check-in, free **upgrades** or trips and use of a private lounge area.

Loyalty program
A customer-reward program used to attract and reward customers, for frequent use of an organisation's services or products.

Upgrade
Moving to a better quality or standard of product.

Members of loyalty programs are usually given a membership card, which they present at check-in. This helps reception staff identify and record specific details about each customer, particularly as it relates to the customer's current trip or stay.

Loyalty programs benefit both the customer and the organisation. The organisation attracts repeat business and word-of-mouth promotion from its customers. Customers not only receive rewards for their membership and loyalty but are also made to feel their value to the organisation.

WORD-OF-MOUTH

It is helpful when customers are so impressed with an organisation that they recommend it to family, friends and colleagues. Customers are only likely to do this if they are certain that the organisation can consistently live up to the high standards they have come to expect. This is another reason why tourism organisations are so concerned with creating a positive image and establishing a high-quality service standard. They use this as a promotional tool.

VISUAL SUGGESTIVE SELLING

Suggestive selling can be accomplished without our personal input. It can be visual. The descriptive words and pictures used in brochures, advertisements, posters or Internet sites create a graphic image to tempt customers; they can appeal to a customer's needs or desires, their wants or their budget.

Some visual suggestive selling aids adopted in many tourism operations include:

- suggestive logos and pictures (sun, beach, palm tree);
- photographs in brochures (exotic or scenic locations; smiling, relaxed people);
- resort/room design (presenting the product features in an attractive or enticing manner);
- use of popular personalities (we like to relate to sports heroes, movie and TV stars); and

Promotional tools
- Sales staff
- Promotional materials
- Promotional activities
- Advertising
- Public relations
- Sales calls
- Mail outs
- Loyalty programs
- Word-of-mouth
- Visual suggestive selling

- exotic displays of food and beverages (we often buy these because they look good rather than because of what is in them!).

The promotion of our products is also contingent on the words used to describe them. We would expect the words to be descriptive and thus persuasive. We therefore use words that conjure up images and tempt us to buy, such as 'excellent quality', 'island paradise', 'turquoise waters', 'tantalisingly beautiful', 'lush forests', 'pristine environment', 'wilderness adventure'.

Thus, visual suggestive selling becomes a powerful tool in the promotion of our products and services.

activity 8.4

▶ Collect a travel brochure from your local travel agent or a travel article from your daily newspaper and highlight the words and phrases used as suggestive selling techniques. Also, analyse the use of the photographs in terms of their main selling points. Which of the products would you buy based on the pictures and descriptions?

check please

17. What are promotional tools?

18. Give two examples of a promotional focus.

19. How do promotional materials vary from promotional activities?

20. What is involved in public relations?

21. How is publicity different from advertising?

22. When might a travel agency use a mail out?

23. What types of organisations do you think might use personal selling as a way of promoting its products and services? Why?

Skills needed to promote products and services

All the promotional activities and tools we have just discussed attempt to lure potential customers. But organisations are still reliant on us to actually 'sell' what is being promoted.

For most people selling doesn't come naturally. If you're one of those people who think selling is hard work, consider this: you already have most of the skills you need to promote products. You have them because these skills are not unlike the skills you need to be a tourism professional and they reflect the attributes discussed earlier of a successful salesperson: good interpersonal skills, enthusiasm, product knowledge and a desire to please our customers. In addition to this we need:

- to be motivated; and
- to have self-confidence.

MOTIVATION

Motivation is the force that induces you to do something. You need to be motivated to finish this course successfully so that you can get a good job; you are motivated to cook dinner so that you have something to eat. At work, you should be motivated to give the customer the best possible service. This means being good at your job, which includes being able to supply the correct information in a courteous and helpful manner so that customers can make an informed decision about their options.

For example, if a customer calls wanting to know the availability of flights to Sydney on Thursday and is only given details about what one airline is offering, they may well be disappointed to learn that an alternative airline is offering flights at a better rate and which meet their travel requirements better.

It is necessary for you not only to know that other options are available but also to be motivated to share this information.

Motivation in the workplace is frequently linked to rewards. For example, we are often motivated to go to work because we are paid for our services (**extrinsic motivation**). We may also be motivated to do our job well because of the satisfaction it gives us (**intrinsic motivation**). From the perspective of promoting products and services, motivation can be either extrinsic or intrinsic.

Motivation
That force within us that induces us to do certain things.

EXTRINSIC MOTIVATION

Extrinsic motivation is related to the receiving of rewards; for example, if we reach a sales target, say $20 000 in sales for a week, we receive a $100 bonus. However, this form of motivation is only useful if you perceive that the $100 reward is valuable. If the reward was only $5 you may not feel that the effort required in achieving the sales target is worthwhile.

In the workplace, other extrinsic motivators include being paid, job security, employment benefits such as annual leave and other 'rewards' that 'pay' us for our efforts.

Employers frequently rely on our intrinsic motivation, however, to do our job well and promote the organisation's products and services.

Extrinsic motivators
· Pay
· Bonuses
· Job security
· Employment fringe benefits
· Pleasant working conditions

INTRINSIC MOTIVATION

Intrinsic motivation relates to our personal satisfaction at having achieved something. For example, the motivation to reach a target of six upgrades in one shift is intrinsic. It is a desire to do well, purely for the pleasure that it brings. We won't immediately get more money or a promotion for intrinsic motivation, but we will feel we have done a good job. We may receive acknowledgement from management and our colleagues for doing a good job and we will feel satisfied that six more customers have had their expectations of the organisation and us met. We will feel good about ourselves and enjoy our work more.

No one can force us to be motivated: it comes from within. However, we can be tempted with motivators, such as rewards, but only when we perceive the reward is worth the effort. The effort will seem much easier for most when targets are set and goals are realistic, as then we have a 'tangible' aim to achieve certain results.

Intrinsic motivators
· Job satisfaction
· Customer compliments
· Praise from our supervisor

activity 8.5

▶ Look at the following rewards and state if they are intrinsic or extrinsic.

- Wage increase
- Job satisfaction
- Employee of the Month award
- Promotion to a higher position
- A satisfied customer

As we have seen, tourism-based enterprises have a common motivating goal—to make a profit. By making a profit the organisation stays in business. Frontline staff contribute to the organisation's goal by offering good service to the customers. By being motivated to promote the organisation's products and services our personal goals are linked to the organisation's, because as long as the organisation stays in business, we potentially have employment.

file this

▶ Our motivation to achieve is strongest when linked to a goal.

INCENTIVES

Some organisations survive on reputation, some on location, while others rely mainly on the range of products and services they offer and their ability to meet the changing needs of their various target markets. But most organisations survive because of the ability of their staff to sell. Many others don't survive at all. Those that do usually have motivated management and staff.

Incentive
A reward for reaching goals or targets.

One way organisations encourage staff to sell is by offering incentives. An **incentive** is a reward for reaching certain goals or targets. For example, an organisation may offer a $500 cash incentive for selling over $20 000 in products in one week (extrinsic motivation). Thus, the sales are usually measured in terms of quantity sold or dollar value, or both, over a set period. The organisation may promote certain products for a specified period, introduce a new service or want to increase the dollar value spent by each customer. In most cases, sales activities are planned and require a team effort for success.

SELF-CONFIDENCE

Confidence is a major contributing factor in being a good salesperson. It develops over time with good training and product knowledge. Confidence comes with believing we can sell and believing in the products and services we are selling.

Imagine working in a travel agency and a customer calls asking about holidays to Bali. They want to fly on a certain day and stay for 10 days. The customer expects an instant reply. They don't expect us to say 'I'm not sure' or 'Have a look in that brochure over there'. This is not helpful and we have potentially lost a customer. Finding out for the customer whether or not the requested product or service is available provides us with the confidence and knowledge for future reference and the organisation with increased revenue, and the customer's needs have been met.

check please

24. What is motivation?

25. How does motivation influence your ability to promote products and services?

26. How does your self-confidence influence your ability to promote products and services?

Differentiation

Tourism enterprises operate in a competitive market. This means that potential customers have a choice between two or more establishments that offer similar products and services.

We need our customers; their need for us is limited only by our ability continually to meet and exceed their expectations. Because the tourism industry's success relies considerably on both attracting and keeping its customers, we are responsible for ensuring our customers want to come back. Even if that customer doesn't return to our organisation, the image they take away with them can make them a valuable ambassador for the enterprise as they tell other potential consumers about us.

But if the products and services are so similar, why would a customer choose one enterprise over another? Other than perceived value for money as a factor in the buying decision, what differentiates one enterprise from another? To differentiate means to make a service or product different. There are three ways in which tourism enterprises can do this and on which potential customers are likely to base their buying decisions:

- Service
- Product
- Price

SERVICE DIFFERENTIATION

Service differentiation is that which makes two or more otherwise identical enterprises and their products different, by providing a service or standard of service that the other(s) does not.

Service differentiation
Where one enterprise is distinguished from another by the services offered.

Obviously, it is not only service that will differentiate one enterprise from another; other factors include marketing and promotional activities, reputation, location, atmosphere, decor and so on. But one key indicator that can often make one enterprise stand out is the skill and attitude of the service providers.

If we put ourselves in the customer's position, what we really want is to be looked after, to feel important. Yes, customers often do want all those gimmicks, products and services offered, but mostly they want to be treated as if they are special; they want us to read their minds, anticipate their needs and exceed their expectations.

Customers want us to sell to them. They want us to sell our products, our services and ourselves. Customers want consistent service standards.

Knowing our target markets assists us in tailoring service differentiation for each market.

PRODUCT DIFFERENTIATION

Product differentiation
Where one enterprise is distinguished from another by the products it offers.

Many enterprises consider the best strategy for differentiation to be that of offering a bigger or better range of products or more of a single product. This is **product differentiation**. A fundamental flaw with product differentiation as the only competitive strategy is that, no matter what product innovation or services an organisation introduces, it will not be long before competitors start offering the same or similar products. A good example of this is consumer loyalty programs that encourage customers to purchase goods from specified suppliers in order to accumulate reward points that will provide additional buying power at a later time. Originally introduced to create a point of difference, there are now numerous programs, each seeking to win customer loyalty through bigger and better rewards.

PRICE DIFFERENTIATION

Price differentiation
When the same product or service is offered by similar businesses but the price differs.

Price differentiation occurs when the same product or service is offered by similar businesses but the price differs. An example is in the airline industry. Airlines frequently compete by offering a range of different prices for the same seat on a flight in order to attract more customers.

If we know what our competitors are offering, we are better placed to compete based on price differentiation. If a customer tells us that our competition is offering the same product at a lower price, it is worthwhile asking our supervisor if we can match that price or better it.

---

paint a picture ▶ Product differentiation

Customer loyalty programs, or frequent flyer programs, were first introduced 15 to 20 years ago by airlines as a way of attracting repeat, regular business, having recognised that it is more cost effective to retain existing customers than to attract new ones. The customer is offered special rates, free accommodation, free flights, express check-in and a range of other 'benefits', which accord them preferential treatment not available from other airlines.

One long-term benefit for the organisation is customer loyalty, while the customer benefits from consistency in the products and services as well as collecting points for later use.

It's difficult to think of any large travel-based company not offering these programs now. Very few organisations held the market for any length of time before their competitors caught on to this scheme.

Do you think these schemes really work? Why? Why not?

file this

▶ Suspects (possible customers) lead to prospects (likely customers), which lead to customers (people using our services) who can become ambassadors (customers acting as salespeople for our organisation)!

activity 8.6

▶ Contact an airline or a hotel group and request information on their customer loyalty programs. What benefits are offered to members? What are the costs? Do you consider these benefits are what customers really want? Are there other benefits not offered that you think should be? Give examples.

check please

27. What does it mean to differentiate?

28. Explain the term 'product differentiation'.

29. What techniques can you use to differentiate your services?

30. How does price differentiation work?

Legislation

Competition is the basis for the economy in which we live and operate. This means that as consumers we can shop around. We want value, quality and service and we are prepared to pay for it. But that doesn't mean we always get what we thought we were getting. And if that happens there has been a potential breach of our rights.

Legislation exists to protect both the consumer and businesses from unfair and misleading trading practices. Unfair practices may also represent unethical practices, but strictly speaking, unethical practices may not necessarily have legal implications.

TRADE PRACTICES ACT 1974

The *Trade Practices Act* has as its objective the enhancement of the welfare of Australians through the promotion of competition and fair trading and the provision for consumer protection. The Act protects individuals, or consumers, rather than corporations, and defines a consumer as a person who buys goods and services for personal use, that is, goods and services that will not be resold.

The main aims of the Act are to prevent anti-competitive competition, promote fair trading and protect consumers. The responsibility for compliance with legislation lies mainly with the owners of the business. Employees, however, also have a legal responsibility to ensure compliance. Penalties apply for non-compliance.

As consumers, we need, and have a right to receive, accurate information about goods and services available for us to purchase so that we can make an informed decision about what to buy. That means that if a menu offers fillet steak, we have every reason to expect that it is fillet steak. If we book a resort hotel, sight unseen, for two weeks, and it was advertised as a luxurious two-bedroom suite with ocean views and within walking distance of all amenities, we don't expect to find a caravan precariously perched atop a cliff and amenities a 45-minute hike away!

The Act prevents businesses from engaging in 'conduct that is misleading or deceptive or is likely to mislead or deceive'. Businesses cannot falsely represent goods or services as being of a particular standard, quality, value, grade, composition, style or model.

Anti-competitive behaviour refers to the actions of businesses to reduce competition in the market place. Price fixing occurs when a business enters into an agreement with its competitors to fix the price of a good or service. Anti-competitive agreements are arrangements that are likely to reduce competition, or have the purpose of reducing competition. Unfair trading refers to behaviour that may mislead or deceive consumers and does not have to be intentional to be a breach of the Act. False representations are any wrongful claims made about the price, benefits, standard, quality, value or grade of goods or services that may unfairly influence a consumer's purchasing decision.

SALE OF GOODS ACT

The *Sale of Goods Act* does not make a distinction between a consumer and a corporation. That is, the Act applies whether goods are purchased for personal use or for resale.

This Act is concerned with defining what goods are, the contract of sale and rules to determine lawful ownership of goods. It specifies the duty of the seller to deliver the goods and the duty of the buyer to accept delivery and pay for the goods.

In a tourism context, we must provide what we say we will provide and, having completed our side of the contract, the buyer must then fulfil their obligations under this contract, by paying for the services and products.

AUSTRALIAN COMPETITION AND CONSUMER COMMISSION

ACCC
The government body responsible for administering consumer protection legislation.

If a customer has a complaint about the way an organisation has conducted its business that they feel has not been adequately addressed by the organisation, they can take their complaint to the **Australian Competition and Consumer Commission** (ACCC), which administers the Trade Practices Act and is empowered to bring action against those who contravene the law.

The commission has the authority under the relevant legislation to investigate complaints relating to the way business is conducted and the way products and services are promoted.

When a complaint is received, the commission determines whether the complaint is covered by the Act and will take action accordingly. The action that is likely to be taken begins with an investigation of the complaint. During this investigation, the commission may or may not tell the business it is being investigated.

There is no fee for making a complaint and a commission office is located in each state. While the commission cannot give legal advice to the person making the complaint, they can explain the underlying principles of the Act and a business's obligations under the Act.

The commission may choose to interview a number of people connected to the business, such as the owners, management, employees, competitors and consumers. From the evidence collected, the commission then decides whether or not to take action against the business through the court system.

It is important to note that it is not only a customer that may make a complaint about our organisation: a competitor may, a current employee or ex-employee may or any number of other 'concerned' bodies may.

---

check please

31. Briefly explain the primary aims of the Trade Practices Act.

32. Apart from legal requirements, why should an organisation deliver the product they promised to sell to the customer?

33. List three practices you consider unethical. Explain why.

34. What is anti-competitive behaviour? Give an example.

35. Explain price fixing. Do you agree/disagree that this practice should be illegal. Explain your answer.

36. In a small town with only two accommodation venues, do you think an anti-competitive agreement may be useful (for the venues)? Why? Why not?

37. How do the principles of unfair trading affect how an organisation represents itself in its promotional activities?

38. What responsibility do you have, as an employee, to ensure compliance with the Trade Practices Act?

39. What is the role of the ACCC? Do you think a regulatory body such as the ACCC is really necessary? Why? Why not?

---

question point

1. Distinguish between add-ons, upselling and upgrades.

2. Why would you sometimes downsell?

3. What are buying signals? How do you recognise them?

4. What use is customer feedback to an organisation?

5. Explain the role of the Trade Practices Act and the Sale of Goods Act in protecting consumers and corporations.

6. How do these two Acts impact on tourism in the provision of goods and services?

7. List five sources where you can find information about your products and services.

8. 'We have the knowledge in us to sell anything.' Do you agree with this statement? Why? Why not?

9. Why is working as a team so important in achieving sales goals?

10. What are the principles of selling success?

11. How do you accomplish each of these principles?

12. What motivates *you*? Why?

13. What are the main techniques used to close a sale?

14. Why is after-sales service important?

15. What is suggestive selling? What techniques can an organisation adopt to suggestively sell its services and products?

16. Explain what promotional activities are and why organisations undertake promotional activities, and identify the key factor that influences their success. Give five examples of the types of promotional activities common to tourism operations.

17. What are the key differences between visual suggestive selling and personal suggestive selling?

Career paths and job-seeking skills

LEARNING OUTCOMES

On completion of this chapter you will be able to:

- identify a range of job opportunities within the tourism industry;
- research job opportunities;
- identify techniques for preparing for job interviews; and
- develop questioning techniques for interview situations.

*In this chapter we take a brief look at some of the positions available in the tourism industry. It is a general guide only as each organisation will have its own **job descriptions** and **person specifications** that prescribe specific requirements for their employees. We have concentrated mainly on the travel operations and visitor services sectors of the tourism industry as identified in Chapter 1 (see Table 1.1) and described the jobs that provide entry-level opportunities with career path possibilities.*

In Chapter 1 we learned that the tourism industry provides some of the most stimulating opportunities for employment available today. Our industry relies on skilled, well-trained employees who are able to meet the growing demands of each market segment in all sectors.

Successful tourism professionals all demonstrate certain characteristics and skills, including:

- *a strong customer focus;*
- *strong interpersonal skills;*
- *good communication skills and cultural awareness;*
- *ability to work as part of a team;*
- *good product and local knowledge;*
- *selling skills;*
- *technical skills; and*
- *the right attitude for a service industry.*

We noted in that chapter also that the industry is divided into different sectors and career paths, all of which offer the possibility of advancement and to become multi-skilled, provided we are prepared to work hard and in a professional manner. This chapter will not discuss job roles in the hospitality sector as these are dealt with exclusively in our previous book The Road to Hospitality *(Prentice Hall, 1999).*

Each role in every operation will vary according to the location, size and other factors impacting on the enterprise. And each role requires skills and knowledge that contribute to the ongoing success of the organisation.

Job opportunities in tourism

The skills we develop for a career in the tourism industry are for life. One of the greatest benefits of possessing these skills is portability. That is, we are able to use these skills in positions offered around the world. Most tourism employment opportunities fall into the broad categories shown in Table 9.1, 'Tourism Industry Sector Career Paths'.

quick thinker

▶ What do you think would be the most attractive jobs in the tourism industry? Why?

TABLE 9.1 **Tourism industry sector career paths**

TOURIST ATTRACTIONS	TOUR GUIDES	WHOLESALE TOUR OPERATIONS	RETAIL TRAVEL AGENTS	INFORMATION SERVICES	MEETINGS
Senior manager	Tour guide owner operator	Senior manager	Senior manager	Regional area tourism manager	Project manager
Manager of: Operations, Sales/marketing, Public relations	Tour manager, Lead guide, Guide coordinator, Specialist guides (ecotourism/cultural)	Manager of: Product, Sales, Marketing, Public relations	Manager of: Small travel agency, Travel administration, Marketing	Manager of: Information centre, Sales, Marketing, Public relations, Strategic planning	Conference manager
Supervisor in: Operations, Sales, Marketing, Public relations	Specialist site guide, Tour guide, Driver guide	Supervisor in: Product, Sales, Marketing, Public relations	Supervisor in: Retail travel and/or corporate international and/or Australian	Supervisor in: Tourism information, Research, Sales, Marketing, Public relations, Strategic planning	Conference coordinator
Groups coordinator	Site guide, Meet and greet guide	Reservation operations	Senior travel consultant international and/or Australian	Senior tourism information officer	Conference assistant
Sales, Reservation agent, Guest service Coordinator		Group tour coordinator	International travel consultant	Travel adviser	Hospitality/travel operations: Functions, Reservations, Group travel
Attractions attendant, Ticket sales officer		Sales, Reservation agent	Australian travel consultant	Tourist information officer	
			Travel sales clerk		

It is important to understand that career movement through these areas can be either horizontally or vertically.

Source: Tourism Training Australia (website). Reproduced with permission of Tourism Training Australia 2001.

JOB ROLES IN TRAVEL OPERATIONS

All types of tourism involve some form of travel to a particular destination. Many different businesses organise and sell such travel. These include tour wholesalers (who package the components of a holiday trip) and retail travel agents who sell holiday and business trips directly to the consumer (the tourist or the business traveller).

Obviously, transport operators like airlines, cruise lines and railway companies need to be involved, as they provide the physical means for the transportation to and between the destinations. There are also ground (and sea) tour operators who provide the transport component for the actual tours within a destination. They are invariably linked to showing tourists the attractions of the area within which they operate. This can include a wide range of transport types—aeroplane, ship, boat, yacht, car, bus, coach, minivan, 4WD vehicle, bicycle, motorcycle, horse, camel, hot air balloon or even space shuttle! However, in this first part of the chapter we will concentrate on those businesses that actually manufacture, distribute and sell the tourism product to the consumer—the tour wholesalers and retail travel agents.

file this

▶ It is not unusual for the principals or owners of travel products (e.g. airlines) also to operate their own tour wholesaling and retail travel agency divisions. For example, Qantas Airways Ltd operates Qantas Holidays as their tour wholesaler and Qantas Travel Centres as their retail agencies. In this way they have more control over the development and distribution of their tourism products.

TOUR WHOLESALERS

The tour wholesaler is the company that packages tourism products and services produced by other businesses into a single offering (a holiday package) to the consumer. In other words, they bulk purchase airline seats, hotel rooms and local transport services to create a holiday package for sale, normally through a retail travel agent, although many will sell directly to the consumer as well. Specialist types of tour wholesalers include **inbound tour operators (ITOs)**, who put together packages (often referred to as *land content*) for use in a destination by overseas travellers. Tour wholesaling companies purchase these 'ready-made' packages from the ITOs and incorporate them into their own programs. Importantly, tour wholesaling companies work on the principle of volume sales in order to make a profit. They may have a range of holiday destination tours to sell but they will require a minimum number of people to purchase the product before a profit is realised. Purchasing the holiday components (transport, accommodation and sometimes attractions) in bulk allows them to offer the product at a cheaper price than if the individual consumers purchased their own holiday components. The job roles and skills required to undertake these tasks fall into two main categories—tour planner and sales representative.

Inbound tour operator
A tour wholesaler who specialises in organising tour packages for use in a destination by overseas travellers.

Tour planner

Tour or trip planning requires careful market research and analysis to ensure that there is market demand for any particular destination (country, city or region within a country). This is a skill in itself, but once satisfied that there is potential demand the tour planner is required to undertake the following tasks:

- Create a concept or theme for the tour.
- Plan and develop the itinerary by timetabling and scheduling each component of the tour.
- Liaise with the suppliers such as hotels and airlines.
- Book all the arrangements for transport, accommodation and attractions.
- Cost out and price the tour, allowing for an acceptable profit margin.
- Create and produce a brochure to promote the product for sale.
- Manage the tour from concept, to sale, to enroute, to post-tour feedback.

As well as creativity, a wide variety of technical skills are required, including organisation, logistics, coordination, financial planning, graphic design and management. Hence, this work is normally done as a team effort by a number of specialists, particularly in larger companies.

Sales representative

Once the tour product is created and developed into brochure format (also displayed on Internet websites) it needs to be marketed and sold. This role is undertaken by the sales representative, who normally works under the direction of a marketing manager who is guided by a strategic marketing plan that outlines particular promotional activities or campaigns. Generally, the tour wholesaler's sales representative will make personal sales calls to retail travel agencies to inform them about the tour product and attempt to convince them it is a worthwhile product (holiday) for them to sell to the consumer.

Apart from sales calls, other activities that can be undertaken include:

- Print and/or electronic advertising campaigns
- Direct mail to potential clients, using a database
- Special consumer promotions (e.g. holiday prizes for competitions)
- Travel trade exhibitions or sales seminars
- Creating media publicity through use of press releases
- Organising a well-known personality to endorse or lead the tour

The skills required for these tasks are creativity, organisation, product knowledge and general selling or sales ability, developed through confidence, personal presentation and communication skills outlined in Chapter 2, 'Work with colleagues and customers'.

RETAIL TRAVEL AGENTS

The retail travel agent is the intermediary that links the suppliers of tourism products (tour wholesalers as well as individual owners or operators of tourism businesses) with the consumer. They normally operate out of a shopfront office and provide travel advice, reservation and ticketing services. They sell packaged holidays (set-itinerary tours) on behalf of the tour wholesalers as well as selling separate components of a trip (airline ticket, hotel room) to individual customers on demand. Often they assist these individual customers or free independent travellers (FITs) to plan and develop their own itineraries to suit their specific individual requirements for the trip. They receive their remuneration from a commission payment on each product sale from the product supplier (airline, hotel, car rental company, travel insurance company). There are three distinct job roles within a travel agency— travel consultant, sales supervisor and office manager.

Travel consultants

According to the Australian Travel Agents Qualifications (ATAQ) program there are three main classifications for travel consultants: Australian (i.e. domestic) travel consultant, international travel consultant and senior travel consultant. Hence, there is a defined career path based on work experience and accredited qualifications.

The tasks of the job role include:

- servicing enquiries from customers;
- assisting customers with itinerary or trip planning;
- advising on and selling travel products;
- making reservations using specialised computer systems;
- issuing documents such as tickets, invoices, itineraries, confirmation letters;
- preparing accountable sales return documents; and
- maintaining brochure stocks and on-line information.

The depth of skills required to perform such tasks is linked to the level of seniority and the passing of exams for each level of qualification. However, the travel consultant is expected to have:

- product knowledge of the destinations they are selling;
- competency in fares and ticketing procedures;
- computer literacy for reservation systems (and database and accountancy packages);
- aptitude for selling; and
- a high level of customer service skills.

The more senior consultants also require leadership and supervisory skills in order to monitor and mentor junior staff.

Travel sales supervisor

In the larger travel agencies this is a more senior position and is normally a step up from senior travel consultant. As the title suggests, this person is involved exclusively in selling. They plan sales campaigns and supervise teams of salespeople. Apart from selling holidays, travel agents can also specialise in the business and corporate markets, including travel for meetings, conferences, conventions, incentive travel to reward employees and exhibitions. Collectively, these are generally referred to as the MICE market—an acronym for each of these different types of travel: meetings, incentive travel, conferences, conventions and exhibitions. The main tasks involved in this role include:

MICE
· Meetings
· Incentive travel
· Conferences/
  Conventions
· Exhibitions

- market research to identify customer needs and level of demand;
- following up customer feedback, particularly complaints;
- recruiting, training, inducting and supervising sales teams; and
- managing the advertising and sales budgets.

Apart from the obvious selling skills, leadership and communication skills are most important. Technical skills in budgeting and marketing are also essential.

Agency or branch manager

Sometimes referred to as the travel manager, this person is responsible for the day-to-day administration of the travel agency. In the smaller independent agencies this would normally be the owner/operator of the business. In the larger corporate chains and franchised agencies an experienced branch or travel manager is in charge. The main tasks of this role would include:

- budgeting and financial management;
- staff supervision including training;
- health and safety issues;
- marketing and promotion planning; and
- managing licensing and accreditation matters.

General business management skills are required to operate at this level, together with an in-depth knowledge and understanding of the travel operations sector of the industry.

JOB ROLES AT THE DESTINATION

While there is a wide variety of businesses and organisations that are involved in the tourism industry, this chapter will deal only with those job roles that are directly related to servicing the tourist or visitor at the local level, as these provide employment opportunities for entry into the industry.

TOURIST OFFICER/MANAGER

Many local governments throughout Australia have formed partnerships with local and regional tourist operators to plan, develop and promote their particular destination. These are commonly referred to as Regional Tourist Associations (RTAs) and are normally headed up by a tourist officer or manager. Many regions have formed their own companies as separate entities from local government and employ destination managers who direct a number of tourist officers. Generally, the role of the tourist officer is to assist the industry operators with the development of their products, service the information needs of the visitors through the management of visitor information centres, and liaise closely with the local communities. The actual job role will vary according to the needs and aspirations of each destination region, but in general terms involves the following:

- servicing the members of the tourist association;
- managing the annual budget, including funding schemes;
- implementing the marketing plan;
- directing and supervising staff (including volunteers);
- developing community awareness and acceptance of tourism; and
- research and development of tourist products.

A high level of skills in marketing and management is required, together with an in-depth knowledge of the tourism industry and its impacts on local communities.

TOURIST INFORMATION OFFICERS

As the job title suggests, the information officers' primary role is to gather, process and disseminate information about the tourist destination within which they operate. This would include information on the range and prices of all accommodation establishments, tours available in the area, all major attractions including shopping opportunities, restaurants and special events. Most tourist information officers operate under the direction of a tourist officer/manager from purpose-built visitor information centres. Many of these centres also act as a central booking agency to assist with the selling of local and regional tourist products. More recently, many of these information centres have installed on-line reservation systems to allow for a more efficient distribution of tourist products from the supplier to the consumer. The skills required for this job role usually include:

- broad knowledge of local tourist products;
- strong customer service orientation to assist visitors;
- clerical and office administration skills;
- competency with computer information systems; and
- ability to communicate with industry operators and the local community.

TOUR GUIDES

Employment opportunities are available with the numerous companies that actually conduct the wide variety of tours in most destinations. Local tour operators conduct river cruises, sightseeing tours, ecotours, bushwalking excursions and the like. Essentially, they provide the means for tourists to experience the attractions of an area through transport services and information about the attractions and the surrounding geographical region. Tour guides play a very important role in the quality of such tours through their knowledge, interpretation and ability to excite and entertain the people on the tour. A number of responsibilities and skills are involved in being a tour guide. For example:

- a duty of care for the health and safety of tour participants
- managing interactions within the tour group and with local people they meet
- exceptional customer service skills, particularly verbal communication
- responding to the needs and expectations of visitors from other cultures or those with special needs
- managing the itinerary and tour logistics.

TOURIST ATTRACTIONS OPERATORS

Most tourists wish to visit various attractions within the destinations they travel to or while en route between a number of different destinations in the same trip or tour. Attractions can be purpose-built features, a showcasing of an element of the natural environment or a special event linked to a theme of cultural/historical display, entertainment, education or pure excitement and novelty. Whatever their purpose or theme they all require staff to service their visitors. Hence, job opportunities will arise in businesses and organisations that market and manage the following:

- historic theme parks
- national parks
- amusement parks
- museums and art galleries
- major and special events
- cultural centres
- specialised tourist shops.

For those staff dealing directly with the visitor, exceptional customer service and communication skills are required, as the job role will normally include meeting and greeting visitors, public speaking to inform and educate about the attraction, and selling the attributes of the attraction to ensure repeat visitation from the visitors and visits from the friends they tell.

JOBS IN THE GOVERNMENT SECTOR

As outlined in Chapter 1, governments at the federal, state and local levels are involved in the tourism industry through the policy development that results in the legislation and regulation within which the industry operates. They are also involved in the planning and funding for infrastructure projects (particularly for transport), research and statistics and destination marketing programs, through the various tourism commissions and regional tourism associations. Hence, there are numerous tourism-related job opportunities within the government sector. For a listing of key tourism government departments and agencies and their contact details refer to 'A few useful contacts' at the end of this book. Entry-level job roles are more likely to involve working in the following areas:

- Information dissemination
- Advertising and promotion
- Public relations and media liaison
- Market research and analysis
- Tourism product development
- Special events coordination

Generally speaking, the government's role in tourism is to advise and assist the private sector operators and developers in building a sustainable tourism industry. By this we mean that the public sector politicians and bureaucrats need to develop tourism policies, regulations and legislation in partnership with responsible private sector operators so that tourism assets and resources are protected and developed for longer-term use and enjoyment. More and more government departments and agencies are streamlining their functions and coordinating their activities to achieve a more commercially viable yet sustainable tourism industry. For example, there are now more cooperative partnerships in investment projects and marketing programs between government and the private sector.

Organisational structure
The way in which roles and lines of authority are arranged in an organisation.

activity 9.1

▶ Contact your State Tourism Commission or Regional Tourist Association and ask them to send you a copy of their **organisational structure.** This is a diagrammatic chart of the management and staff levels and their functions under specific divisions or departments. Check for entry-level jobs (or above this if you have more experience) that you think would be suitable for you, then contact the human resources manager and/or the person in charge of that division or department and ask what job opportunities are available.

Getting a job in tourism

The growth of tourism in Australia means that more and more opportunities for careers in tourism will arise. Both employers and customers are placing greater emphasis on the skills of tourism professionals.

To improve the chances of getting a job, and indeed to make a career in the tourism industry, it will be necessary to meet these challenges through education and training, preparing ourself for the world of work and being motivated to achieve our goals.

RESEARCHING JOB OPPORTUNITIES

Most of us at some point in our career will need to seek employment and, like any other task, finding employment within the tourism industry takes effort!

Locating the job isn't the end either—we then have to apply for the job, prepare for an interview, attend the interview, sometimes have a second interview, and then, quite often, wait a long time before we hear if the job is ours.

Like most things in life, however, there are steps to follow that help maximise our chances of success.

RESEARCH

As covered previously, research can be simple or complex. In looking for a job, the most obvious first place to look is in the local newspapers. But there are also many other ways. Having almost finished this book, you should by now have identified the areas of tourism that most hold your interest. This can help in your search for the right job.

Newspapers

Each city has its major newspapers, including *The Age* in Melbourne, *The Sydney Morning Herald, The Courier-Mail* in Brisbane, *The West Australian* in Perth, *The Mercury* in Hobart and *The Advertiser* in Adelaide. Nationally, *The Australian* newspaper also advertises job opportunities, as do many of the travel and tourism trade magazines, like *Travel Trade* and *Travel Week*.

All contain an employment section on either a daily or weekly basis and most devote a section to employment opportunities within the tourism industry.

Internet

If you have access to the Internet, a search in your area of career interest will yield amazing job opportunities throughout Australia. Good places to start include **www.monster.com.au** and **www.employment.byron.com.au**.

SOLICITED APPLICATIONS

The jobs advertised in newspapers are what we call solicited applications. That is, employers are soliciting for (inviting) suitable candidates to apply for the position(s) advertised.

While we may think that we should apply for all jobs advertised in our area of interest, we should avoid sending our résumé to every employer that advertises. Before sending a standard letter in the hope that someone may offer an interview, we need to ask ourself:

1. Is this the type of job I am looking for?
2. Is this the type of establishment I want to work in?
3. Do I have the relevant qualifications and experience?
4. Does this position move in the direction of my career goals?

If you can honestly answer yes to these four questions, then write a letter of application.

When looking at an application, employers will consider its professionalism, the language used, whether it has addressed the job criteria and whether the applicant has the relevant skills. In other words, they are matching the letter of application with a predetermined specification about the person they want to fill the job.

Keep letters short, to the point and consistent with what was requested in the advertisement. Highlight personal strengths and always type letters of application unless otherwise specified. While we may think we have beautiful handwriting, a potential employer may consider it indecipherable, or unprofessional because it is not typed, and throw it away.

EMPLOYMENT AGENCIES

A number of companies specialise in finding staff for employers, ranging from temporary positions to executive roles in tourism. While these generally target senior staff, there are also occasionally opportunities for entry-level staff.

Employment agencies are listed in the telephone directory and often in daily and local newspapers. It does not cost anything to register with an employment agency, although they will require an up-to-date résumé and will often conduct an interview to determine your suitability as an applicant for positions that become available.

Many agencies also offer valuable advice on personal presentation and résumé presentation, help identify skills and offer advice on how to update skills.

GOVERNMENT ASSISTANCE

Previously, the government employment services also aided in job search. This is still available; however, it is now privately managed through a number of companies. The government's Centrelink service is still able to advise in terms of benefits available for both employers seeking employees and employees seeking a job.

UNSOLICITED APPLICATIONS

An unsolicited application occurs when we apply to an organisation for a position without knowing if one exists. In other words, our letter is uninvited but not necessarily unwelcome.

An unsolicited application can give a potential employer a good indication of who we are and what skills we can offer the organisation. It also shows we have initiative.

If sending, or delivering, unsolicited applications, following a few rules can increase the chance of getting the letter read:

- Type the application (professional presentation).
- Find out the correct name and title of the person to whom the letter should be addressed, and double check all spelling, especially people's names.
- Include a typed, up-to-date résumé.
- If you say you will call, call!
- Specify the job you want. If you are not sure, identifying the strengths you have and how you can assist the organisation will help the reader decide if you are worth speaking to.

Keeping applications to the point, and not making any bold promises that you can't keep, go a long way to making a good first impression.

TELEPHONE CANVASSING

Using the telephone is a time-effective way of sourcing employment opportunities. The local *Yellow Pages* and *White Pages* will list a host of tourism businesses and organisations from which we can select potential employers. Most professional tourism and travel trade associations also publish directories listing member organisations with contact details (refer to 'A few useful contacts' at the end of the book for a list of these professional associations and their contact details).

Once we have identified possible employers we can call for the information necessary for the unsolicited applications (e.g. name of manager, address, etc.) or we can ask the appropriate person about the availability of work, and whether or not we can arrange to meet with them.

Before calling, we need to consider what we are going to say. In other words, follow the general rules of making outgoing calls, covered in Chapter 4, 'Communicate on the telephone'.

FOOTSLOGGING

There is no doubt that when all else fails, walking around and just calling in to potential employers is a good way to look for work. We may receive ninety-nine knock-backs, but it may be that one-hundredth call that does it.

By physically calling in on employers, it shows we have initiative, are keen and committed, and it gives employers an opportunity to see us as well, which won't happen over the telephone or by letter.

No matter which option we take, if we are prepared, present professionally and behave professionally, people will treat us as a professional.

Preparing for job interviews

Once we have been granted an interview, it is then vitally important to prepare, both mentally and physically.

We may be only one of several (or several hundred) people being interviewed, therefore we need to ensure that we are ready to stand out from the crowd.

Some of the ways to do this are:

RESEARCH

The more we know about our potential employer, the more impressed they will be as to our abilities. Many interviews include at least one question about our knowledge of the organisation.

It is not difficult to find out about almost any organisation. We can call and ask for the information or their brochures, or we can ask friends or colleagues what they know. In general terms, we need to find out:

- How large the organisation is
- Who owns the organisation
- What other states/countries they operate in
- Who their main market is
- Their general reputation

If possible, also try to talk to current or previous employees of the company to get a feel for the organisation, and find out what the job entails.

This knowledge, this homework, gives us more ammunition to show them how they will benefit from employing us.

file this

▶ Over-confidence in an interview can be just as damaging as no preparation.

ANTICIPATE QUESTIONS

There is no definite way of knowing what any or all of the questions are that we may be asked in an interview. Nonetheless we can prepare ourselves by anticipating what they might be.

General questions will depend on the level of experience we have (if any), the position to be filled and the needs of the organisation. Likely questions include:

- Schooling: what level did we achieve? Specialist subjects?
- Hobbies: what do we like doing in our spare time? Why? Employers also use this as a determinant of our ability to work in a team.
- Experience: what previous experience would we bring to this job? Did we like past jobs? Why? Why not? Why did we leave?
- What are our strengths and weaknesses?
- What do our friends think are our strengths and weaknesses?
- Where do we expect to be in two years, five years . . . ?
- What are our career goals?
- What can we offer this company?
- Why should the company employ us?
- How will working here interfere with our social/sporting life?

Occasionally, we may be thrown an unusual question that doesn't seem to relate to our work (e.g. What is our favourite book and why?); often the employer is trying to work out what motivates us or what our values are, to ensure that they match those of the organisation or them personally.

Please note, however, that it is never appropriate—and is usually illegal—for an employer to ask us about our personal life, such as marital status, number of children, religion, sexual orientation, criminal record (unless in the gaming industry) or other personal details, if it has no relevance to the job. These types of questions should be delicately avoided or deflected. Should this come up in general conversation, so be it; however, questions of this nature, that have no bearing on the job, can be deemed discriminatory.

By being prepared with the answers to the above questions, we can respond effectively and confidently, giving us the maximum possible chance of employment.

PREPARE QUESTIONS OF OUR OWN

Most of us go into an interview believing we are prepared, having practised responses to the general questions, knowing we look great and feel great and otherwise expect to do well. Some of us think it strange when we are asked if we have any questions. At this point we may look a little lost, feel a bit confused and mutter something about having covered everything. And indeed, everything may well have been covered. But surely we have at least one question up our sleeve? By asking questions, it again shows that we are interested and have prepared for the interview.

A few suggestions to get started are:

- What career opportunities are available within the organisation?
- Are there opportunities for further training?
- How many people work in the office or organisation?
- Does the organisation have a standard dress requirement?
- When would I start?

- What will my main duties entail?
- Does the company have plans to expand?

If we don't know a lot about the organisation, this may also be a good time to ask a few questions in terms of size, corporate goals and so on.

Depending on the position and the organisation, it is not generally recommended that we ask about wages/salary and benefits at the first interview unless a position is being offered then and there.

BE PHYSICALLY PREPARED

When being interviewed, it is important to be mentally and physically alert. If we haven't had enough sleep, or are run down, then naturally our responses to questions will be sluggish and we may appear uninterested. Being physically on top of things usually also improves our mental ability.

The way we present ourselves and how we carry ourselves will say a lot about us to an interviewer. When attending an interview:

- dress appropriately;
- remember poise, posture, courtesy and appropriate body language;
- use active listening skills;
- respond to questions in some detail but not at great length;
- display interest;
- take a copy and the original of your résumé and any supporting documents and references; and
- take notes. Even if you throw them away afterwards, at least it showed you cared enough to write down information!

activity 9.2

▶ On a piece of paper, draw a line down the middle and on the left write down all the reasons someone should employ you (i.e. your strengths). On the right, list all the reasons why they may not employ you (i.e. areas for improvement). Now think of all the ways in which you or a potential employer can help improve your skills.

file this

▶ Was the organisation's first impression of me a positive one?

EVALUATION

After every interview we should consider our performance as objectively as possible. Learn from mistakes. We should ask ourselves: 'What did I do right/wrong?' 'What didn't I know the answers to?' 'Why not?' 'What do I need to do better next time?' 'What was their impression of me?' 'Was my grooming appropriate?' 'Did I use all of my interpersonal skills?'

This critical evaluation is not meant to be a tortuous exercise. It is intended to allow us to reflect on both the positive things that happened in the interview and the things that can be improved upon. And next time we attend an interview, we are able to use the skills developed as a result of this evaluation.

Where to from here?

A major challenge for tourism enterprises is to attract and retain the right mix of skills, and commitment to service excellence. Our personal goals, motivation to achieve those goals and recognising opportunities as they arise are the only things that limit what we can offer a potential employer.

You may have used this book as part of formal training or as a step in your personal development. But your potential does not end here. Further study and experience is probably needed to achieve your goals. If that is what you need, then that is the next step to take.

If you already have considerable experience, those skills can be formally recognised in one of two ways.

ACCESS

ACCESS is the hospitality and tourism industry workplace assessment system. The system is administered by state and territory tourism training authorities, which provide for skills assessment of employees in their place of work. The employee is assessed in a range of skills learned in the workplace, based on the national competency standards.

For further information, contact your local tourism training authority.

RECOGNITION OF PRIOR LEARNING (RPL)

RPL replaces the original exemption system used by educational institutes to recognise prior learning. The main advantage of RPL is that it not only recognises studies previously undertaken, but also work experience and life experiences. RPL can be used to exempt from or credit a student with studies in a particular unit or a range of units.

The student does not necessarily have to have had their skills assessed previously through ACCESS, although this can help.

For further information, refer to your course counsellor, careers adviser or director of education.

A few useful contacts

ACT

Australian Government Info Shop
10 Mort Street
Canberra, ACT 2601

ACCC
National Office
470 Northbourne Avenue
Dickson, ACT 2602
www.accc.gov.au

Tourism Training ACT & Region
PO Box 2092
Canberra, ACT 2601
www.ttact.com

Australian Bureau of Statistics (ABS)
PO Box 10
Belconnen, ACT 2616
www.abs.gov.au

Bureau of Tourism Research (BTR)
Level 4, 20 Allara Street
Canberra City, ACT 2600
www.btr.gov.au

Tourism Forecasting Council (AFC)
C/- Dept Industry, Science and Resources
GPO Box 9839
Canberra City, ACT 2601
www.isr.gov.au

Sport and Tourism Division
C/- Dept Industry, Science and Resources
GPO Box 9839
Canberra City, ACT 2601
www.isr.gov.au

Canberra Tourism and Events Corporation
Level 13, SAP House
Cnr Akuna and Bunda Streets
Canberra City, ACT 2601
www.canberratourism.com.au

COMCARE Australia
(Commonwealth OHS Agency)
Corporate Centre
Cnr Rudd & Moore Streets
Canberra, ACT 2601
www.comcare.gov.au

ACT WorkCover
3rd Floor FAI House
197 London Court
Civic, ACT 2601
www.workcover.act.gov

Standards Australia
Gallery Level, The Boulevard
City Walk
Canberra, ACT 2601
www.standards.com.au

**Liquor, Hospitality & Miscellaneous Workers Union
 (LHMU)**
Unit 5, 2nd Floor
40 Brisbane Avenue
Barton, ACT 2600
www.lhmu.org.au

Environmental & Indigenous Tourism
Office of National Tourism
GPO Box 1545
Canberra, ACT 2601

Australian Hotels Association (AHA)
Commerce House
24 Brisbane Avenue
Barton, ACT 2600
www.aha.org.au

NEW SOUTH WALES

Australian Government Info Shop
32 York Street
Sydney, NSW 2000

ACCC
Level 5, Skygardens
77 Castlereagh Street
Sydney, NSW 2000
www.accc.gov.au

Australian Tourist Commission (ATC)
Level 4, 80 William Street
Woolloomooloo, NSW 2011
www.australia.com
www.aussie.net.au

Tourism New South Wales
GPO Box 7050
Sydney, NSW 2001
www.tourism.nsw.gov.au

Australian Federation of Travel Agents (AFTA)
Level 3, 309 Pitt Street
Sydney, NSW 2000
www.afta.com.au

Australian Tourism Export Council (ATEC)
Level 2, 80 William Street
Woolloomooloo, NSW 2011
www.atec.net.au

Pacific Asia Travel Association (PATA)
Pacific Division
PO Box 645
Kings Cross, NSW 1340
www.pata.og

Council of Australian Tour Operators (CATO)
Level 3, 309 Pitt Street
Sydney, NSW 2000
www.cato.asn.au

Australian Liquor, Hospitality & Miscellaneous Workers Union (ALHMU)
National Office
7th Floor, 187 Thomas Street
Haymarket, NSW 2000
www.lhmu.org.au

NSW WorkCover Authority
400 Kent Street
Sydney, NSW 2000
www.workcover.nsw.gov.au

Worksafe Australia
92 Parramatta Road
Camperdown, NSW 2050
www.worksafe.gov.au

NOHSC
GPO Box 58
Sydney, NSW 2001
www.nohsc.gov.au

Tourism Training NSW
Level 6, 1 Chandos Street
St Leonards, NSW 2065
www.ttnsw.com

Standards Australia
Head Office
286 Sussex Street
Sydney, NSW 2000
www.standards.com.au

The Australian & New Zealand Community Clubs Council
(Administered by the Registered Clubs Association of NSW)
RCA House
499 Kent Street
Sydney, NSW 2000

Tourism Training Australia
GPO Box 2493
Sydney, NSW 2001
www.tourismtraining.com.au

Hotel, Motel & Accommodation Association (HMAA)
Level 3, 551 Pacific Highway
St Leonards, NSW 2065
www.hmaa.com.au

Australian Hotels Association (AHA)
Level 5, 8 Quay Street
Sydney, NSW 2000
www.aha.org.au

Meetings Industry Association of Australia (MIAA)
PO Box 1477
Neutral Bay, NSW 2089
www.miaanet.com.au

NORTHERN TERRITORY

NT Government Publications
13 Smith Street
Darwin, NT 0800

ACCC
Level 8, National Mutual Centre
9–11 Cavanagh Street
Darwin, NT 0800
www.accc.gov.au

Northern Territory Tourism Training Board
PO Box 359
Darwin, NT 0801
www.nttb.org.au

Northern Territory Tourist Commission
GPO Box 1155
Darwin, NT 0801
www.nttc.com.au

Work Health Authority
Minerals House
66 The Esplanade
Darwin, NT 0800
www.nt.gov.au

**Liquor, Hospitality & Miscellaneous Workers Union
  (LHMU)**
38 Woods Street
Darwin, NT 0801
www.lhmu.org.au

Australian Hotels Association (AHA)
Unit 20, 24 Cavanagh Street
Darwin, NT 0800
www.aha.org.au

Standards Australia
C/- Territory Construction Association
191 Stuart Highway
Parap, NT 0820
www.standards.com.au

QUEENSLAND

Australian Government Info Shop
City Plaza
Cnr Adelaide and George Streets
Brisbane, Qld 4000

ACCC
10th Floor, AAMI Building
500 Queen Street
Brisbane, Qld 4000
www.accc.gov.au

Division of Workplace Health and Safety
(Department of Training and Industrial Relations)
Forbes House
30 Makerston Street
Brisbane, Qld 4000
www.detir.gov.au

Standards Australia
232 St Paul's Terrace
Fortitude Valley, Qld 4006
www.standards.com.au

Ecotourism Association of Australia
GPO Box 268
Brisbane, Qld 4001
www.ecotourism.org.au

Queensland Tourist and Travel Corporation
Level 36, Riverside Centre
123 Eagle Street
Brisbane, Qld 4000
www.qttc.com.au

Queensland Tourism & Hospitality ITC Inc
PO Box 98
Roma Street
Brisbane, Qld 4003

**Liquor, Hospitality & Miscellaneous Workers Union
  (LHMU)**
74 Astor Terrace
Spring Hill, Qld 4004
www.lhmu.org.au

Tourism Training Qld
GPO Box 1974, Roma Street
Brisbane, Qld 4001
www.ttq.org.au

**Hotel, Motel & Accommodation Association (HMAA)
  of Queensland**
Alexandra House
201 Wickham Terrace
Brisbane, Qld 4000
www.hmaa.com.au

Catering Institute of Australia
Queensland Division
PO Box 7263
Cairns, Qld 4870

**Australian Institute of Hospitality Management (AIHM)
  (South Qld) Inc**
PO Box 3421
South Brisbane, Qld 4101

Queensland Hotels Association (QHA)
Level 3, 160 Edward Street
Brisbane, Qld 4000
www.aha.org.au

Tourism Queensland
GPO Box 328
Brisbane, Qld 4001
www.queensland-holidays.com.au

SOUTH AUSTRALIA

Australian Government Info Shop
60 Waymouth Street
Adelaide, SA 5000

ACCC
14th Floor, ANZ House
13 Grenfell Street
Adelaide, SA 5000
www.accc.gov.au

South Australian Tourism Commission
GPO Box 1972
Adelaide, SA 5001
www.tourism.sa.gov.au
www.southaustralia.com

WorkCover Corporation
100 Waymouth Street
Adelaide, SA 5000
www.workcover.com

**Liquor, Hospitality & Miscellaneous Workers Union
(LHMU)**
101 Henley Beach Road
Mile End, SA 5031
www.lhmu.org.au

Tourism Training SA
PO Box 8071, Station Arcade
Adelaide, SA 5000
www.ttsa.com.au

**Hotel, Motel & Accommodation Association (HMAA)
of South Australia**
18 Angus Street
Kent Town SA 5067
www.hmaa.com.au

Australian Hotels Association (AHA)
60 Hindmarsh Square
Adelaide, SA 5000
www.aha.org.au

Standards Australia
63 Greenhill Road
Wayville, SA 5034
www.standards.com.au

TASMANIA

Australian Government Info Shop
31 Criterion Street
Hobart, Tas 7000

ACCC
3rd Floor, 86 Collins Street
Hobart, Tas 7000
www.accc.gov.au

Tourism Tasmania
GPO Box 399
Hobart, Tas 7001
www.tourism.tas.gov.au
www.discovertasmania.com

Workplace Standards Authority
30 Gordons Hill Road
Rosny Park, Tas 7018
www.wsa.tas.gov.au

**Liquor, Hospitality & Miscellaneous Workers Union
(LHMU)**
165–167 Davey Street
Hobart, Tas 7000
www.lhmu.org.au

**Hotel, Motel & Accommodation Association (HMAA)
of Tasmania**
511 Brooker Highway
Glenorchy, Tas 7010
www.hmaa.com.au

Australian Hotels Association (AHA)
176 New Town Road
Newtown, Tas 7008
www.aha.org.au

Standards Australia
10 Barrack Street
Hobart, Tas 7000
www.standards.com.au

VICTORIA

Australian Government Info Shop
190 Queen Street
Melbourne, Vic 3000

Information Australia
75 Flinders Lane
Melbourne, Vic 3000
www.infoaust.com

Aboriginal Tourism Australia
Level 2M, North Rialto Tower
525 Collins Street
Melbourne, Vic 3000
www.ataust.org.au

ACCC
Level 35, The Tower
360 Elizabeth Street
Melbourne, Vic 3000
www.accc.gov.au

AAA Tourism
Level 6, 131 Queen Street
Melbourne, Vic 3000
www.aaatourism.com.au

Tourism Victoria
55 Collins Street
Melbourne, Vic 3000
www.visitvictoria.com
www.tourismvictoria.com.au

Office of Fair Trading
3rd Floor, 500 Bourke Street
Melbourne, Vic 3000

Australian Chamber of Commerce & Industry
Level 4, 55 Exhibition Street
Melbourne, Vic 3000
www.acci.asn.au

Information Victoria
318 Little Bourke Street
Melbourne, Vic 3000

Australian Council of Trade Unions
ACTU House
393–397 Swanston Street
Melbourne, Vic 3000
www.actu.asn.au

Victorian Smoking and Health Program
25 Rathdowne Street
Carlton South, Vic 3053
www.quit.org.au
www.tobaccoreforms.vic.gov.au

Standards Australia
19–25 Raglan Street
South Melbourne, Vic 3205
www.standards.com.au

Victorian WorkCover Authority
Level 3, 485 Latrobe Street
Melbourne, Vic 3000
www.workcover.vic.au

WorkCover Conciliation Service
Level 3, 624 Bourke Street
Melbourne, Vic 3000

Tourism Training Victoria (TTV)
7th Floor, 189 Flinders Lane
Melbourne, Vic 3000
www.ttvic.com.au

Liquor, Hospitality & Miscellaneous Workers Union (LHMU)
117–131 Capel Street
North Melbourne, Vic 3051
www.lhmu.org.au

Hotel, Motel & Accommodation Association (HMAA) of Victoria
1st Floor, 21 Burwood Road
Hawthorn, Vic 3122
www.hmaa.com.au

Licensed Clubs Association of Victoria (LCAV)
PO Box 306
Kew, Vic 3101

Australian Institute of Hospitality Management Inc (AIHM)
PO Box 1055
Elsternwick, Vic 3185
http://home.vicnet.net.au/~aihm/

Australian Aboriginal and Torres Strait Islander Corporation for Tourism
Level 6, 230 Collins Street
Melbourne, Vic 3000

Australian Hotels Association (AHA)
1st Floor, 322 Glenferrie Road
Malvern, Vic 3144
www.aha.org.au

WESTERN AUSTRALIA

Australian Government Info Shop
469 Wellington Street
Perth, WA 6000

ACCC
3rd Floor, East Point Plaza
233 Adelaide Terrace
Perth, WA 6000
www.accc.gov.au

Worksafe Western Australia
1260 Hay Street
West Perth, WA 6005
www.safetyline.wa.gov.au

Standards Australia
165 Adelaide Terrace
West Perth, WA 6004
www.standards.com.au

Western Australian Tourism Commission
6th Floor, St Georges Court
16 St Georges Tce
Perth, WA 6000
www.tourism.wa.gov.au
www.westernaustralia.net

WA Hospitality & Tourism ITC
PO Box 1794
Perth, WA 6872
www.wahtitc.com.au

Liquor, Hospitality & Miscellaneous Workers Union (LHMU)
Level 13, 251 Adelaide Terrace
Perth, WA 6000
www.lhmu.org.au

Australian Hotels Association (AHA)
38 Parliament Place
West Perth, WA 6005
www.aha.org.au

Glossary

AAA Australian Automobile Association.

ABN Australian Business Number.

ABS Australian Bureau of Statistics.

ACCC Australian Competition and Consumer Commission.

ACCI Australian Chamber of Commerce and Industry.

Accident report A written record of injuries sustained by an employee during their working hours.

Accommodating A conflict resolution technique that plays down the differences and plays up the similarities between conflicting parties in the hope of smoothing things over.

Active documents Documents in current use.

ACTU Australian Council of Trade Unions.

Add-ons A selling technique used to persuade a customer to buy additional products or services.

Advertising Any paid-for space or air time in the mass media for the promotion of a product or service.

AFTA Australian Federation of Travel Agents.

Agenda A list of points or topics to be discussed at a meeting.

Aggressiveness Forcefully imposing our views and ideas without regard for the other person.

AHA Australian Hotels Association.

Archiving The practice of removing a file or record from everyday use and storing it in another location.

Assertiveness The ability confidently to express thoughts and feelings with regard to other persons' point of view.

ATAQ Australian Travel Agents Qualifications.

ATC Australian Tourist Commission.

ATEC Australian Tourism Export Council.

Attractions Sights and activities at a destination that will attract tourists.

Australian Competition and Consumer Commission (ACCC) The government body responsible for administering consumer protection legislation (such as the Trade Practices Act).

Australian workplace agreement (AWA) Certified agreement between an employer and employees relating to working conditions and rates of pay.

Avoiding A conflict resolution technique whereby one or both parties to the conflict ignore the conflict issues in the hope that they will go away.

Award A code that sets out minimum working conditions and pay rates in a given industry for a defined category of workers.

Biodiversity The range of living organisms, particularly plants and animals, that make up our natural environment.

BSP Bank Settlement Plan.

BTR Bureau of Tourism Research.

Client Another name for a customer.

Closed questions Questions requiring 'yes' or 'no' answers. They make it easy for a customer to say 'no' or make other non-buying decisions.

Code of practice A practical and flexible guide for meeting legislation and standards in the workplace.

Cold stress This occurs as a result of exposure to severely cold working conditions. Cold stress can begin when the body temperature falls below 18°C.

Collaboration A conflict resolution technique. It is the most effective and direct technique for achieving win–win results as it uses problem-solving techniques to resolve the issues of each of the conflicting parties.

Competing A conflict resolution technique that results in victory for one party to the conflict through force, authority, domination or superior skill.

Compromising Conflict resolution technique that requires each party to the conflict to give up something they value to resolve the conflict.

Conflict Usually any situation where disagreement occurs between two or more parties.

Correspondence Written communication such as letters between an organisation and other entities.

Cross-cultural communication Communication that takes place between two or more people from different cultures.

Cross-cultural conflict Conflict that may occur because of cultural differences and ignorance or misunderstandings arising from those differences.

Cross-cultural understanding Learning about and understanding other people's cultures and lifestyles.

Cultural stereotyping The categorisation of all people who originate from a particular culture or background as being exactly the same. It does not recognise any individual characteristics.

Culture The collection of beliefs, rituals, morals, values and attitudes among a group of people. It can also be a way of life, accepted behavioural pattern, religion, law and habits among a group of people.

Customer A person who pays for goods or services. Also referred to as a client.

Customer profile A record of a customer's personal details and spending history with the organisation. Is likely also to contain information about the customer's preferences.

Demographics Identifies groups of people according to age, gender, family size, income, occupation, education and marital status for the purpose of market segmentation.

Designated work group (DWG) Representatives from a specified section or department of an enterprise, or a group representing the collective interests of all employees, who liaise with management and Occupational Health & Safety officers on OHS issues.

Destination Where a traveller is intending to visit.

Diplomacy The ability to manage personal relations tactfully and intelligently.

Discrimination The treating of one person differently from or less favourably than another in the same situation, based on race, sexual preference, gender, marital status and other characteristics that have no relevance to the situation.

Disturbance Any event or occurrence that interrupts the usual activities within an organisation.

Domestic tourism Tourism undertaken by Australian residents within Australia, either interstate or intrastate.

Downselling Sales technique used to sell an item by suggesting the highest priced item first then progressively offering similar products in the lower price range.

DWG Designated work group.

Duty of care The legal and moral obligation one person has for the safety and wellbeing of another.

E-commerce Conducting business transactions via the Internet.

Ecotourism Concerned with maintaining the natural and cultural integrity of certain tourism areas. It is an attempt to provide a link between the economic development of tourism and the conservation and protection of the natural areas.

Ecotour A small-scale, low-impact, nature-based tour used as a learning experience.

EEO Equal employment opportunity. Legislation designed to ensure that people are not discriminated against on irrelevant characteristics (such as race, gender, nationality, etc.).

Empathy Attempting to understand another person's feelings.

Enterprise agreement An agreement negotiated between the employer and employees that sets out terms and conditions of employment, and pay rates, for that enterprise.

Enterprise standard The standard set by an individual enterprise for the delivery or production of services and goods.

Export Goods and services sold by a business within a country to other countries to earn foreign currency.

External customers All customers that are not colleagues. That is, people who pay for the services and facilities offered by an organisation.

External-use documents Those documents that are coming into or being sent out of the organisation (used by staff and other parties).

Extrinsic motivation Motivation to do something because it is linked to external rewards, such as pay and bonuses.

Familiarisation trips Free trips offered by airlines and/or other tourism providers to travel agents to sample the products offered by those companies.

Filing The process of arranging and storing documents according to a particular classification.

First aid The application of emergency care, in the first instance, to an injured person.

FIT Fully or free independent traveller. A traveller who makes all their own travel and accommodation arrangements.

Formal communication Structured communication that includes passing information through accepted channels such as letters, memorandums, procedures, etc.

Formal groups Groups whose common link is usually work related.

Formal research Involves systematically gathering and analysing information from primary and secondary sources relating to a product or service.

Grapevine Informal communication channel, usually by word-of-mouth. The information obtained in this way is often not reliable.

Group A collection of people in the workplace who are brought together because of a common link, for example similar skills.

Group dynamics The way members of a group interact and behave towards each other.

Guest A person who visits a hospitality or tourism establishment for the purpose of using its facilities and services. Guests are also termed customers because they pay for the products and services they use. Can also refer to people accompanying other customers.

Hazard management The identification of hazards in the workplace that pose a potential threat and the implementation of steps to eliminate those hazards.

Hazards Anything that can potentially cause harm to anyone working in an organisation or the public.

Heat stress Occurs as a result of working in hot conditions. Heat stress begins when more heat is absorbed by the body than can be dispersed by perspiration and other means.

IATA International Air Transport Association.

Import Goods and services purchased by businesses within a country from other countries.

Improvement Notice Written notification requiring an organisation or individual to fix a breach of OHS legislation.

Inactive documents Documents not in current use (likely to be archived).

Inbound tour operators Organisations that arrange in-country tours for overseas visitors.

Inbound tourist Visitor to Australia whose main place of residence is not Australia.

Incentives Rewards offered to staff for reaching certain sales goals or targets.

Incident report Written report that records the details of an incident.

Industrial agreement An agreement negotiated collectively between employer and employee representatives that sets out minimum working conditions and terms and pay rates and applies to a specified industry or sector.

Industry standard A standard that is established that can apply across an entire industry.

Informal communication Information communicated

through unstructured means, such as that which is communicated orally.

Informal groups Groups whose common link is more likely to be based on personal characteristics, such as tastes, personality, ideals, preferences, etc.

Informal research Involves the collection of information from secondary sources.

Internal customer Colleagues in the workplace. The concept of internal customers identifies colleagues serving customers to whom we provide a service.

Internal-use documents Documents used within an organisation (by staff only).

Interpersonal skills Those skills that enable us to communicate and interrelate effectively with others.

Intrinsic motivation Forces that motivate us to do something for personal satisfaction (internal) such as doing well for the pleasure of it.

Itinerary Detailed record of scheduled travel arrangements.

ITO Inbound Tour Operator.

Job description Outline of duties to be performed and a list of the technical skills required to undertake the job tasks.

Launch party A special event or party specifically designed to launch (introduce to the market place) a new product or service.

Loyalty programs A customer-reward program offered by many organisations to attract and retain customers. The program offers rewards for frequent use of the organisation's products and services (such as free flights, free upgrades, and express check-in) to customers for their loyalty.

Mail merge A function in computer software that allows you to insert the customer's personal details, contained in the database, into a standard letter.

Mail out Term used to describe a sales letter sent to a large number of existing or potential customers on the organisation's mailing list.

Manual handling The physical manoeuvring of any item (pulling, lifting, pushing, bending).

Market segmentation Separating of the market into distinct groups or categories according to their special characteristics, needs and wants.

Media release An informative, newsworthy article, written to promote a new service or product.

Memorandum An internal-use document used for communicating a brief message to a lot of people at once.

MICE Meetings, incentive travel, conferences, conventions and exhibitions market.

Minutes Written record of a meeting (detailing what was discussed and by whom, and what action is required).

Motivation The force within us that induces us to do something.

Multicultural society The co-existence of several cultures in one community.

Multiplier effect Flow of spending through the community as a result of tourism activities.

Nationality Indicates a person's country of origin.

Near miss An incident whereby an accident almost happens.

Niche market (Small) segment of a market sharing very similar characteristics.

NOHSC National Occupational Health and Safety Commission.

Non-verbal communication Body language. One of the three elements of communication that aids interpretation of a message. It is the use of gestures and other body movements to help communicate a message.

OHS Occupational Health and Safety.

Open-ended questions Those that require more than 'yes' or 'no' answers.

Organisational structure The way in which roles and lines of authority are arranged in an organisation. It is also a diagrammatic chart outlining management and staff positions showing functions under divisions and departments.

Outbound tourist Tourist, whose main place of residence is Australia, travelling outside Australia.

Package holiday Usually an inclusive holiday, booked in advance, which can include some or all of the components of the trip such as transportation, accommodation, some or all meals and sightseeing tours or activities at the place of destination (for one all-inclusive price).

Passiveness Submissive behaviour that demonstrates a willingness to allow others to dominate and impose their viewpoints without consideration for their own.

Person specification Usually part of a job description. Describes the personal characteristics and attributes required by job applicants.

Personal selling Oral presentation made to a customer for the purpose of selling products and services. Can be face-to-face or on the telephone.

Personal space The distance required between two people in which both feel comfortable, when interacting.

Physical hazards Those hazards that impact on the body including noise and vibration, ultraviolet radiation and heat and cold.

Policy A (written) course of action or statement about the enterprise's position on an issue.

Prejudice A preconceived, unfavourable opinion about something or someone formed with (or without) personal knowledge or experience.

Price differentiation The differentiation of a product or service based on price.

Primary research sources Research sources that provide us with first hand information.

Procedure The steps required to complete a task or duty; usually written.

Product differentiation Features or characteristics of a product that distinguish it from other similar products.

Prohibition Notice Written notification to an organisation or individual preventing the carrying on of an activity that is or has the potential to be a risk.

Promotional activities Activities undertaken by an organisation to increase exposure in the market place of particular products or services.

Promotional materials Printed or electronic information about the products and services an organisation is selling.

Promotional tools The ways in which an organisation promotes its products and services.

Psychological hazards Hazards that impact on our mental wellbeing.

Public relations A range of activities designed to portray the organisation in a positive light through 'publicity'.

Publicity Gaining exposure on the radio, on television or in the newspaper for free or minimal cost to gain public support.

Purpose of travel The reason people travel, whether for business, pleasure, education, pilgrimage or other special interest. Knowing the purpose of travel can help identify target markets.

Race The population or group of people sharing a distinct ethnic origin.

Racial discrimination Occurs when a person is treated less favourably than another in similar circumstances because of their race, skin colour or nationality.

Racism A belief that one person is inferior to another based on race.

RCA Restaurant and Catering Association.

Responsible tourism development Organising tourism activities in an attempt to balance the needs of local communities with those of the tourists.

Retail travel agency The intermediary that links the suppliers of tourism products with the consumer.

Right of entry The right an OHS inspector or member of the police force has to enter premises for the purpose of inspection and to ensure compliance with OHS obligations.

Risk The likelihood that a potential hazard will result in injury or disease.

Risk control The elimination or reduction of the likelihood of an injury occurring if exposed to a hazard.

Risk management The identification of incidents that may or do occur as a result of the same risk and putting in place procedures to prevent further injury.

RPL Recognition of prior learning.

RTA Regional Tourist Association.

Sales calls Also referred to as personal selling. Face-to-face (or over the telephone) promotional activity undertaken by the organisation's sales representatives to promote a product or service to a potential customer.

Secondary research sources Sources of information that have already been collected and analysed.

Sector One distinct operating area of an industry.

Service The provision of goods and services to customers by individuals. Service is an action, an activity.

Service differentiation Features or characteristics of the services provided by an organisation that distinguish it from other organisations.

Service ethos The desirable qualities, attributes and characteristics possessed by individuals in the delivery of service.

Services Intangible activities or actions, offered by organ-

isations and individuals to meet customer needs and wants.

Sexual discrimination This occurs when one person is treated less favourably than others because of their gender, marital status, sexual preference or pregnancy, in otherwise similar situations.

Solicited applications Advertised job positions (the organisation is 'soliciting' for suitably qualified applicants).

Standard letter A pre-formatted letter that contains the same basic information but requires the input of the recipient's personal details.

Standard or standardisation The setting of a minimum level of performance for completing each task to ensure a consistent quality.

Stereotyping The categorisation of groups of people according to a single characteristic that limits the idea of those people as individuals.

Suggestive selling Selling products or services by suggesting alternatives. Most effective when the alternatives are described in a way that creates desire.

Suspicious person Any person who gives the impression something might be wrong by their behaviour or appearance.

Sustainable development Achieving a balance between tourism development and the protection of the natural environment for use by future generations.

Target market Category or group of people with similar characteristics and buying habits that an organisation wants to attract.

Teamwork This is achieved when the members of a group collectively contribute to the achievement of goals set by the team.

Template A blueprint for text (font, type sizes), graphics or layout, or a combination of all three.

TFC Tourism Forecasting Council.

Tour wholesaling Companies that purchase tourism products from different suppliers and package them for sale to consumers either directly or through travel agents.

Tourism Those activities that take people away from their usual place of residence for pleasure or holiday, other than for work. The tourism industry is comprised of a range of other industries which are required to support the needs and wants of those people who travel.

Tourism sectors One area of the industry, comprising those industries or business enterprises that provide goods and services to tourists, visitors and all types of travellers, while they are travelling.

Tourist A person who travels for pleasure and reasons other than for employment or business more than 40 kilometres from home, over a period of 24 hours.

Trade union An organisation that represents its members, being employees of a specific trade or industry, and aims to improve their working conditions and protect their rights.

Travel sector Sector of the tourism industry (companies and businesses) that manuafactures, promotes, sells and distributes travel products.

Trip A journey that requires a stay away from home, being at least 40 kilometres in distance and of at least 24 hours' duration, but not more than three months.

Unsolicited applications Applying for a job without knowing if one exists (in other words, the letter is unsolicited).

Upgrade Refers to the situation when the customer chooses to pay the higher rate for a better quality or standard of product or when the organisation sometimes provides a free upgrade.

Upselling Sales technique used, through suggestion, to persuade a customer to buy a more expensive product or service. Start at the lowest priced product or service and progressively move up the price and quality levels.

Visit As a component of a trip, is defined as 'being made to each place where one or more nights is spent while on the trip'.

Visitor services A sector of the tourism industry that is involved in attractions management (including special events), tourist information services, tourism agencies involved in destination marketing and the MICE market.

Waste management The management of waste disposal in a way that minimises harm to the environment, reduces costs to enterprises and reduces pollution.

World Wide Web (WWW) Global network of Internet websites.

Bibliography

Anderson, Kristen (1992), *Great Customer Service on the Telephone*, The Worksmart Series, American Management Association, New York.

Australian National Training Authority (1997a), *Hospitality Training Package, Hospitality Industry National Competency Standards*, Vol. 1 and Vol. 2, Australian Training Products Ltd, Melbourne.

Australian National Training Authority (1997b), *Tourism Training Package, Tourism Industry National Competency Standards*, Australian Training Products Ltd, Melbourne.

Axtell, Roger E. (1991), *Gestures: The Do's and Taboos of Body Language Around the World*, John Wiley & Sons Inc., New York.

Bambrick, Susan (ed.) (1994), *The Cambridge Encyclopedia of Australia*, Cambridge University Press.

Becker, Dennis & Becker, Paula Borkum (1994), *Customer Service and the Telephone*, Business Skills Express Series, Irwin Publishing, New York.

Bedson, Trudy (1991), *Sales Techniques*, Travel Career Development Series, Australian Travel Agents Qualifications Unit.

Blanchard, Kenneth & Johnson, Spencer (1994), *The One Minute Manager*, HarperCollins, London.

Bull, Adrian (1997), *The Economics of Travel and Tourism*, 2nd edition, Longman, South Melbourne.

Bureau of Tourism Research, International Visitor Survey, March quarter (1997).

Clarke, Dr Peter B. (ed.) (1993), *The World's Religions: Understanding the Living Faiths*, Readers Digest, Pleasantville, New York.

Cole, Kris (1998), *Supervision: Management in Action*, Prentice Hall Australia, Sydney.

Cordato, Anthony (1999), *Australian Travel and Tourism Law*, 3rd edition, Butterworths, Sydney.

Davidow, William H. & Uttal, Bro. (1989), *Total Customer Service: The Ultimate Weapon*, Harper Perennial, New York.

Declan, Kenny (1991), *Customer Relations and Sales Techniques*, Regency Institute, SA, Regency Hotel School, Regency Park, South Australia.

Durrant, Mark (ed.) (1997a), 'A Healthy Outlook for Inbound Tourism', *Forecast: The Sixth Report of the Tourism Forecasting Council*, Canberra, Vol. 3, No. 2, pp. 5–15.

Durrant, Mark (ed.) (1997b), 'Measuring the Economic Significance of Tourism', *Forecast: The Sixth Report of the Tourism Forecasting Council*, Canberra, Vol. 3, No. 2, pp. 29–30.

Dwyer, Judith (1997), *The Business Communication Handbook*, 4th edition, Prentice Hall Australia, Sydney.

Ellis, Raymon C. Jr & The Security Commission of the AH&MA (1986), *Security and Loss Prevention Management*, Educational Institute of the American Hotel & Motel Association, East Lansing, Michigan.

Finch, Lloyd C. (1990), *Telephone Courtesy and Customer Service*, revised edition, Crisp Publications Inc., Menlo Park, California.

First Aid in the Workplace, Code of Practice (1996), No. 18, 1 June 1996, AGPS, Melbourne.

Gardner, Margaret & Palmer, Gill (1992), *Employment Relations, Industrial Relations and Human Resource Management in Australia*, Macmillan Education Australia Pty Ltd, South Melbourne.

Gerson, Richard F. (1996), *Beyond Customer Service: Keeping Customers for Life*, Crisp Publications Inc., Menlo Park, California.

Guidance Note on Passive Smoking in the Workplace (NOHSC: 3019 [1994]) July 1994, Worksafe Australia, AGPS, Canberra.

Hall, C. Michael (1995), *Introduction to Tourism in Australia: Impacts, Planning and Development*, 2nd edition, Longman Australia Pty Ltd.

Harris, Robert & Howard, Joy (1996), *Dictionary of Travel and Hospitality Terms*, Hospitality Press, Melbourne.

Harris, Robert & Howard, Joy (1999), *The Australian Travel Agency*, 2nd edition, McGraw-Hill Australia Sydney.

Health Act 1958, Reprint No. 8 (Victoria).

Hinton, Tom & Schaeffer, Wini (1994), *Customer Focused Quality: What To Do on Monday Morning*, Prentice Hall, Englewood Cliffs, New Jersey.

Hunwicks, Mark (1994), *Cultural Awareness, Hospitality Perspective*, Regency Institute, SA, Regency Hotel School, Regency Park, South Australia.

Innkeepers Act 1968 (NSW).

Johnson, Dawn (1998), *Introduction to Travel and Tourism*, The Travel and Tourism Series (Book One), McGraw-Hill Australia, Sydney, NSW.

Johnson, Dawn (2000), *Sales and Marketing in the Tourism Industry*, The Travel and Tourism Series (Book Four), Irwin/McGraw-Hill, Sydney, NSW.

Kruitnof, Johan & Ryall, Jeff (1994), *The Quality Standards Handbook*, The Business Library, Information Australia, Melbourne.

Mathews, John (1993), *Health and Safety at Work*, 2nd edition, Australian Trade Union Safety Representatives Handbook, Pluto Press, Sydney.

Metropolitan Fire Brigade (1997), *Fire Prevention, Fire Safety in the Work Place*, Fire Prevention Department, Melbourne.

Nutting, John, Cielens, Marty & Strachan, Jenny (1996), *The Business of Communicating*, 3rd edition, McGraw-Hill Australia, Sydney.

O'Sullivan, Kerry (1994), *Understanding Ways: Communicating Between Cultures*, Hale & Iremonger, Sydney.

Occupational Health and Safety Act 1985, Act No. 10190/1985 (Victoria).

O'Shannessy, Vivienne and Minett, Dean (1999), *The Road to Hospitality*, Prentice Hall, Australia.

O'Shannessy, Vivienne, Haley, Sheryl & Richmond, Pania (2001), *Accommodation Services*, Prentice Hall, Australia.

Patterson, James G. (1995), *ISO9000 World Wide Quality Standard, Criteria for Documentation and Performance*, Crisp Publications Inc., Menlo Park, California.

Pease, Allan (1982), *Body Language: How to Read Others' Thoughts by Their Gestures*, Camel Publishing Company, Sydney.

Pendleton, Wayne & Vickery, Roger (1997), *Australian Business Law: Principles and Applications*, Prentice Hall Australia, Sydney.

Peters, Thomas, Waterman, J. & Robert, H. Jr (1990), *In Search of Excellence*, Harper & Row Publishers, Sydney.

Prescott, David & Lang, Barbara (1993), *Communicating at Work*, Harcourt Brace Jovanovich, Sydney.

Richardson, John I. (1995), *Travel and Tourism in Australia: The Economic Perspective*, Hospitality Press, Victoria.

Standards Australia, Tourism Training Australia & Standards New Zealand (1994), *Excellence in Hospitality, Quality System Guidelines—Guide for the Hospitality Industry*.

Trade Practices Act 1974, Reprint No. 8 (Commonwealth), AGPS, Canberra.

Travel and tourism—and the Trade Practices Act, Australian Competitor and Consumer Commission, November 1999.

Vallence, Keven & Wallace, Laurie (1993), *Quality Concepts*, Nelson Australia, Melbourne.

Victorian WorkCover Authority (1996), *Reduce Manual Handling Injuries*, Ergonomics Unit, ISBN 07306 7497 5.

Victorian WorkCover Authority (1997), *Getting Started with Workplace Health and Safety*, 'An Introduction to Hazard Management, Workplace Inspections and Selecting a Health and Safety Consultant', 'An Introduction to Workplace Health and Safety Policies, Procedures and Evaluation', 'An Introduction to Health and Safety Responsibilities, Roles and Functions, Training, Information and Records', 'An Introduction to Workplace Consultation'.

Workplace Relations Act 1996, AGPS, Canberra, 1997.

Worksafe Australia (1996), *Organising Health and Safety Training for Your Workplace*, AGPS, Canberra.

Index

Numbers in **bold** indicate a margin definition.

241